GT
4803
.L82

Ludwig, Jack Barry
The great American
spectaculars

BRADNER LIBRARY
SCHOOLCRAFT COLLEGE
LIVONIA, MICHIGAN 48152

THE
GREAT AMERICAN
SPECTACULARS

Also by *Jack Ludwig*

CONFUSIONS

ABOVE GROUND

A WOMAN OF HER AGE

THE GREAT HOCKEY THAW

GAMES OF FEAR AND WINNING

THE
GREAT AMERICAN
SPECTACULARS

The Kentucky Derby, Mardi Gras,
and Other Days of Celebration

JACK LUDWIG

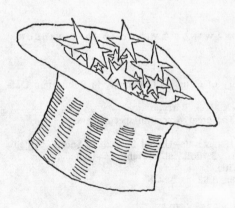

DOUBLEDAY & COMPANY, INC.
GARDEN CITY, NEW YORK
1976

GT
4803
.L82

DRAWINGS BY RAYMOND DAVIDSON

Library of Congress Cataloging in Publication Data

Ludwig, Jack Barry.
  The great American spectaculars.

    1. Festivals—United States. 2. Sports—United
States. 3. Political conventions—United States.
I. Title.
GT4803.L82   394.2

ISBN: 0-385-06670-8
Library of Congress Catalog Card Number: 73-83598

Copyright © 1976 by Jack Ludwig, Brina Ludwig and Susan McLaughlin
ALL RIGHTS RESERVED
PRINTED IN THE UNITED STATES OF AMERICA
FIRST EDITION

FOR
Sam Vaughan
AND
Angus Cameron

Contents

This day then, let us not be told,
That you are sick, and I grown old,
Nor think of our approaching ills,
And talk of Spectacles and Pills;
To morrow will be Time enough
To hear such mortifying Stuff.

> —Jonathan Swift,
> "Stella's Birth-Day
> March 13, 1726/7."

THE
GREAT AMERICAN
SPECTACULARS

Preface

For a long time I wondered what made certain events in American life different from all others. They existed as goals people wanted to reach—as soon as possible. They were charged with almost magical power: the event was always more than the sum of its statistics. Outstanding among these unusual happenings was the Kentucky Derby. On the face of it, the Derby was just a horse race —glamorous, exciting, important, yet not the best of all possible horse races. In any given year, for instance, many hundreds of three-year-old horses were eligible for the Derby. A smaller number—still in the hundreds—were actually entered in the race. Of these, a large number were listed as possible starters. Finally those going into the starter's gate would number about a dozen.

Those horses, in any given year, could be undistinguished. A potential winner might not have trained up for the race; or been injured; or simply soured. It could well turn out that the three-year-olds of a certain year did not represent the great breeding lines of racing. The horses could have mediocre records as two-year-olds, could have accomplished little in their first four months as three-year-olds. Yet, were the worst to happen, and the worst of all possible fields go to the post, the Derby as an event, as a happening, as a great day in the American sporting and social calendars, would be largely unaffected. In 1972, when Riva Ridge dominated the Derby field; in 1973, when one of the greats of racing, Secretariat, easily won the Derby on the way to a Triple Crown, the Derby was the number one racing event in the country; in 1971, when the eventual winner, Canonero II was so undistinguished he had to be lumped with a string of nothing horses as a field entry, the Kentucky Derby set both new attendance and new betting records. Had all twenty horses in 1971's Derby been scratched and twenty others substituted, the new records would still have been set. People came from all over the country and the world not only to see, but to be at, the Derby.

This existence as an event largely independent of its participants marked the Kentucky Derby as something crucially different from, say, the World Series, the Super Bowl, Stanley Cup hockey, or National Basketball Association championship play. In all of those contests the nature and stature of the participating teams was very important. Were two mediocre teams by some fluke able to sneak into these sporting finals, interest would fall off drastically. The special quality which differentiated a Kentucky Derby from other sports championships needed, I thought, much looking into. From studying the Derby, and using it as a model by which to measure other special days and events in the country, I came to my consideration of what I began to call the great American spectacular.

Obviously the Kentucky Derby was not just a horse race. It was *the* American horse race, with a dimension all its own: it marked a very special date—the first Saturday in May—on all kinds of calendars, social, sporting, political. Yet look at it objectively: it isn't the richest race in America. Many other races have as big a purse. A number have purses much larger. The Derby can't qualify as a real championship race: in fact, May is too early in a thoroughbred's year for the race to be a true test of even three-year-olds. There are better ways of establishing the horse-of-the-year: a true championship race would be open to horses with the most distinguished stakes records—regardless of age, regardless of where they were bred. What points up the extraordinary role of the Kentucky Derby is the failure of the other two races that make up racing's Triple Crown—Baltimore's Preakness and New York's Belmont Stakes—even to approximate the Derby's position as the great American racing spectacular. The Derby is probably the one American sporting event recognizable on every continent in the world. It is a goal for people outside the United States. People anywhere in the world who want to be in on something special, want—someday—to attend the Kentucky Derby.

Apart from its pre-eminence as a sporting event, the Kentucky Derby existed as a station, something to experience, something not to miss. Louisville, Kentucky, the first Saturday in May was one of the important dates publicists recognized. Existentially, Churchill Downs on Derby Day was a "there" one simply had to get to.

The Derby's "thereness" was a matter of spring, and a matter of instant recognition. Put a movie star or a politician in front of Churchill Downs's twin spires and that identification needed between people and a place registers. The blanket of roses thrown over the Derby winner was another national and international signature. Or the almost corny Kentucky colonel image complete with white suit, white Stetson, black string tie.

Exploitation of the Derby worked both ways: everyone who used the Derby to pep up his or her recognition factor was also giving the Derby added publicity and exposure. A dress designer or car manufacturer using the Derby as backdrop was intensifying the Derby image—which meant that the next designer or manufacturer would find the Derby as a medium that much stronger.

There was another dimension to the events I began to cluster with the Derby as great American spectaculars: each was held in a fairly ordinary place utterly transformed by its spectacular. I wanted to see, for instance, what Louisville was like when the Derby didn't dominate every aspect of its urban existence. What, in a word, was Capistrano like when the swallows left? What were the causes of a place's transformation from a city like any other city to a place like no other place in the land?

Many questions were on my mind before I attended the Kentucky Derby in 1972. The Derby could be a reward—political, industrial, commercial. It could also be used to signal the importance of a certain meeting: I knew, for instance, that the famous conversation between then-Attorney General John Mitchell and ITT's Dita Beard (subject: mergers, antitrust implications, the gifts of Sheraton Hotel space to the GOP in San Diego—hot political items at the time) had taken place at a pre-1971 Derby party given by Kentucky's governor, Louis Nunn. I knew, too, that Kentucky's newly elected Democratic governor, Wendell E. Ford, had invited Senator Ed Muskie of Maine, the early frontrunner for the Democratic nomination, to use the Kentucky Derby backdrop to kick off his expected victorious run against Richard M. Nixon.

You get the picture. I began then to consider what other events had the same national impact as the Kentucky Derby. How would a great American spectacular calendar be constructed? If one started with the Derby early in spring, what would follow—and where? I didn't confine my search to sports events. I began by asking the questions the Kentucky Derby's status as a spectacular suggested: *was this a place or a thing one was dying to experience?* Did people put themselves in hock in order not to miss out on this essential American thing? What was the difference between the spectacular experienced by those coming in from the outside and those who lived in a place all year round?

Using the Derby, then, as guide, I constructed my spectaculars calendar. As it turned out, every spectacular I included was a first time experience for me.

I'll list some of the events I didn't put on the calendar and say that comparison with the Derby was what usually made the difference between an *out* and an *in*. I should also add that in making that comparison I was not knocking the events excluded: the Cheyenne Rodeo—or any other rodeo that attracted the top riders and steer wrestlers—was an outstanding event, one I personally liked very much. But the Rodeo, unlike the Derby, even in the 1970s came off as a regional event. The exclusive sports definition of the World Series, Super Bowl, Stanley Cup, NBA championship I've already referred to—and who would knock those things as important events in American life? Or the Miss America contest, which wasn't excluded because Atlantic City, New Jersey, was regional. The site of the Miss America contest, as a matter of fact, is almost irrelevant. Nor did I cut out the contest in order to avoid Bert Parks' annual toothy dirge. Atlantic City during the Miss America contest was Atlantic City unchanged—storm-worn, wave-threatened, one-foot-in-the-watery-grave. The Kentucky Derby was available to anybody who wanted to attend—locals, outsiders, women, men, young people, middleaged people, old people, whites, blacks, the rich, the middle incomes, the poor, highbrows, middlebrows, lowbrows, etc. Not so the Miss America contest with its emphasis on middleclass, second-hand joys—rote presentations, swimsuit strutting, evening gown fashion displays, make-up, smiles, tears, and chiffon.

The considerations that kept the Miss America contest off the spectaculars calendar argued against the inclusion of the Oscar ceremonies, Tony, Emmy, Grammy awards. An industry-defined studio audience made participation far too restrictive.

What should be and must be included is more relevant to what will follow: Memorial Day, at the end of May, marked the next stop on my spectaculars calendar, Indianapolis, for the Indianapolis "500." Every other big car or stockcar race stood a distant second to the "500" just as every other horse race lagged far behind the Kentucky Derby. The Pocono "500" and the Ontario "500" made up automobile's Triple Crown—a concept that didn't quite catch on as racing's Triple Crown clearly had. The Daytona "500" was a very big event for stockcar drivers but had somehow never made it as spectacularly as Indianapolis. In spite of television coverage it continued to be largely regional.

The third event I chose was the Rose Bowl. Unlike the Super Bowl, it was rooted in one place—Pasadena, a city that resisted transformation as much as Indianapolis and Louisville seemed to encourage it. The deciding factor in my choice was the Rose Bowl's position in college sports as well as in year-end Bowl games. The Rose Bowl, like the Derby, didn't depend totally on the stature of the teams competing in any given year. People wanted to "see a Rose Bowl game" the way people wanted to "see the Derby" or "see the Indianapolis '500.'" The Rose Bowl had restricted participation on New Year's Day to the Big Ten and the Pacific-8 conferences alone, without substantially altering the game's position as the number one Bowl attraction. Even higher stood the Tournament of Roses Parade, perhaps the gaudiest show in the country—watched by as many or more people than watched the Rose Bowl game proper.

Once I selected a college bowl game I decided to take another look at college sports, the NCAA track meets, for instance, and swimming championships. None could make it in the Derby–Indianapolis "500"–Rose Bowl climes. I considered the Masters Tournament at Augusta, Georgia, perhaps golf's best-known event and much more of an event than the equally prestigious PGA championship or the United States Open. The Masters was no longer regional but, compared to the Derby and the "500," appeared rather tight, even parochial. The same tight classbound quality attended the Forest Hills tennis championships and the America Cup yachting challenge race.

What else were Americans "dying to attend"? In 1972, not an annual but a leap year spectacular claimed a place on the calendar —the national nominating conventions which, it turned out, were both to be held in Miami Beach. Richard Nixon as the incumbent was not being challenged. The Democratic nominating convention, on the other hand, was wide open. I decided to make it the political spectacular in this book. Miami Beach was a place that kept popping up in American political and sports history: the transformation of a city being invaded off-season interested me, too.

The fifth event I constantly heard someone was "dying to attend" was Mardi Gras, in New Orleans, something that had started as a local festival and, during the past twenty or thirty years, become a recognized national event.

My spectaculars year had a pleasant, natural round to it. I began in spring at the Kentucky Derby and ended just before spring at Mardi Gras. My year which ended with Mardi Gras days of misrule began with similar days of misrule in Louisville and Indianapolis. My calendar moved from May 6, 1972, Derby Day, to May 20, when I attended the second leg of the Triple Crown, the Pimlico Preakness. On May 27 I experienced the Indianapolis "500," and, on June 10, was in New York for the third leg of the Triple Crown, the Belmont Stakes. July I spent at the Democratic National Convention in Miami Beach. On January 1, 1973, I was in Pasadena for the Rose Bowl. My spectaculars year ended in March with Ash Wednesday, which began Lent and ended Mardi Gras.

Doing this book, I began to understand, I think, the importance of pastimes and circuses in modern American life. I'll elaborate on the subject, but for now I should say that the necessity of circuses rose in my estimation to be almost the equal of the necessity for bread. I also saw that in this complicated country a brilliant idea may be followed almost instantly by its commercial exploitation, its parody, its denigration, and that things can thrive in the presence even of their opposites. The small children wildly excited by the Indianapolis "500" or Rose Bowl or Mardi Gras were little affected by the massive commercial exploitation of the spectaculars. No matter how successful the local event became nationally, it remained for children, for families, a special holiday, a great day to be in town—when all the action comes rolling in.

I look at the events I attended with a novelist's eye. The way a drunk sings "My Old Kentucky Home" may be as important to a writer as who won the Kentucky Derby. At no time could I ignore what was happening nationally and internationally—not even during Mardi Gras. Every spectacular occurred in a specific historical setting. Political, military, economic, cultural counterpoint plays against the spectacular throughout the book.

The day I began, Friday, May 5, Kentucky Derby eve, the Louisville *Courier-Journal* headlined two page one stories. The first was datelined Paris:

PARIS TALKS—APPARENTLY
SECRET AS WELL AS OPEN—
HALTED BY U.S. AND SAIGON

The other, a local story, commanded a headline the size given to the Vietnam War:

EVERYBODY'S HAPPY AS FIELD
OF 16 ENTERED IN 98TH DERBY

Derby-goers had only to raise an eye to see the larger, sober, unspectacular Vietnam reality troubling everybody's circuses. That reality will wind in and out of my Great American Spectaculars tale.

1

The Very Rich *Are* Different

Long before F. Scott Fitzgerald discovered the socially mysterious East, land of the very rich, he could ponder high midwestern social riddles in his hometown, St. Paul, a Boston that never quite made it to San Francisco: why, for instance, St. Paul socialites, like proper Bostonians, had not one, two, but three, four, or more addresses; why a tight social caul was thrown over upperclass St. Paul children till they were old enough to be shipped out to the safer New England boarding school spaces. At birth rich St. Paul children were imprinted with money images and the Boston sound, which were supposed to keep them forever safe from the twin plagues of poverty and provincialism. Children prepping in the St. Paul area were exposed to imported teachers fluent in Basic Back Bay. In the carefully constructed Midwest social ghetto one could still be guaranteed life with "one's own kind." Social isolation was costly, but money, which was society's object, was no object.

Fitzgerald lived on Summit Avenue, the main drag of upperclass St. Paul, "in a house below the average/ Of a street above the average," according to his own social barometer. St. Paul had local robber barons who buffed at crudeness with crisp thousand dollar bills. To guarantee their children freedom from the potentially corrupting parental model, they sent kids East for sanctuary in the *real* Social Ghetto.

No matter where the very rich went, or when, they controlled the environment in order to mingle only with their own kind. Everyone was governed by the First Law of the Social Thermostat: "Be not in town *after* New Year's Day, return not to town *before* Labor Day." Social Baedekers didn't have to prescribe the exact spot the rich should head for: wintering in Florida, they almost instinctively avoided Miami's black slums.

The Social Commandments, unlike the Mosaic Code, had never been carved in stone—not that the rich couldn't have afforded it. The rich, from birth, understood, respected, and obeyed the compact. For instance, during the season (which began twenty-four hours after Labor Day and lasted till twenty-four hours after Christmas Day) everyone was expected to be in town and wear recognizable town clothes. Fashion designers were admirably accommodating and timed their shows so that the rich could get a two or three month jump on the Social Seasons. These were Town, Christmas, Cruise, Easter, Tour, and Spa.

The diurnal round, too, was full of nuance: day and night were designated by before-six and after-six clothes. Town and Cruise were separated by a thinness of white dinnerjacket.

The very rich, who, as Fitzgerald found out but Hemingway did not, were "very different from you and me," emphasized their difference hourly. They had twice a hundred social decalogues but didn't have to commit a single one to memory. They had only to remember to hire the maids, valets, and social secretaries whose existential definition derived from keeping the rich pointed in the right direction. Devout secular guardian angels, the hired help, like social ornithologists, made sure no stray bird flapped off course when the specially bred flocks migrated to the approved strands and islands.

After Christmas, to be warm, the unimaginative went to Florida, the ailing to Arizona. The very best summer place was simply any thirty-room villa as far from the intersection of Park Avenue and Fifty-seventh Street as possible. One might sail one's oceangoing yacht to the dream spot, or have a spare sixtyfooter out on charter waiting till one arrived on a luxury liner (New York–Le Havre) in posh quarters not even the ship's captain could enter.

Easter and Christ's Passion signaled a new injunction to travel. One would revisit (no socialite was ever anywhere a first time)

London, Paris, Rome, the stations of the transatlantic cross. Late June one had to be settled in one's summerhouse, which to St. Paul provincials meant nearby Lake Minnetonka, a favorite summer address for Bostonians (thus proper for St. Paul). Chicago socialites did their freshwater sailing in Wisconsin or took over uncharted chunks of Canadian Ontario. Detroit and Indianapolis socialites in summer occupied northern Michigan.

Once in the East, Fitzgerald experienced the enlarged address syndrome: Park Avenue, Fifth Avenue, Sutton Place, and their 50s, 60s, 70s, 80s side streets served as addresses *in town*. The weekend house on the north shore of Long Island, or in Westchester County, or in Dutchess County was the second address. During the season one did the town's charity balls, museum openings, symphony concerts, its theater, ballet, and that most important of all social events, opening night at the Metropolitan Opera. On weekends one filled one's country house with several railroad cars of one's own kind.

That Metropolitan opening night is an early model of the great American spectacular performing its primary aristocratic function —restricted, exclusive, mandatory, eleemosynary, expensive. Cotillions and coming-out parties were dependent on the very young; only the Met could sound an adult mustering call. No matter how far one wandered in summer, the deadline for return was that first operatic night. Something like the annual initial meeting of the Soviet Politburo, the Met opening with its satellite pre-Opera and post-Opera parties provided an absolute power register. From who was invited where, from who had risen an invitational notch, and who was down, or out, one could interpret social auguries without slicing open a single prognosticating pigeon. Like a bestseller list, opening night gave everyone an objective numbered social ranking, a social Dow Jones.

One extremely important Social Commandment was, *Neither sweat nor shiver*. In search of the perpetual temperate zone, a New Yorker, keying on the Social Thermostat, moved from Manhattan to Europe to the Hamptons to Saratoga and back to Manhattan with only a few proper climatic sidetrips in between. To avoid the merely rich, the very rich followed a Thermosocial Law which said, *Never sail in summer, never ski in winter*. Mostly, one strove not to be anywhere ever, but perpetually *just having arrived, or just leaving.*

That commandment to be in town during the season antedates the founding of the Met. Genuine operalovers, in pre-Met days, wanted both to be in town for the season and in Milan for the opera. Solutions were found. If Manhattan couldn't come to the mountain, the mountain would have to come to Manhattan: that is, robberbaronial money could easily sail a boatload of warbling Italians right into New York the moment a stage existed for Italians to sing on during Prime Social Time. The Met was founded. Twenty years earlier a summer-season problem was solved in Saratoga Springs: billeted in enormous unmoveable summerhouses and grand hotels, the very rich needed a good horse race. So Saratoga Racetrack was built, within walking distance of the posh retreats.

Fitzgerald knew of similar aristocratic problem-solving: Back Bay society built a railroad from Boston to Lake Minnetonka to accommodate the obligatory summer move. Convenient railroads ran to the Hamptons, to Long Island's northern Gold Coast (which Fitzgerald used as setting for *The Great Gatsby*). Limousines could facilitate the very rich, but trains were needed to transport servants. Along the Hudson River's east bank, huge estates were serviced by railroad track which carried important houseguests needed to stock megaroom manses.

The reason the very rich could build special railruns was that they already owned the railroads, and lots of railroad laborers. Thousands of darkhaired low-wage Italian immigrants were available all over the East to drag around heavy steel rails, massive wood ties, and, when necessary, pound rock into a proper levelgrading fineness. These workers were of the same sturdy ethnic stuff that built those picturesque New England stone fences whose origins I don't remember Robert Frost asking about much, or even Henry David Thoreau. The work was extremely hard, the men died young, which left a lot of orphans, needed, of course, to fill the rockwalled institutions supported by charity balls. The rich also built hospitals soon full of terminally ill workers from the carcinogenic industries and oxygenless sweatshops busy generating the fruits of risk capital.

A thorough review of America's glorious years would doubtless connect the movement of empire with the inclination of the rich to own forever whatever they played on once. Earlier Caesars, we know, blew Rome for cool Alpine retreats when things got hot in town. When Rome turned chilly, the Caesars tried warming in Egyptian sand. American imperialism was almost casual—a grab here, a grab there, usually through climatic options. An eventually raped banana republic encountered its fate because some rich kid, sailing, got lost, like Crusoe, and ended up on a stretch of choice oceanfront beach. When rescued, the kid told his daddy. The launching of yet another U.S. flotilla soon followed. Imperialism looking for new worlds to conquer could do worse than end up in temperate zones.

Society ideologically hung together even when it frolicked apart. In the Social Diaspora everyone spoke a standard tongue. Portland, Maine, had no difficulty communicating with Portland, Oregon. In winter, though, socialites could be thousands of miles apart. Summer's clustered colonies ranged from northern Maine, Cape Cod, Newport, the Hamptons, Saratoga right across the choice lake and mountain regions of the country to Lake Arrowhead, Lake Tahoe, and Puget Sound.

So widely scattered, society, to survive, needed more class re-unions. The Met was its maximum dress-up affair. Ladies were expected to put away Pinkerton paste. Robberbarons who lived as exiles while filching Montana's silver or draining Texas's oil, for the Met affairs got into what Jiggs of the socialclimbing comicstrip "Maggie and Jiggs" called his "soup and fish" in order to spend a few uneasy nights bowing to a batch of busted Bulgarian barons. Women put on their diamond tiaras and, like Maggie, flaunted pearly lorgnettes. This symbiotic night of nights jewel thieves lived for: the morning after, one scanned either the society or crime columns of the New York *Times* and the New York *Herald Tribune*.

Other mandatory Met-like roll calls were needed—clothes just as expensive as the ball get-ups could then be worn, though less showy, less formal.

On June 9, 1973, I sat in the Trustees' Room at Belmont Racetrack waiting for Secretariat to win the Belmont Stakes *and* racing's Triple Crown. The room was full of the season's social returnees fresh back from their scattered sunny holdings, everyone bronzed as babyshoes. The dominant sound was a mixture of high St. Paul's and tight Miss Porter's School, which made everyone seem to be imitating Nelson Rockefeller. People were named Tish, Gav, Hedge, Trish, Pudge, Dev, Wend, Crawf, Biff, Reege, Sissie, Chickie, Buffie.

At the Belmont table next to mine, Tish's, Reege stopped by, so Tish asked her husband, Gav, if he and Reege had ever shaken hands.

"Reege," tanned Gav said, "you and I haven't had that pleasure, but I feel I know you. I mean I *know* that delicious boat of yours—almost in the biblical sense."

"God yes, Reege," said Tish with such effusion I concluded he must be at least ten times richer than Gav, "it's obscene, he positively *lusts* after her."

"She's a filly, Ree," said Gav, "sleek, a beautiful animal. I look at her and drool."

"Mary Jim feels the same way, Tish," said Reege. "She gets hot flashes thinking her sweet boat is chartered to some little Greek millionaire."

"I understand Ma'Ji's feeling," said Tish, "someone oily padding over *that* white deck *barefoot?*"

The Fitzgeralds, all their lives, wanted what Reege obviously had. The French flag flying over Antibes, for instance, had no more political significance to Reege than a regatta pennant. The very rich belonged to only one nation, Class. Reege had more in common with a White Russian count than with any American laborer. Both he and the count lived by a cheery credo:

Let *Us* Eat Cake.

Social imperialism asserted society's first refusal rights to all the world's turf. Choice play-spots could be denied the masses with laws, walls, fences. The Metropolitan Opera inner circle could be tightly sealed off from middleclass contagion: Saratoga built cabana-like enclaves closed off from the general public. The public could participate, but only in plebeian pleasures confined to the plebeian section.

The Met and Saratoga were two society Wailing Walls. The calendar obviously needed a spring event. A prime take-over candidate was the Kentucky Derby.

First run in 1875, eleven years before the first running of the Met, the Kentucky Derby didn't become something special until its managers decided the U.S.A. needed a Big Race such as The Derby (at Epsom Downs in England) and the even more formal, more social Royal Ascot Gold Cup race.

The Epsom Derby was a great day, a carnival, a picnic, a sideshow for both Britain's society and its workingclass, combining plebeian bread and circuses with patrician tea and watercress sandwiches. In 1973, over three quarters of a million people attended The Derby at Epsom, the world's most spectacular spectacular. Half a million people turn its infield into a combination of Coney Island and Battersea Park lined with multicolored tents fit for a medieval jousting tourney. That infield is full of open air pubs, streetcriers hawking sausages, stands selling fish and chips, hardboiled eggs, Cornish pasties, Devon creamcakes. Bookies, like carny sellers of snakebite oil, stand above the crowd shouting their odds as thousands of children run around, playing tag, scraping knees, galloping between oblivious lovers. Infants suckled, fed from bottles, armed with lollipops and icecream-on-a-stick are held up to be imprinted by the vital action. Acrobats tumble through narrow spaces, soccerplayers waggle "headers," cricketers try to bowl without pinging a dozen strolling nonplayers. The old sit in their folding chairs and watch the rides whipping by overhead. From their vantage point there's no way to see the race. So they listen to the ratcheting and the delighted screaming. Everywhere it's a live Breughel "Children's Games."

But, in the midsts of Epsom, the toffs are having their day. The parking lots hold hundreds of Rolls-Royces massed together as if The Derby were a limousine rally. Inside, the aristocratic Royal Enclosure is closed off. Lords and ladies from time to time train their glasses on the lowerclasses. Horseflesh one can touch in the paddock; the masses are a good two furlongs away, kept behind wood and metal barriers.

In The Derby's cooler inner reaches, dress is not optional, though the social directives suggest that. Women wear long dresses and fancy hats, the same costuming one sees at Royal Ascot when the Queen has her Gold Cup day. Epsom, on Derby Day, is, like the Met opening in New York, a time for designers. Women wear name clothes and, tastefully, the right jewels. Royal Ascot gray shows up in toppers and swallowtail coats and doublebreasted vests and spats. Some men actually use monocles.

The Royal Enclosure at Royal Ascot displays no token masses. Royalty, aristocracy, and the very rich own this day. Ascot men show modernity with variations on the theme of topper, tailcoat, vest. Style mutants wear the traditional coats but in mod colors, mod patterns, mod fabrics. The year I attended Royal Ascot the Queen had her own horse running for the Gold Cup. Before every race she made a Queen's progress into the saddling area, a fluttering behind her as of gulls following a fishing boat.

Royal Ascot's social privacy, its just-among-us exclusiveness, made it much like, say, a Queen's posh, yet secret, garden party. The Kentucky Derby had only to imitate Royal Ascot to attract Reege, Tish, and Gav; for the masses it needed to add the Epsom Derby's public carnival spirit. When Charles Hatton combined the Kentucky Derby, the Preakness, and the Belmont Stakes under the catchy rubric of the Triple Crown, the Kentucky Derby's significance escalated socially *and* publicly. To win the Triple Crown a horse had first to win the Derby, so, in effect, the Derby was two races—its own race and the first leg of the Triple Crown.*

Few events in the United States resemble the Kentucky Derby. Its winners, no matter how ordinary their subsequent racing records, fall into the most exclusive breeding category. A victory in the Kentucky Derby is worth more to a stud fee than three, four, or more wins in top-money stakes. Any history of thoroughbred racing in the United States—and the rest of the world—celebrates Kentucky Derby winners. Horses who win the Triple Crown form an exclusive racing category, but even among those horses the great achievement remains winning the Derby.

Socially, the Kentucky Derby, unlike the Met or Saratoga scenes, which were largely New York affairs, belonged to no par-

* Society never could get terribly excited about the second leg, the Preakness, held at Pimlico in Baltimore. The Belmont Stakes was an *our crowd* thing and marked the official end to the New York social season. Socially it was more relevant than the essentially plebeian Memorial Day.

ticular social set. Louisville, Kentucky, couldn't begin to compete with New York or Boston social power. Kentucky, however, created a democratic illusion of being hospitable to any millionaire with one week free in May. The Derby became the most important date on the Spring Social Calendar. Louisville society could live with the illusion that it hosted the Derby's festive parties. New York and Boston society allowed the illusion to persist, and, for the most part, ran things the old New York-Boston way. Co-hosting was common, but the finer seasonal snubs specifically excluded all locals. A New York hostess might take over local space, servants, and dollars. The grateful but ripped-off Kentucky hostess would feel it was all worth it if the New York lady remembered the Kentucky lady's name next time they saw each other in the lobbies of the Met.

In other parts of the country, take-over of the Kentucky Derby created new society dreams. Couldn't Far West, Deep South, Midwest society co-opt some local happening? The fall belonged to the Met, spring to the Kentucky Derby, summer to Saratoga. Local socials would have to book the inbetween.

Indianapolis society, for instance, took a long time to realize the potential of a local event, the Indianapolis "500," a motorcar race. Horses are easily connected with society because horses, like their owners, are bred for genealogical improvement. The manufactured automobile was noisy, filthy. The rough foreigners in the car pits were totally different from the displaced dukes society honored at the opera. Car owners didn't much resemble the rigidjawed owners of thoroughbreds and polo ponies. Car people spoke with those raspy twanging southern or midwestern accents Fitzgerald and his chums had been brought up to resist.

And yet, to the para-Whitneys of Indianapolis—and, later, to the putative-du Ponts of Pasadena (who socialized the Rose Bowl), or the meta-Mellons of New Orleans (who secularized Mardi Gras)—taking over a public event was a brilliant social coup. Quite independent of their status as national events, important sports dates, public spectaculars, the Kentucky Derby, the Rose Bowl, the Indianapolis "500," and the New Orleans Mardi Gras became significant dates on the Social Calendar.

The Great American Spectacular became an important date on

the criminal calendar, too. Jewel thieves soon realized that a spectacular was like the Met opening. An accommodating partnership such as exists between sadists and masochists developed between society and those jewel thieves: the spectacular guaranteed the attendance of a certain number of rich pigeons. Sexual artists could also turn up and find takers for even the most occult specialties. Hucksters, con-men, petty thieves, and pickpockets joined in a criminal minispectacular.

In time the spectaculars came to dominate a certain part of the country at a certain time of year. The rest of the country and the rest of the world ceased to exist. Every city I visited was oblivious to war, unemployment, inflation, crime while its spectacular informed the town. Every spectacular wanted to be idyllic as Eden. The good-guy values, "enjoyment," "relaxing," "having a ball," "never bothering your head about politics and such stuff," presided over them all.

The time I cover, from May 5, 1972, the day before Riva Ridge won the 1972 Kentucky Derby, to March 6, 1973, before midnight ended 1973's Mardi Gras, may turn out to have been one of this century's most significant periods. A despised war was being fought, some of it in secret. A weird election featured Watergate, Richard M. Nixon's Pandora's Box, which was opened only a few weeks after the Indianapolis "500."

The Louisville *Courier-Journal* on May 5, 1972, Derby eve, seen from 1976's perspective, points up the strangeness: it contains Richard Nixon's funeral eulogy for J. Edgar Hoover, who was buried the day before:

> "The American people are tired of disorder, disruption and disrespect for law. America wants to come back to the law as a way of life. . . . 'Great peace have they which love Thy law.' J. Edgar Hoover loved the law of his God."

But as far as the Derby crowd was concerned, the *real* news was that Al Hirt of Mardi Gras, the New Orleans spectacular, had come to Louisville for the Derby spectacular. A *Courier-Journal* cultural observer commended Al's rapport with the audience, yet wondered what had happened to the old Kentucky spirit in the last couple of years:

The spontaneity was evident when Hirt's five-piece band began a few bars of "My Old Kentucky Home." Virtually the entire audience was immediately on its feet, singing along.

The band then lapsed into "Dixie," which roused a crowd at Freedom Hall when Hirt last played here in 1970. But last night the song of the South didn't have that effect. About half the audience sat, with the rest standing a little uncertainly.

During Derby Week "half the audience" comes from the *North,* where "Dixie" could never make the Top Forty: "My Old Kentucky Home," on the other hand, was an apolitical nostalgic anthem.

Al Hirt playing the Derby prepared me for many a *déjà vu.* A person, band, float, TV cameraman, network reporter, AP writer I had seen at an earlier spectacular would turn up again, and again. The parades ultimately ran together to become one seemingly endless procession. I saw Reege, Tish, and Gav (or their bronzed equivalents) everywhere. American archetypes appeared and reappeared, too predictably stereotypical for even a comicstrip: the sentimental drunk, for instance; the trivia bore; the nostalgia noodnik; Jesus Freaks who hadn't memorized their spiel; people who bragged of how much they "smoked" or "tripped."

Images appeared, then reappeared: the tall strutting storklegged hand-on-hip drum major furred in a busby, braided all over, flashily booted. The Shirley Temple-headed drum majorette gold-and silver-sequinned, chainmailed, forever twirling with jawfixed smile and rigid pelvis. My spectaculars nightmare was the sousaphone-player, female or male, waggling a dead white ceramic horn overhead like a floating bidet. The instrument wound boa-like round the blower's Laocoön body. Marching with a sousaphone meant lots of heavy sweat, and troubled counting. And, evidently, bad eyes. Every sousaphonist seemed to be wearing wirerim glasses over a scrunched-up nose, below a worried brow. I saw this marching martyr first in Louisville, the initial of his school worn on a middy. As school succeeded school, those letters began flipping by like random flashcards. Out-of-time sousaphonists wound in an unbroken line from Louisville to Indianapolis to Miami Beach to Pasadena to New Orleans. The sousaphone flatulated against pitchedsharp trumpets, flat French horns, flatter saxes, offkey clarinets tuned to the key of selfdestruct. Simple American cacophony, amplified by unsynchronized speakers, turned into Nuremberg roar.

From coast to coast I marveled at how such bands and other marching sodalities, petty militia units, family rifle groups, drill clubs were always able, in the 1970s, to grab a much bigger chunk of a school or town budget than the local library. Each uniform cost a set of Shakespeare. The braid and flash, however, packed the somber menace of U.S.-equipped military juntas. The country's military cum militaristic posture dominated the spectaculars. Parade grand marshals, no matter what parade, were, invariably, admirals, retired admirals, generals, retired generals, Bob Hope, John Wayne, or other essences of western law and order. As the Kentucky Derby's Pegasus Parade grand marshal, Lorne Greene flashed the peace sign the length of the marching route. Greene was a staple of the pacifist Thanksgiving Day Santa Claus Parade in New York City, but his salute didn't get too much photo coverage in even so liberal a paper as the *Courier-Journal*.

For every spectacular a civilian archetype, American grotesque, male or female, turned up holding a card penciled over with "Parking," "Beds," "Box Lunch, Breakfast." Shills beckoned on every spectacular's street, waving motorists into driveways and onto lawns. On non-spectacular days these same people threatened to have children arrested for so much as a toe touch of precious bluegrass. For the day of misrule, "Keep Off the Grass" and "Trespassers Will Be Prosecuted" signs disappeared. Sodgouging widetrack deeptread steelbelted mini-earthmover wheels were solicited to come rip up a little Kentucky turf at the going rate of $10 to $15 per car. Mattress space on the floor went for $20 to $45 a night—*minimum* three nights. A lean breakfast cost five bucks, a box lunch the same. It's almost mystical, this rip-off fever, this folk instinct for the jugular lode. Dealers deal quicker, hookers trick faster, dips pick pockets more crisply. Everybody agrees: "We don't make it this week, then when?"

Spectaculars, in the spirit of the higher rip-off, suspend even the higher prejudices. Three hundred and sixtyfour days a year a community will lament the bare feet of the "hippie," but not when the "hippie" can be ripped off. *Hair,* with its "Age of Aquarius," was almost instantly turned into a marching-band hymn, or a tune scrubbed-face middleclass kids could plink out on their shiny electric guitars. *Hair,* at the Great American Spectacular, becomes just another show, like *Snow White* or *Dumbo,* and other Walt Disney halftime staples.

The Mardi Gras Parade had the usual "Great Movies" theme with one really strange float in it. The Tournament of Roses parade can afford new floats every year. Not Mardi Gras. The same floats are used year after year with paint added here and tinsel tacked up there. In 1973 somebody goofed. The fairy tale float supposed to represent Walt Disney's *Gulliver's Travels* presented Gulliver in reverse drag, stretched out, collar open to reveal two maidenly cleft breasts which, in 1972, before undergoing a sex switch, belonged to Sleeping Beauty.

Spectacular "themes" stick close to safe fairy tales and movies. Add these floats to the unbroken line of marching bands and you get the true spectaculars *gestalt,* a nightmare such as Bosch painted. All the country's halftime shows go off simultaneously—all the twirlers, highkickers, locksteppers, animal mascots, cannonshooters, pranksters, balloonreleasers, barebackriders, handstanders, trampoline tumblers, cardsection writers, honor guards, flagbearers, bandleaders, Spectacular queens, Spectacular princesses, cheerleader courts, parade marshals.

Hieronymus Bosch provides a way into the spectaculars' lower latitudes. On pageant days, the earth releases its blind, its lame, its halt. Though Bosch could see that side of the Spectacular, Breughel would see the other—its color, vitality, pattern, and, above all, variety.

2

Everybody's
Old Kentucky Home

Going from New York to Louisville was like flying to a strange country and finding it in the middle of a war. New York's images of midtown women and men are fashionably formal or fashionably casual. Women wear hats, and gloves that rarely match their shoes. Men wear their hair long, their lapels wide, and in early May wander affluent midtown in Gatsby outercoats, sheepskin, or suede.

My first sight of Louisville was nothing but brushcuts and uniforms. Every head was inclined toward the Hertz, Avis, and National counters, not, as I first imagined, because randy Vietnam returnees hadn't seen an American woman in months. These were recruits, clamoring for mere cars (in order to get back to Fort Knox before being counted AWOL). Rows of competing civilians stood tiptoe, waving tendollar bills, twenties, fifties. The accents I heard were Indiana—only a few miles away—Maine, Vermont, the deeper South, the Far West.

One drunk, in the gang rush, had been turned around a full 180 degrees. His back was to the Avis counter as his waving twenty bucks implored Kentucky to come up with a "dewlap." His forehead was flour white, his cheeks beet red; he had just left his Nebraska farm. In addition to his "Kentucky dewlap" he bawled for:

a) a car
b) a room

c) a bath
d) a woman
e) an "x-rated all-black show"

Most of the other civilians similarly waved money at the rent-a-car women, shouting like stock exchange pitmen. The Avis girls were themed up in red-and-white jockey silks and jockey caps. Around them everything was red roses. A Hertz girl gave a customer a Gulf map of Louisville: the guy left a tip of twenty bucks. That Nebraska drunk, just for being pointed in the direction of a bar ten feet in front of him, wanted to buy the Avis girl a "whole pail of dewlaps."

No cars were available. No hotel or motel rooms were available. Yet almost everyone would somehow end up sleeping somewhere Derby eve. Close to Churchill Downs, and all over Greater Louisville, not-quite-finished apartment buildings added an army surplus cot and a straight chair to a bare flat and socked it to everyone for a flat minimum of $100. People left their own apartments, or houses, in order to convert space into bucks. Cars—some with, some without, drivers—materialized. University of Louisville students told me they made several hundred dollars each day of Derby Week driving five or six people at a time in broken-down jalops. The going rate was a flat five bucks a ride. The drivers expected, and got, additional tips. During a spectacular, everybody seems anxious, even grateful, to be overcharged.

All around the airport, people turned up tagged with name cards like priceticketed window display dummies. Some were organizers, some the organized. Tour leaders, program directors, travel agents waited for new planeloads of Derby groupies to print out. Unions, sales teams, big and small business used the Derby to reward initiative, productivity, a good sales graph. Million-dollar-a-year insurance salesmen ("writers," they are called) were one class the Derby served to honor. Waiting for my rented car, I watched numbers of slightly depressed, excessively grateful insurance men arrive, uniformly collarpinned, tieclipped, nameplated, logo-tagged. But only two businesswomen. Firstnaming and other Dale Carnegie ploys began instantly. The sales stars were swiftly herded into company vans and stationwagons and packed off for the microsecond-precise scheduled spontaneity programmed to be fun.

Scattered around the airport were the slightly stoned young, barefoot, tousled, in Abercrombie & Fitch backpacks hung on Abercrombie & Fitch aluminum frames. Mother or Dad must have bought the plane tickets, which forced many a street beggar to travel first-class. Forty-buck jeans designers had skillfully faded, and just as skillfully frayed. What marked the young heirs of the very rich was their footwear. Pampered feet never learn to slum. Hundredbuck boots provided posh pedestal for the poverty pose. Even more noticeable was when the *pauvre* went barefoot, and hung the fancy leather from a ragged neck. Two months later, at McGovern headquarters, I saw the casual workshirts and denim pants again combined with topgrain hide of cow. The rich have this ultimate hold over their children: kids will give up class, religion, join communes, vow poverty, silence, chastity, nudity, yet remain fiercely loyal to leather.

When I looked outside the Louisville airport terminal, I thought I was in Fort Lauderdale. Mesomorphic jocks in safari shorts, bare chested, were doing a beer dance, surrounded by people in T-shirts advertising "Miami of Ohio," "Bowling Green," "Slippery Rock," "Jesus," and "Hair." Women in oversize college sweatshirts and short shorts showed the bare brown leg, badge of Fort Lauderdale (on a par with frisbees and Boone's Farm syrups).

The men, positively reinforced during football season to *think bodycontact,* regularly fell into a crouch, reached for the nearest woman to heft, tussle, and toss. The women held horizontal, high above some beery muscleman's head, went stiff, shouldered like an oxen yoke before being wigwagged back and forth severely. There was also a warm-up version of the Scottish sport, tossing-the-caber, in which a woman is pitched by her feet stiffly upward and forward, to be caught—most of the time—by the next aspiring tosser. During the football season women fare better; scrimmaging and ball chasing drains off unsublimated male ergs. But this was spring, in a sporting society, where one turns *to* sex for sublimation.

A rounded square of arms-linked Fort Lauderdales was doing a barefoot heelandtoe in the parkinglot as I drove off to downtown Louisville, in a gaggle of out-of-state campers. The camper was once a retired people's conveyance; in the seventies it's the hip caravan, owned by collectives, communes, gays, and straights. In New Orleans' French Quarter after a heavy rainstorm I saw *fifteen* people do a Barnum and Bailey clown exit from one mediumsize camper. Campers turned up at every spectaculars site, often the very same ones I had seen earlier. Young camper people were living my spectaculars circuit from Kentucky to Louisiana in a parody version of society's always-just-coming or always-just-going thing.

My Louisville "hotel" was an apartment building called The Adams House, converted for Derby Week full occupancy and fast turnover. Its doors were kept locked, guarded by a uniformed trooper with loaded gun. When I asked about the armor, I was told that during past Derby weeks, drunks and others had been known to rush a building and use its toilets, its towels, its beds. To get in, one had to sound one's name through a locked door and hope someone would turn up and open.

After signing in, and coughing up my hundred, I walked bellboyless to the elevator, which ultimately came down. Out stepped a beautiful black girl with blush-red cheeks (the color combination of movie Indians). Her clothes were Bergdorf expensive, salon stuff, flashy white sharkskin. With her was a tall thin paleface wearing a fedora—pinchcreased, slightly stained, perched on his head like an apple. His shirt was buttoned to the neck, he wore no tie, his eyes were slightly crossed, his tongue hung between his lips as though he had just run a fourminute mile. His arms, however, stayed at his sides, recruit-rigid. The elevator door slid fully open, he slowmarched out straight ahead, aimed by his womanfriend at the front door the understanding trooper unlocked quickly. The woman hurried to a waiting car, and drove off. Out in the bright sun, the guy leftrighted it up to the sidewalk, marked time, then made a sharp left onthedouble, and marched off.

During the next forty-eight hours I spent most of my time at Churchill Downs, yet saw that same girl go up with a redfaced sailor whose knuckles cracked in hillbilly-band spoons rhythm; I saw her next with an elderly gentleman who smiled beatifically, fit for El Greco. The woman was always cheerful, always fresh, always stylish. I saw her go up or come down with six or seven other males, and once—a score for the equal rights amendment—she cuddled an attractive blonde woman.

The guiding principle of the spectaculars I first heard enunciated at the Indianapolis "500" by a woman responding to her huckster husband's question about a plastic trinket's price:

"Hit him, Johnnie," she said, "there's no tomorrow."

The night before the Kentucky Derby I was supposed to meet Ron Turcotte, Riva Ridge's jockey, and some New York Racing Commission people, but in the jam of traffic and communication we never made contact. I traced Turcotte to a restaurant, called him; the hostess said she would page him, forgot, and left the phone off the hook. I again heard the characteristic sounds of the spectaculars—clamoring, begging, threatening, bribing, hollering offers to the maître d' of twenty, thirty, fifty bucks if he came up with a table now.

When, the next morning, I went to the Churchill Downs jockey room to find Turcotte, I walked in on what looked like a production of *Little Men*. Everyone stood about five feet high, some an inch less, some inches more, many with George Raft sharplyparted hair, sharplycut dark sideburns, a few with afros. A couple of tousled lighthaired guys like Turcotte looked out of place in the room.

In the heat of day, these small grown men wore bathrobes, like movie extras in hopes of a call. Or stretchy T-shirts, like kitchen boys trying to *avoid* a call. Their pants, though, were uniformly white, shiny, plastic, and their boots, black or dark brown, had the tops cuffed over. On the wall pegs and in valet rooms, jockey silks showed in profusion. It was a Dufy scene. Apart from crash helmets, jockeys in the 1970s dressed much like jockeys of the late nineteenth century.

The small men moved in and out of showers, in and out of sweatboxes. No jockey could pass a scale without stepping on. On his way to take a phone call a jockey would weigh himself, and, coming back, weigh himself again. The unlucky jockeys who read heavy news on the scales sipped black coffee and stared sullenly at their metabolically blessed brothers chomping on thick hamburgers. The clerk of scales, the jockeys' herdboss, an ordinary-sized man, stood above the jockeys like Gulliver among the Lilliputians.

In 1972 some of racing's most colorful jockeys weren't riding in the Derby: Willie Shoemaker, Braulio Baeza, Angel Cordero, Jr., Lafitte Pincay, Jr., Jacinto Vasquez, Jorge Velasquez. Their absence meant the sixteen-horse field contained only four or five colts with either the record and/or the breeding to go in a Derby. The rest didn't merit expensive name jockeys.

The jockeys at Churchill Downs were the central figures in the Kentucky Derby spectacular for about two hours. The race itself was only one small part of the spectaculars complex I began to recognize in Louisville. The spectaculars syndrome, the spectaculars model, the spectaculars formula has to be described part by part.

3

The Formula

I. THE FESTIVAL

The Kentucky Derby Festival, which led up to the big race, had been going on since the fourth week in April. The Festival brochure said, rather proudly, that "what began as just a parade in 1956 has grown into a ten day celebration climaxed, of course, by the running of the world's most famous racing spectacular—The Kentucky Derby."

The Festival featured, among other things:

1. An Air Show (sponsored by the low-flying Yellow Cab Company of Louisville)

2. A middlelowbrow unrock concert, starring Roger Miller (still "King of the Road" to the Festival PR people)

3. A "Welcome Wagon Boat Cruise" for nostalgics, at $10 a couple, on the *Belle of Louisville*

4. The Great Steamboat Race between the *Belle* and the *Delta Queen of Cincinnati,* this at twenty-five dollars per couple.

With cigarette advertising cut out of television, Philip Morris, and Marlboro (its bestselling label), moved in wherever the masses gathered. Philip Morris presented Roger Miller free; Marlboro sponsored a three-dollar "chuckwagon breakfast" which added southern grits to the usual western offering of flapjacks, eggs, bacon, sausage, ham. These Festival events were open to the public, but the calendar also listed events with admission "By Invitation," foremost among these the Derby Festival Queen's Coronation Ball (sponsored by a women's charitable organization called "The Fillies"). Not listed at all were the Derby society parties, the Kentucky equivalent of the before and after New York Opera parties.

A couple of other affairs were designated "By Invitation," a Knights of Columbus Derby Dinner and "Ad Club Day at the Races," sponsored by the Advertising Club of Louisville through its special men's group called "The Thorobreds." More socially and politically significant were two events sponsored by the powerful Kentucky Colonels organization; "By Invitation" one could get to their dinner on Derby eve, or to their daylong barbecue the Sunday after the race.

The year 1972 was not a good one for the Kentucky Colonels. The organization had issued an invitation through the new Kentucky governor, Wendell H. Ford, to Senator Ed Muskie when polls showed Muskie leading not only his Democratic rivals but the incumbent, Richard M. Nixon. Then some of Mr. Nixon's friends went to work on Muskie. By May "dirty tricks" had wiped out Senator Muskie, but Wendell Ford's, and the Colonels', invitation was not withdrawn.

I remembered a similar incident at Williams College: Williams' president, Jim Baxter, had pulled off a brilliant coup, he thought, by getting an early commitment from Thomas E. Dewey, the guaranteed next President of the United States, to be the college's 1949 commencement speaker. But the Senator Muskie who arrived in Louisville hadn't even made it into the finals.

Muskie wasn't the Colonels' only unfortunate pick: for some reason the organization had decided to present Danny Thomas as their featured entertainer. Thomas's success was roughly equal to Muskie's, or so the *Courier-Journal* report of the Colonels' dinner seemed to suggest:

> An impassioned plea for American patriotism was made in Louisville last night by entertainer Danny Thomas, who, after delivering jokes tirelessly for about 30 minutes, brought some 750 persons to their feet at Convention Center to sing, "America the Beautiful."

The reporter couldn't completely hide her own (or the affair's) general depression and gamely assured her readers that "the evening wasn't all one of sober considerations."

II. SOCIETY

The year's most stylish social shut-out, the kind of thing F. Scott Fitzgerald might have considered too improbable as fiction, was scored by the C. V. Whitneys, who chose as their guest-of-Derby-Week one of New York's then Beautiful People, Marion Javits (who brought along her Senator husband, Jacob). Only one social element was seemingly barred from the Whitney party, or, at best, sparsely represented—Kentucky locals. The Whitneys were hosting a huge Derby party at Churchill Downs race day, but gave their exclusive society party in Lexington, on their horse farm, not walking distance from Churchill Downs. To make sure the party would stay exclusive, the Whitneys flew their guests in on the Whitney family jet, just as, in earlier days, the stately manse on the east or west bank of the Hudson River used trains to haul in socially registered houseguests.

Starred along with Marion Javits was C. V. Whitney's cousin, Joan—the late Mrs. Charles S. Payson—then owner of New York's baseball Mets. Mrs. Payson, an operalover as well as a society superstar, had given her Mets the very best New York social name. Baseball was Mrs. Payson's third-best charity. She owned the Greentree Farm Stable in her cousin C.V.'s Lexington.

The Whitneys had that grand society talent for converting any turf into one's own. Lexington, Kentucky, soon resembled a floating chunk of New York's Sutton Place. Mrs. C. V. Whitney made one quiet concession to Kentucky, however: her menu listed a regional favorite, Kentucky corn grits soufflé.

Her party was an updated Jay Gatsby dream, with 112 guests seated in the Whitneys' atrium and a smaller table of twenty set up on the bridge over the Whitneys' not-in-use swimmingpool. For her spring party motif, Mrs. Whitney creatively chose an artificial-bird theme. Every table had its own stuffed cardinals, American goldfinches, doves, and/or owls motionlessly perched alongside tall cages filled with real, not artificial, flowers. In case any of the guests retained a little Zelda Fitzgerald zip and might want to dive into the family swimmingpool, Mrs. Whitney offered discouragement in the form of floating swans made of pristinely white mums and Christmas-y twinklelights. A cheery yellow-and-white marquee decorated with wisteria-covered arbors, weepingwillow trees, and little house plants connected Mrs. Whitney's atrium (where Cliff Hall's Palm Beach orchestra made socially proper Meyer Davis-Lester Lanin sounds) to a vista of Kentucky bluegrass.

To make certain that people who weren't invited would know they weren't invited, Eugenia Sheppard, the society columnist, was invited to write about who was invited. Mrs. Whitney herself got home just in time for the Derby, it seems, by interrupting her Tour season in Spain, where she, and equally committed friends, were reconstructing a walled medieval city. This meant buying up decayed houses and, with the help of the director of the Prado, restoring them. The walled city was close to a modern city, which had been given the name of Generalissimo Franco's greatest admirer, Trujillo. Mrs. Whitney in a pre-party interview explained that the only obstacle to the old walled city becoming itself a kind of Prado was "what we might call squatters in this country, who live among the ruins." She evidently hadn't yet heard of the original Trujillo's solution to squatters in Dominican Republic slums: warnings, bulldozers, and dynamite.

Derby Day everyone, not just Mrs. Whitney, seemed to be having a party. Hippies, jocks, holy rollers, hookers, Kentucky Colonels, admen, sodalities, sororities, fraternities. Breakfast parties began early. Governor Ford himself invited about a thousand guests, who had to eat in four separate shifts. Breakfast organized social clusters which remained together the rest of the day, turning into lunch parties, picnics, dinner parties. Clubhouse tables were booked years ahead, or, for some, like the Whitneys, were considered lifetime commitments. A "good table" at Churchill Downs was another register of someone's social Dow Jones.

Infield parties, too, were well organized. At Epsom Downs for The Derby, the crowd seemed to consist of village friends, pub

friends, and, more common, families. In Kentucky, blankets
spread under fraternity and sorority banners recreated for the
Derby a spirit of clubby Panhellenic close-out to demonstrate that
the American campus was still safe from democracy.

III.   THE MEDIA

Up in the press box, some of the old Derby hands had already
blocked out their stories. They allowed for chance, should chance
in some way affect the Derby running. The set story ran something
like this:

> *Before a* [huge   disappointing   sparse
>   amazed   silent   stunned   roaring
>   dumb   astonished]
> *crowd of over 125,000* [Riva Ridge   Freetex
>   Hold Your Peace   No Le Hace]
> *owned by* [Meadow Stable   Middletown Stable
>   Maribel G Blum   J R Straus]
> *won* [going away   in a thrilling stretch duel
>   by a whisker   by a nose   by a neck
>   by twenty lengths   coming from behind
>   as he pleased   coming through on the far outside
>   sneaking through on the rail]
> *paying* [get mutuels off mimeo track chart].
>   *Said jockey* [Ron Turcotte   Chuck Baltazar
>   Carlos Marquez   Phil Rubbico]
> *my* [colt   horse   gelding   mount   bay   chestnut]
> *run* [pretty good   like lightning   like the wind
>   his own race   just like the trainer told me]
> *and had* [plenny left   nothin' left   lotsa daylight
>   just enough racing room].
> *Our strategy was to* [save ground till the speed
>   come back to me   break on
>   top and steal it].
> *The track was* [slow near the rail   fast in the middle
>   lightnin' on the outside].

My colt's the best three-year-old since   [Citation
                                               Nashua
                                               Native Dancer
                                               Man o' War
                                               Rin Tin Tin].

One turfwriter had prepared *five* possible leads the night before the race. The fact that one horse was favored over the rest of the field—Riva Ridge at overnight odds of 8–5—perhaps suggested this pre-write. The writer told me, however, that he never went to a race without his leads already written. Horses, he said, do one of five things 99% of the time. In rare instances a favorite may stumble and throw its jockey. Such acts of God deserved a fresh writing. He assured me that with only a touch-up here and there his prewritten models were what he almost always filed. He used the time saved, he said, at the bar.

IV. THE SCENE

In May, morning shadows are sharp black cut-outs. A lover of shadows like the blind writer Borges, were he still able to see, could have spent Derby Day watching the brightly striped milepole's shadow. It shortened till noon, acting as a sundial.

A gray haze then hung in the sky; the infield's deepspring green shone in contrast. That infield was mini-Epsom, lacking only Epsom's midway rides. A rock band up on a small infield platform seemed as isolated as a circus sideshow. Singers gyrated, the band grooved, but nobody was watching.

Children made red, green, black, yellow disks and dots on the infield green. Closer to the rail, bandmembers of various Louisville high schools lolled on the grass. Fairfield Senior High had placed its bright red school flags on the hedges; they looked like the U.S.S.R.'s.

That spring of '72, a huge security detail manned the roofs above the infield. Soldiers, national guardsmen, local police, track securitymen seemed everywhere. Less obvious were civilians in CIA shades and FBI double-o glasses. Olive drab contrasted with the crowd's primary colors. Did Churchill Downs expect a black-white riot? An antiwar demonstration? A Fort Lauderdale orgy? Armed, uniformed men represented one half of an American allegory, halfnaked young people in the infield represented the other half, those all-but-disappeared flower people who had vanished into commune or collective hills and ravines.

As the afternoon advanced, picnics ended, the bands put their uniforms back on, the pompom girls stretched and primped. Chaperoning parents, who had been serving food, left. Instruments tuned with riffs, fanfares, jazz bursts. Once up, everybody was ready to go. The all-white Fairfield High band and pompom girls lined up next to the all-black band from Male High, who were next to a slightly "mixed" band from Thomas Jefferson High. The long, thin Male High drum major was stylishly dégagé in a white beret and gold vest: his lead drummer wore his hair in a wild afro and covered his eyes with applegreen put-on bubble sunglasses.

In the infield six or seven kids rotating on a blanket salaamed faster and faster. Communal joints were passed. Those who dragged deepest fell back zonked-out, prone. Others who seemed to have been tripping would presumably see a Derby for pterodactyls. Veteran dealers kept their backs to the roofed soldiery and peddled pills and pot like popcorn. The counterculture did its thing eye-level with the Silent Majority. Sororities and fraternities entertained the odd smoker, but, on the whole, loyal to America, featured Fort Lauderdale jocks loudly baying for beer.

V. FRANCHISES

Looking at the band, the pompom girls, the trippers, the smokers, the beerguzzlers, the Boone's Farm drunkards, I thought of the 1970s word which covered them all, *franchise*. I was in Colonel Sanders country; Kentucky had sent out fried chicken franchises to multiply and prosper. Franchising was the American landscape's Act of Uniformity. The buildings and merchandise were always the same. Employees were interchangeable. A uniform McDonald's, Midas Mufflers, Howard Johnson's were independent of regional American uniqueness.

Not only food but fun was franchised and programmed. The Derby parade, the Indianapolis "500" parade, the Rose Bowl parade, the Mardi Gras parade were almost totally franchised. Music came out of Central Arranging; so did marching-band strategies—wheeling, sleeving, weaving, reversing. Descriptions were franchised. Themes were franchised. What the Beatles did in the early 1960s, once commercially co-opted, became franchised Arthur Fiedler Boston Pops and marching-band arrangements.

Franchising is best explained by a formula: in areas of North America that have never seen a Mexican, for example, a taco franchise will be bought by someone who has never tasted a tostada, an enchilada, a tamale, a taco, or even a refried bean. The franchisee is sent a scale, a ton of ingredients, and a sheet, with instructions to take a tortilla out of a can (luckily labeled "tortilla"), heat it this number of minutes, add one-half ounce meat from the can labeled "meat," one-half ounce cheese from the package labeled "cheese," etc. *Franchising* does the same for marching bands, sousaphonists, drum majors, pompom girls. A Norman Vincent Peale franchising service distributes sheets of nondenominational or varidenominational sermons.

The franchised instruction sheet for marching bands says take about thirty drummers, add about thirty trumpets, twenty trombones, twenty clarinets, twenty saxophones, ten tubas, six sousaphones, four glockenspiels, four cymbalists, one drum major, and—pouf!—tacos.

The Fairfield High girls at the Derby used a few audibles to keep their plays together; the formula said onetwothree bump (chastely), onetwothree grind (chastely), grin, anklediddle to the left, anklediddle to the right, turn in chaste cancan, flash panties, face around, show teeth as if for a chewing-gum commercial. In their franchised patriotic climax, the girls unfurled a fortyfoot flag.

Almost out of sight, in the backstretch, grooms and exercise boys led horses out for the pre-Derby races. Curried colts and fillies reared in track dirt. Some, in a sweat, seemed stained, dark, shining. Without numbers to mark them, without differentiating racing colors, or jockeys, the horses seemed pastoral, ahistorical in the surrounding track dirt and green.

Around the stables, nothing was plastic or franchised. Real

horses switched real tails at real flies. Horses stretched, stood still, or nibbled real grass. At dawn, waking horses whinnied as if Derby Day were a first under the sun. In the middle of programmed Festival fun and social hype, the horses, and the men and women around them, stood their ground, asserting the primary, the actual, the real.

VI. PASTIMES

Looking at the Fort Lauderdale jocks now flopped out on their groundsheets, zonked, or feigning, I thought of Breughel's "Land of Cockayne," in which a spreadeagled scholar with swollen cod-piece stares up at the sky; a farmer, his flail pitched aside, is sleeping; a knight has dropped his lance, and his Sancho Panza. A pig moves with a knife threaded through its hide, as if someone fell asleep in mid-skinning. Something more than theme or moral is on Breughel's canvas—gesture, with shape, color, is humanly there. So it was in Louisville. The unspontaneous, the lax, the boring together became something different. The bands, the Fort Lauderdales, the Hare Krishnaites and Jesus people picking their way among the fallen Derby revelers, the hip and the square created an infield of games, circuses, and pastimes. Sober John Milton digressed from epic theology to describe bad angels playing at ordinary human games. Froissart interrupted a serious allegory to detail the sixty games he used to play as a child in Valenciennes. Breughel's "Children's Games" is an acting-out catalogue of pastimes; and Rabelais, as part of Gargantua's growing-up, lists 217 games he could play. Watching the Derby, the Indianapolis "500," the Flamingo Park and Convention Center games in Miami Beach, watching the Rose Bowl and Mardi Gras, I changed my attitude toward pastimes. I began to understand how important they were for sustaining *life*. Man, I began to see, lives not by bread alone; humankind also lives by circuses.

Rabelais has Gargantua play his medieval and Renaissance games—almost all of which, I realized, I was seeing, in modern form, on the Derby's infield green—and later, in Indianapolis, Miami Beach, Pasadena, New Orleans. Almost anyone can translate Rabelais' games into what she or he plays, played, or has seen played:

At the beast
At trump
At the fib
At the ivory bundles
At the tarot
At the torture
At the handcuff
At love
At chess
At the lottery
At the dice
At the chance
At the lurch
At even and odd
At bob and hit
At pull yet a little
At trudge-pig
At pinch without laughing
At prickle me tickle me
At rill madam, or grapple my lady
At belly to belly
At the quoits
At tip and hurle
At the veere and tourn
At hide and seek
At whip top
At I take you napping
At bum to buss or nose in breech
At swagay, waggy, or shoggyshou
At blindman buff
At cricket
At the pounding stick
At jack and the box
At knock-pate
At the crane dance
At bobbing, or the flirt on the nose

In the stands and in the various spectacular site infields the recognizable games analogous to Gargantua's were:

> Piggy-back
> Various card games
> Can-you-top-this
> Pick-up-sticks
> Chess and checkers
> Dice
> Numbers
> Buck-buck-how-many-fingers-up
> Odd-and-even
> Shadow boxing
> Tug of war
> Tickle-me-you-can't-make-me-laugh
> The Fort Lauderdale woman hoist
> Chesting, blocking, belly banging
> Hide-and-seek
> Spin-the-top
> Pretend-you're-sleeping
> Blindman's buff
> Tag
> Kick-the-can
> Catch ball
> Fly kite
> Float frisbee
> Nudge, pinch, jab, trip, up-end, wrestle, pound
> Jam-the-hat-over-the-eyes
> Pull-out-the-tie
> Pull-out-the-shirt-tails
> Truss-the-head-in-the-wearer's-sweatshirt
> Rip button
> Zip-down-the-fly.

In the Kentucky Derby infield I was reminded many times of Gargantua, who, when he had "well played, shuffled, clogged, and thrown away his time, . . . thought fit to drink a little . . . and stretch . . . and . . . sleep. . . ."

VII.   THE EVENT

In the clubhouse and press area the serious pastime was drinking. The infield was deeded watery juleps and Boone's Farm wine; classic drinkers were on pure Bourbon and branch water. One guy, an unsouthern Montrealer, was a sobbing Bourbon drunk three hours before the race.

"Man," he announced to the press box, "it's beautiful Mickey Mouse—in the world's entire history I give you twenty to one there's never been anything more pure Mickey Mouse. I love it. I love it—I go straight home every year and tell my little old mother how everybody cries singing 'Kentucky Home,' and *she* cries. Fourteen years. Everytime I swear it's going to be my everlovin' last, but man, when they play that 'My Old Kentucky Home,' I'm up on my feet, crying *and* singing."

As the day warmed, spaced-out smokers frazzled beside fraternity-sorority folk loudly harmonizing Glenn Miller nostalgics in an infield overwhelmingly white. Blacks for the most part clustered together near the fence around the parking lot, as if that space, assigned to them years ago, had been little affected by court decisions. A few small dice games were in progress. Younger kids were having fun pitching nickels close to a wall.

In Louisville, in Indianapolis, in Pasadena, side-betting for nickels, dimes, and dollars livens a spectacular. Pools are big. Amounts bet can run from a dime to several hundred or even thousand dollars. The exact order of finish—three horses, four, the entire field—was the basis of one kind of Derby pool; there was in-betting based on the winning horse's two furlong, four furlong, six furlong, etc. fractions with penalty points assigned to each missed one fifth of a second. Time pools at Indianapolis, on the other hand, were based on the first ten finishers estimated to the 1/1,000th of a second. Huge Rose Bowl pools fixed on the exact time of the first touchdown, of the last touchdown, and on the usual pool matters—total score, exact score, and variations.

Compared to what was happening on the Derby tote board, Churchill Downs pool betting was paltry. One can roughly estimate the handle of a good American track on a stakes day by multiplying the attendance by $100–$130. The Derby, which has the heaviest total betting action of any race in the country, doesn't come close to the expected figure (multiplying its "estimated" attendance by, say, $100). Obviously, then, the Derby attracts at least 40,000 to 50,000 token bettors, and people who don't bet at all. The Derby, unlike other "big" horse races, is heavily attended by people who just want to be there, don't want to bet, and have little interest in any specific horse winning. The low per capita betting figure of around sixty dollars a head also indicates that the Derby attracts a far younger *and* far older crowd than most other American stakes races. The very young and very old don't go in much for betting. The Belmont Stakes, which has been run longer, and is better situated (fifteen miles out of Manhattan, and on the edge of Long Island's heavily populated Nassau County), has never come closer than a distant second to the Derby attendance in recent years. Its best attendance figure is always 40,000–60,000 shy of the Derby's; yet its betting, working out to the predicted multiple of $100–$130 per patron, falls only a few hundred thousand shy of the Derby record.

At five o'clock, half an hour before the big race, that Derby betting action became very heavy. Riva Ridge, 8–5 on the morning line, went down, then up, never higher than 2–1. Hold Your Peace was next at 7–2, No Le Hace right behind at 4–1: the "field" lumping was fourth at 8–1—mostly because Canonero II, a 1971 "field" entry, had won the Derby at $19.40 for every two-dollar bet.

Just after five, sun broke through the haze, penetrating the mists over distant hedges. Afternoon shadows stretched long, thin, dark. The crowd below the press box moved closer to the rail. Infield lollers woke or were poked awake. Goodnatured shoving and squirming followed at the infield fences.

Churchill Downs looked like an early nineteenth-century tinted etching of itself. The track outriders in their red coats were picture-card Dickens. The outrider horses, dark and stifflegged, looked oversized, formal, not of this time.

Kentucky's breeding farms add significance to Churchill Downs and the Derby. As much as the Keeneland Yearling Sales and the

August auctions at Saratoga, Derby time generates spring horse talk, offers to sell, promises to come see. Breeding farms are located on the edges of Churchill Downs. When one looks out from a beautiful plant like New York's Belmont Park, one sees what Aubrey Beardsley called America's "beautiful dreck"—suburban schlock guaranteed to obliterate the pastoral. New York's Aqueduct overlooks JFK Airport, and shares JFK's screeching flight pattern. Every other American track suffers airplanes, but Aqueduct is constantly under the shadow of massive jets. Churchill Downs is near an airport and part of a city, but seems only an extension of open grass country.

Its pastoral setting is perfect for the Derby's secondary role as the American horsebreeder's spectacular. The list of Derby winners is dominated by horses bred in Kentucky, not very far from Churchill Downs. So, too, for other unrestricted major stakes: the Preakness, for instance, and the Belmont. Riva Ridge, 1972's favorite, was bred in Kentucky by Meadow Farms, Christopher Chenery's stable (in 1972, and after, managed by his daughter, Penny Tweedy).

Mrs. Tweedy entered her box early, shortly after five, when $463,000 had already been bet on Riva Ridge's nose, and the Montreal guy was well into his third Bourbon hour.

"Listen," he shouted to nobody in particular, "get ready. When they play 'My Ol' Kentucky Home' every one of you cynical son-of-a-bitches is going to feel your spine turn into an icicle."

In the infield the Fairfield High pompom girls raised their chins in a grand chesty uplift show. Mrs. Tweedy, watching them, seemed cool. Her dress was Meadow Stable's racing blue and silver-white, in polkadot compared with her jockey's checkerboard pattern.

All over the infield the barechested and barebacked were having blobs of white Noxzema applied to inflamed sunburnt places. Out cold on blankets and groundsheets, some celebrants would clearly not make it up to watch this Derby. Kids climbed on parental shoulders. A few little children were held on stepladders. A peculiar pre-rain stillness settled over the crowd. The quiet was broken only by the urgent last-minute cry, "Juleps, full-up!"

Owners left their boxes for the saddling-up ritual in the paddock. Little Lucien Laurin, Meadow Stable's trainer, was adjusting Riva Ridge's cinch strap and giving jockey Ron Turcotte last-minute orders. Bending forward, clasping fingers, cupping, he gave Turcotte an easy leg-up into the saddle.

When the first fanfare blew for the horses to come onto the track, $2,700,000 had been bet on the Derby, over half a million of that on Riva Ridge to win.

The National Anthem was played, with singing quite restrained, but the first note of "My Old Kentucky Home" sent a roar over the stands and infield. A national ritual was being observed, and celebrated.

As the horses moved on to the track, Mrs. Tweedy hurried back to her box, smiled at several nearby people who waved a good luck wish her way. Having a horse in the Derby is an achievement all by itself. Many horse owners and breeders never come up with a contending horse to run in the Derby. Bad luck eliminated Hoist the Flag, one of the most promising two-year-olds in recent racing history (who broke a leg but wasn't destroyed because of his stud value). Hoist the Flag would have been a Derby favorite; another contender slow to mature, Key to the Mint, the Rokeby Stable's Three-Year-Old-of-the-Year in 1972, just couldn't train up for the 1972 Kentucky Derby.

In the middle of the field, slowly parading, was Mrs. Tweedy's Riva Ridge (named after an Italian World War II campaign in which her husband, John Tweedy, had fought). On Riva Ridge's saddlecloth was a lucky devil's red "7," his program number for the Derby. Ron Turcotte sat quite still, calmly talking to George Davis, the Meadow Stable lead rider. When Davis finally let go, Riva Ridge eased into a canter, loping, then changed to what track charts call "breezing." Turcotte separated Riva Ridge from the rest of the field, slowing down, then walking this smallish dark horse that Mrs. Tweedy called "funny ears" (unlike her huge handsome charismatic Secretariat, Riva Ridge's younger stablemate, who, at this point in 1972, had not raced).

Unhurried, Turcotte headed toward the starting gate, his blue and white silks sparkling against the far green hedges. Turcotte had been first in the 1965 Preakness on Tom Rolfe for his only win in Triple Crown racing. Turcotte had made his commitment to

Riva Ridge early—a whole year earlier—on a day when his most successful mount up to that point, Shuvee, was running her last race. Mike Freeman, Shuvee's trainer, who had called Shuvee "Ron's horse," understood Turcotte choosing Riva Ridge: Turcotte's eye, in 1971, was already on the 1972 Kentucky Derby.

Several months before the Derby, in the Everglades, Riva Ridge, outrun at the start, and bounced around, lost. Turcotte wasn't going to let that happen again. The moment the field broke out of the gate he raced Riva Ridge hard to the first turn, then dropped in on the rail a length and a half in front. Turcotte's hands were down low, a sign his horse was running easy. Raised up out of the saddle, head up, Turcotte seemed to be measuring the distance between Riva Ridge and the second horse, Hold Your Peace, as if he wanted the solid safety of that intervening space. Once Hold Your Peace feinted a run at Riva Ridge, but Turcotte wasn't buying. Again Hold Your Peace spurted, and still Turcotte held his easy pace.

The third motion was for real: Hold Your Peace made its move; Turcotte looked back, tightened his reins, and Riva Ridge responded with a rush. As the racing charts would sum it up, Hold Your Peace was quickly "disposed of." In the stretch, No Le Hace skidded into contention like a little kid chasing a missed bus. By the time No Le Hace righted himself, Riva Ridge was winner. Mrs. Tweedy was up and cheering, hugging elfin Laurin, a man who would be perfectly cast as a pixie uncle in a French-Canadian TV series.

Winners sparkle on the tip of an iceberg, losers glubglub in the murky deathclimes below: Ron Turcotte, with Riva Ridge's win, began an incredible string of Triple Crown victories—winning five of a possible six races, all for Mrs. Tweedy and Lucien Laurin. Mrs. Tweedy, by winning the 1972 Derby, turned the fortunes of Meadow Stable right around. In 1971 and early 1972, Meadow Stable was having financial problems: Upper Case, Riva Ridge, and, of course, the 1973 Triple Crown winner, Secretariat, changed everything. Secretariat was syndicated out for $6,080,000. Her 1972 Derby winner, Riva Ridge, was syndicated for $3,000,000— this in addition to their purse earnings.

The Churchill Downs pressroom the moment Riva Ridge won

looked like party headquarters for a victorious political candidate. Reporters crowded the podium set up for Mrs. Tweedy. Lucien Laurin joined her, and, eventually, a freshly showered, dressed-up Ron Turcotte. Post-race press conferences, like a Boston Pops summer concert, are quite predictable. This one included the following questions:

> Q. [to someone who has just won the Kentucky Derby for the first time] Is this your biggest thrill in racing?
> Q. At any point in the race did you think your horse might not make it?
> Q. Is this the best horse you have ever owned?

Mrs. Tweedy, smiling widely and waving a silver stirrup cup, reminded everyone that some reporters had suggested she run Upper Case, who had won the Wood Memorial in New York, and not Riva Ridge, in the Derby. Others had suggested she run them both.

"I guess that settles," said Mrs. Tweedy, hoisting her stirrup cup, "the question of whether we had the wrong horse in the race."

The press gang cheered.

After Mrs. Tweedy answered the usual questions, Lucien Laurin stepped up. The contrast between him and Mrs. Tweedy pointed up the social meaning of the Derby spectacular. Penny Tweedy belonged to the clubhouse and trustees' world—the society circuit; Lucien Laurin was part of the backstretch world.

A few weeks later, when I was in Baltimore for the Preakness and talking with Elliott Burch, trainer for Rokeby Stable, owned by multimillionaire socialite Paul Mellon, a reporter interrupted to ask Burch, "How does Mellon feel about Key to the Mint?"

"*Mister* Mellon," Burch said—I think the put-down word for his tone is "icily."

If trainers were not the social equals of owners, then neither were newspaperpeople. During the big race, or other sporting event, class striations may be ignored—temporarily. It's all democratic. But just as the Met and Saratoga are class segregated, so, too, the Derby. Owners and socialites generally are allowed twenty-four hours to mingle with those out there. The model observed at the Kentucky Derby travels all over the country—upper-class, middleclass, steerage—a great land ship temporarily touched down at a spectacular, but, in essence, a vestige of those luxury liners which carried America's class structure intact from social New York to social Europe, and back.

Two weeks later, during the Preakness, in Baltimore, the social compact was the same one observed in Louisville and New York. Here were the jockeys, trainers, backstretch workers, differentiated from one another only by success—i.e. money. The jockeys drove Mercedes or Cadillacs, Lincolns, Imperials, and the successful trainers, for the most part, did, too. The odd jock or trainer even went in for the Bentley or Rolls-Royce, in imitation of their social betters, the owners.

But no jockey or trainer in 1972 imagined that owning a Bentley and dressing in Saville Row clothes opened the way into society—old or new. That kind of social breakthrough might have been possible—or imagined possible—in Fitzgerald's day. Post-race parties in Baltimore were as exclusive as the C. V. Whitney Lexington party. The New York–Boston–St. Paul rule of "one's own kind *only*" was observed.

The Preakness—unintentionally, I know—pointed up the success of the Kentucky Derby as racing's number one spectacular. Baltimore's a big city, Washington and Philadelphia aren't that far away, nor, for that matter, is New York City, and yet the Preakness didn't even approach the Derby's attendance (or its betting handle). Key to the Mint added class absent in the Derby field. Riva Ridge was now interesting as a possible Triple Crown winner. Yet Pimlico race track on an admittedly unpleasant wet gray day could only come up with an attendance announced as 48,000 (and which, to me, looked lighter than 35,000). The contrast with the Derby's 130,000 plus was startling.

At the pre-race party a sheltered-indoors Mrs. Tweedy was gay and confident; outside rain was falling. By eight in the evening Baltimore was covered in mist; midnight, the air was thick, liquid. The track was pocked with pools and ponds. By noon the track was officially rated "sloppy." Nobody wanted to use nasty but more accurate words like "emulsive," "soupy," or "oozy." Pimlico on Preakness Day would have been a great setting for a film on Napoleon's retreat from Moscow.

By post-time for the first race the infield looked deserted, as though the track were officially dark for the day. A few stubborn people huddled under umbrellas, hunched up in raincoats. It was cold and nasty. A rock group boogied on a tiny infield stage. Any comparison with Louisville was uncompromisingly invidious. The track turned to a brown gunk, like soggy toffee. After the first race several people tried to ignore the track footing and cross over to the infield. One man found his shoe firmly stuck in the watery muck, hopped free (like John of the nursery rhyme) and perched like a stork, waiting for rescue. A rubberbooted attendant slogged in, freed the lost shoe bearded with mud. A few gallants, instead of spreading their coats uselessly on the mucky water, grabbed up stranded women, who with a sudden flash of thigh broke Pimlico's cast of solid gray.

Between races the track's outriders on their dripping wet horses splashed around the track spraying water like rain. The rail position, sometimes preferred under sloppy track conditions, rippled in the wind like a shallow canal. On the far outside, rain welled up dangerous pools.

Just before the Preakness, a horse called Smokey Johnny, cutting in to that usually drier rail spot, skidded suddenly, was pulled up, skidded again, slamming into the rail, throwing its rider and snapping its foreleg. It loosed a shrieking cry high above the shocked crowd's groan. Its rider had been thrown free, and was unhurt. The horse stood motionless, the rain still falling. Its foreleg dangled, swaying slightly, twitching out of control. A horse ambulance churned up through the mud; track attendants gently tried to load the horse aboard. Pain made the horse scream out again, louder, a terrifying cry that hung in the air over the horses coming out on the track for the Preakness. A local horse, Bee Bee Bee, a long shot ridden by a small-time jockey familiar with Pimlico mud, beat Riva Ridge, beat Key to the Mint, beat 'em all. Mrs. Tweedy's dream of a 1972 Triple Crown was over.

Rain only partly explained why the Kentucky Derby overshadowed the Preakness *and* the Belmont Stakes. When I got on an Amtrak Metroliner in New York's Penn Station to go to

Baltimore, the contrast between the Preakness and the Derby was instantly apparent. No lines in New York, no excited talk about "the race." My car wasn't even full. A husband and wife, unconcerned about the Preakness, were trying to follow a Mets baseball game on a transistor with lousy batteries.

The first real race talk I heard was from an eighty-year-old gent I had somehow missed meeting in Louisville. The old turfwriter was full of racing tales about "niggers" and "guineas."

The Kentucky Derby was clearly in a class by itself, and, from all indications, pretty sure to remain so. Years of studying the Derby's success formula had not produced for any other larger, wealthier track a racing spectacular to threaten the Derby.

Three Saturdays after the Preakness, as I watched Riva Ridge win the Belmont Stakes in New York, the New York Mets were at home in Shea Stadium, and drew a crowd as large as Belmont's. Macy's and Gimbel's each probably had as many horseplayers in their respective stores as turned up for the Belmont. Belmont had its own "Sidewalks of New York" signature to put up against "My Old Kentucky Home," but otherwise didn't make it. New York was perhaps just too cool for a sports spectacular.

In Kentucky the Derby is *the* Day of the year, but in New York the Belmont Stakes is just another Saturday stakes race on the New York Racing Association calendar. In a year when a horse has won the Derby and the Preakness and a Triple Crown is possible, the Belmont picks up added interest. In 1973, with Secretariat running and winning the Triple Crown, interest could not have been higher. Yet compare Riva Ridge's or Secretariat's Kentucky Derby with Secretariat's Triple Crown-winning Belmont Stakes *as a spectacular* and the Derby in both years comes out far ahead. The Belmont Stakes that Secretariat won was the most dramatic race I have ever seen; Riva Ridge's Derby win was fairly ordinary. The one and only great American racing spectacular quite obviously was the Kentucky Derby.

In the year I saw Riva Ridge's winning Derby and Belmont (and losing Preakness), I watched the filly Triple Crown (the Acorn, Mother Goose, and Coaching Club American Oaks run in New York), the Wood Memorial, the Suburban, the Jockey Club Gold Cup, all, again, run in New York. I attended the 113th running of the Queen's Plate, *the* Canadian racing spectacular, at Toronto's Woodbine track—and perhaps a dozen other $100,000—or higher—stakes races. The Derby was unthreatened by them all: wherever I went, if the Kentucky Derby were mentioned, someone was sure to say either, "Oh, *I*'ve been to the Derby," or, "That's one thing I really want to do before I die—see a Kentucky Derby." Nobody said the same thing about the Preakness or the Belmont; even in Canada, the Derby meant more than the older *Canadian* Queen's Plate.

Again, people who wanted to go somewhere special, or do something special, thought of the Derby as that special thing. The politicians, entertainment people, business executives, society leaders who used the Derby as stage paralleled the business organizations who used the Derby as reward. Anyone selling the most cars, or tires, could not only brag about attending the Derby but know that the person bragged to shared the Derby awe. As experiential point-scoring, the Derby stood highest among American spectaculars.

In the American "deal," an interdependence exists between bread and circuses. The teleology of work is, over an entire life, "betterment"; during any one year the sharper goad is "enjoyment." People set their calendars for vacations to coincide with the Derby, the Indianapolis "500," Mardi Gras. The calendar is marked off week by week—much in the same way that people count down to birthdays.

America, in addition, is hyped on "firsts"—the first kiss, the first car, the first sexual experience, the first house. People also rank "my biggest" this, or "most exciting" that. The Kentucky Derby is a recognized American objective, a special place to be at a most particular time, a Mount Everest, which, "because it is there," has to be experienced. Killjoy Gertrude Stein said, "What if when we get there we find no there there?" Muttery muttering too subversive for happy-ending America. Having been "there" is an important American need. Along with the Grand Canyon, Yellowstone Park, the Redwood National Park forest, Niagara Falls, the giant sequoias in Sequoia National Park, The Great American Spectacular took its place as a "there" everyone must get to, or die uncompleted.

4

The Big Car Race

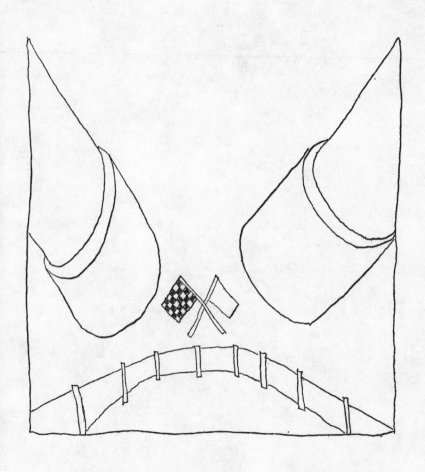

In Louisville only the Avis girls, off the track, dressed like jockeys; in Indianapolis during "500" week almost everybody, including sportswriters, wore a crested cap, a crested jacket, or any other crested thing in order to look like a racing pro. Husband and wife "teams" wandered the Speedway Museum in twin nylon jackets slashed with racing stripes. One woman balanced an astronaut's scrambled-egg longpeaked cap on top of her pink plastic curlers; her jeweled prescription bifocals were shaped to simulate a driver's. Her husband wore the same cap tipped forward over aviator sunglasses gleaming with military metal. White socks gaping between his race-driver shoes and too-short nylon trousers were, however, reassuringly civilian.

In Louisville the Churchill Downs red rose—on a card, a sign, a program—was usually small and delicate (the Kentucky Derby was as frequently represented by the track's twin spires); in Indianapolis the "500" crossed white and checkered flags were everywhere, in all sizes. Sponsor decals that covered almost every inch of a "500" car also covered the jackets of fans, collectors, and imitators—oil crests, tire crests, gas crests, valve crests, battery crests, piston crests, ring crests, shock absorber crests, windshield-wiper crests were set in a scatter of U.S.A. and white-and-checkered flags.

That white-and-checkered-flag motif showed up on bracelets,

earrings, cigarette cases, lighters, crucifixes, panties, brooches, cufflinks. High on the Indianapolis petty porn scale was a peek-a-boo bra with one cup white, the other checkered—cut out where it counts, ostensibly to give the wearer racing room.

Checkered flags, white flags as pennants, triangles, oilcloth and plastic tatters fluttered from strung wire and clothesline. Flags decorated gas stations, auto shops, garages, supermarkets, mobile homes, hamburger shacks, bicycle banana seats, motorcycle handlebars, car aerials. Department stores stocked checkered shirts, trousers, skirts, nightshirts, boxer shorts, swimsuits, sportscoats, which, when sold, were packed in checkered paperbags or checkered boxes and carried in checkered shoppingbags. Checkered flags substituted for the more accurate plague "X" to mark disaster stations pushing the usual Spectacular wares— "rooms," "eats," "parking."

Car racing fans, a special breed, wear racing gloves as genuine (and expensive) as Bobby Unser's, carry hundred-buck stopwatches, hundred-buck binoculars, multihundred-buck cameras they aim at anything in decals and crests. Stopwatches, like racing caps and jackets, express the professional status of spectators. The more expensive the stopwatch, the more profoundly knowing the fan. Before the Speedway tower with its minisecond electronic timing device was built, the stopwatch could have been considered an essential part of "500" spectatoring. The stopwatch, however, means more than its function. It supposedly stands as status, emblem, token, fetish, fraternity pin. The racing aficionado doesn't want you to think he's just one more lousy tourist or dumb sports fan. The measure of who he is resides with his stopwatch.

That stopwatch has another function. It is the staple of trivia collection. A "500" aficionado speaks in 1/1000 second differentiations. A horse racing "in" man ticks off only one fifths. At the Kentucky Derby early morning workouts those carrying stopwatches will be track clockers, handicappers, turfwriters, trainers, owners, jockeys, and perhaps a very few fans. At the time trials for the Indianapolis "500" almost everyone carries some kind of stopwatch. It's a standard Christmas or birthday present in Indianapolis—kids get them for graduation, for their Bar Mitzvah. One can guess at the status, age, or "betterment" index of a stopwatch-carrier by checking out the price of the timepiece. Some people collect stopwatches. Some keep the watches they replace so that the full run becomes a personal stopwatch museum. At the time trials the overwhelming majority of those doing the timing have nothing at all to do with the race. The stopwatch is the recognized local symbol of true "500" participation.

Fans rate their success as "participants" not by the usual gauges alone—autographs, signed pictures, noncommercial souvenirs—but by how deeply they penetrate the Dantesque inner reaches of Gasoline Alley (where racing cars are worked on and stored). One may, on special days, buy tickets or otherwise get them, so that gawking and peeking become legitimate. Points are scored whenever one penetrates an impenetrable barrier, or passes beyond a proscribed gate; high standing is awarded anyone whose camera focused on the dark recesses of a stripped-down engine. The different colored tags and badges which allow closer and closer access on Race Day are soon known, quickly recognized, greatly admired, envied, yearned for, and, sometimes, "rented," borrowed, or snatched. A commercial, industrial, or financial enterprise using the "500" to reward its employees can't simply follow its Kentucky Derby model—transport 'em, house 'em, feed 'em, amuse 'em, booze 'em. Businesses must deliver those acknowledgedly hard-to-come-by ribbons and badges to differentiate those *they* are rewarding. Tire companies compete with oil companies *and* with other tire companies to see who can—officially or unofficially—open the closed-off professional car racing world to those who will talk up the "500" experience the rest of their lives.

In Indianapolis the code slogan is not only "I was there," but "I was almost a part of it." Pacific-8 Conference or Big Ten alumni at the Rose Bowl may identify with alma mater's doing-or-dying, yet recognize the obvious distinction between doer and watcher. Indianapolis sets the aficionado up in a special limbo somewhere in between. As the cop who directs traffic may develop the delusion that his wave powers cars, so the aficionado may come to believe that without his or her presence the "500" could never get started.

There's also a Guinness Book of Records mania that works in Indianapolis as it does in Churchill Downs: "This is my fiftieth consecutive Derby," one is told, and proudly. Tradition is even more important than statistics trivia: an old gentleman told me he "started comin' to the '500' when I was five 'cause my daddy was a car man. Been comin' ever since. Sooner missed m'own weddin' than the Race."

Nobody, in my own experience at Louisville, trotted up to Churchill Downs on a horse got up to look like a Derby entry; in Indianapolis people play "pretend '500.'" Their cars carry "STP" decals plastered over everything, and frequently are fitted with supplyhouse gadgets and "extras" that make every Middle American's car his chariot. Dragsters with the ass end of their Fords flipped up power their extra-wide extra-heavy whitewalls out of hidden driveways into the gaggles of Speedway traffic rpm-ing through Indianapolis at two miles an hour.

In Indianapolis a portion of the "500" crowd looked like sidemen to Bill Hayley's Comets, or Sha-Na-Na (with no put-on). The 1970s duck-tailed haircut was modified long, but sharp shaped sideburns still marked the in-crowd as members of the Elvis society. Tattoos were rare in Louisville, plentiful in Indianapolis—only 100 miles away. On the interstates around Indianapolis "racers" tried out their "500" strategies—riding the draft, slingshotting, tailgating on the straightaway, gunning for the inside lane, circling the field on the outside. Mufflers were considered sissy, but even mufflerless cars scutcheoned a full set of muffler-manufacturers' decals.

On the Speedway approaches during trial days or Race Day democracy prevails: jalops, limousines, sportscars, campers, trailers, sandbuggies, antique cars, buses, cabs, cop cars, trapped ambulances, hemmed-in fire equipment, tow cars, "rescue units." In this unprogrammed chance parade, motorized pimps and camper-housed hookers frequently draw alongside their prospective driver-goggle-wearing Johns determinedly respectable next to their driver-goggle-wearing wives.

Twenty-four hours before the big race, the great American spectacular time of misrule begins—for outsiders. The "500" for Indianapolis residents means something totally different—a wonderful local holiday, the best picnic of the year, the week everybody seems cheerful and excited. For children, the "500" means fun and a change in who or what is in town. Kids in Indianapolis take up a watch on the streets that continue US or Interstate highways through the city and see if they can spot license plates from all fifty states and all the Canadian provinces. Children cover their tricycles and bicycles with "STP" decals and careen over the sidewalks, making their own soundtrack. Toy "500" cars are crashed, slammed, hurled over imaginary tracks. Slot-car play gets wild. Motorcyclists on only two wheels feel only half there Race Week. Time has to be ticked off in 1/1000th seconds all week long in order to penetrate Race consciousness.

In 1972, however, Indianapolis, wrapped up in the "500," couldn't completely close out what was happening elsewhere. Between the running of the Kentucky Derby on May 6 and the Indianapolis "500" on May 27, Arthur Bremer, on May 15, had tried to kill Alabama's Governor George Wallace. On "500" eve, network news broadcasts showed President Richard Nixon in Leningrad, Henry Kissinger in Moscow. While outsiders began the hours of misrule in which the old would pretend to be young, the middle-aged come on as swingers, the young pretend to be what their elders believed about them, the un-spectacular world went on.

> New York (UPI)—Vice-President Spiro Agnew, in accepting an award as father of the year, yesterday defended American involvement in Vietnam, saying it was "immoral to turn a deaf ear to the weak."

The Indianapolis *News,* cordially unisolationist, chose for Race Day an editorial "Salute to Armenia," not usually a high interest topic for most Midwest newspapers.

> It was on May 28, 1918, that Armenia was declared an independent, democratic republic. Its freedom was short-lived, however, and after two years it became Soviet Armenia. Memory of that moment of freedom still lingers among Armenians everywhere.

The "500" chose as its theme "Those Wonderful Years," encompassing, among other things, flappers, the growth of the movie industry, and, unmentioned, the rise and fall of Mussolini, Stalin, Hitler, the 1929 Crash, the Great Depression.

In the forty-acre "Field of Action" off 30th Street, next to Gate 10, where mesomorphs, preparing for the race, risked herniation with ice-filled coolers piled on top of hefted cases of canned beer— and where potsmokers, gluesniffers, winedrinkers huddled under blankets—something special happened on "500" eve:

> Terry Lee Wissinger and Karen Gwyn Hawkins . . . used [their] time to marry.
>
> Standing in a field of cars, circled by hand-holding friends and watched by dozens of curious strangers, Terry told Karen, "I promise to be a faithful husband through all of the worldly problems we will encounter . . ." and she in turn answered, "I want to spend my whole life as your wife."
>
> After selections from poet Kahlil Gibran's "Meditations" and "The Prophet," the Rev. David Turnbull pronounced the couple man and wife. . . .

In the *Star* on Race eve that same action field caused cranky speculations. One long-time "500" observer said that "the race crowd is largely good people," except that too many even good people dumped into a forty-acre dimly lit field made for a "tremendous amount of problems":

> A multitude of Speedway residents and merchants have experienced some unpleasant cleanup jobs annually. But portable toilets placed in convenient locations outside the race track in the town have eased the sanitation problems considerably, police report.

Something else the police didn't report:

> Speedway Police Department statistics do not completely reflect the abrupt increase in crimes which occurs each May, because many different police agencies always are working within their jurisdiction and each department makes arrests and investigations as needed. . . . In April 1971 a total of 35 offenses were reported to the Speedway police: in May the total jumped to 65 crimes and then in June . . . 30. . . .

One Indianapolis reader, who still blamed Chief Justice Earl

Warren's "permissiveness" for just about everything, suggested a way out:

> The best way to start making our country reasonably safe again, and to protect citizens from being victims of violence, is to get rid of those among us who commit acts of violence. The lives of a thousand criminals is not worth the life of one innocent victim. With that common sense thought, I for one call for the annihilation of the murderers among us.

Another reader went even further and described precisely what was inciting crime in America:

> I watched the Emmy Awards on television, and enjoyed it to a point. . . . The Johnny Mann singers gave a beautiful patriotic presentation, making a comment about the importance of working together, and pulling together. Then Johnny Carson came on with his remark "War Bonds on Sale in the Lobby!" and all the stupid people applauded him! Strange, strange humor!
>
> The next afternoon, Governor George Wallace was shot.

As sops to normalcy the "500" Festival Parade presented such well-displayed entertainment kewpie dolls as Phil Harris and Dick Clark. TV and film loveables were represented by Jim Nabors and Andy Devine, but the lower celebrity ranks didn't do too well, featuring one Gary Collins, star of a doomed ABC television series, his wife, Mary Ann Mobley, an actress and former Miss America. Joining the Collinses were Bob McGrath, an actor on Sesame Street, and Gail Fisher, who, the program notes said, "plays the secretary on the ABC television show 'Mannix.'" Colonel Harlan Sanders, ubiquitous founder of the fried chicken franchises, turned up in Indianapolis as he would at most spectaculars.

In contrast to the posh Kentucky Derby party of Mrs. C. V. Whitney was the democratic "500" Festival Queen's Ball held at the new Indiana Convention-Exposition Center. The Center was suitably decorated with 7,400 square yards of black and white checkered carpet, according to a *Star* team of reporters who further described the decor thus:

> Rising 12 feet above the tables were shimmery metal "fountains" kept in graceful motion by air currents. In the base

of each flickered white votive candles, and tiny electric
lights twinkled in silverleaf arches bordering the dance floor.

The reporters added reassuringly that "no 'hot pants' were in evidence," a fact Eugenia Sheppard thought not worth a mention at Mrs. Whitney's Derby party. "Several Orient-influenced gowns" and a woman with "diamond-studded eyelashes drew many comments" according to the *Star*. John Walsh, vice-president of the Indiana National Bank, appeared in "a display of honorary medals —the Order of the Tower, Indiana Society Medal and the Indiana University Medal." Even more "sparkling in the candlelit room were the lighted earrings, powered by tiny batteries, worn by Miss Pat Cronin." Not at the Queen's Ball, and not in the "500" parade because "technically it wasn't a float," was Miss Cronin's most obvious rival, "a 12-foot-high motorized Schlitz beer can [that] honked at incredulous spectators from a parking lot at Pennsylvania and Michigan streets."

More restricted than the Queen's Ball was the Borg-Warner Corporation party at the Indiana National Bank Auditorium on Race eve, at which "most of the 350 guests roamed the terraces where the breeze was gentle and checkered flags in flower beds snapped smartly at attention." The *Star*'s reporters remarked how "Indianapolis society leaders wearing safe, neat business suits and their wives" came up against the "race crowd who were wearing some pretty jazzy outfits." More exclusive yet was a party at the Columbia Club given by Mrs. Roscoe Turner for 160 guests and featuring as stars bandleader Stan Kenton and Dr. Denton Cooley, the Houston heart specialist. The *Star* also reported four formal weddings on Race eve. The big "Concerning Women" item announced that Dolly Coles, wife of the president and chief operations officer of General Motors Corporation, would be the very first woman ever to ride in an Indianapolis "500" pace car:

Dolly had evidently told her good friend Tony Hulman [bossman of the "500"], "One of these days women's liberation will get to the Speedway. When you pick the first woman to ride in the pace car on race day, please think of me." He did.

Tony Hulman was the subject of the *Star Magazine*'s "Hoosier in Profile" Race Day feature:

> The man of a dozen fiscal facets, veteran of thousands of board meetings, passenger in speeding pace cars, flier, golfer, fisherman, hunter, recipient of a dozen sports accolades from hallowed Yale University, is scared—but courageous enough to admit it.
>
> "I'm really kind of shy," he says. "I really just hate to almost do anything, just the same way I hate to be interviewed—just scared to death."
>
> You sense that a man so true to himself will never treat you falsely.

In *Autoweek* for Race Day one Mike Knepper was reporting on "An All-Time Low in Broadcasting," the ABC Wide World of Sports presentation of "the fatal crash of Jim Malloy" during the "500" time trials:

> Thankfully, for some time now, the periodic clamor to ban auto racing as barbaric, deadly and all the other adjectives applied to the sport by the lunatic fringe that stalks the chambers of state and federal government and wields the gavel at DAR meetings has not raised its asinine head. But armed with the morbid treatment of Malloy's accident and the special segment on [Billy] Vukovitch and [Gary] Bettenhausen, both sons of famous drivers who were killed at Indy, the clamor could start anew. . . .
>
> [S]ensationalizing death is a philosophy best left to the National Observer or the Police Gazette. It is not accepted by racing enthusiasts and it is not accepted by the general public which can see all the violent death it wishes on the evening report from Viet Nam.

The *News* for Race Day reported in the midst of its promotional go-go that "Al Unser, winner of the last two 500-Mile Races, last night revealed the rear wings on all the cars can cause two problems":

> "You can't see over or under them so you cannot see two cars in front of you," he said.
>
> The second problem concerns "drafting." This occurs

when one car rides in the jetstream of another car, enabling the rear car to conserve fuel without sacrificing speed.

"But with the rear wing the wind goes over the top and misses your front foils," he explained. "This makes your front lighter than your rear and can cause some control problems."

Other drivers, Al's brother Bobby among them, wondered about those wings, too. Wally Dallenbach and many other drivers were suddenly asking aloud if human reflexes could adjust to a car traveling at average speeds of 190 mph or more. Dallenbach had been a close friend of Jim Malloy, who had just been buried in Denver.

"Nobody likes to talk about it," Dallenbach said, "but how much correction time did he [Malloy] have at 190? A quarter of a second? There's a difference between 170 and 190. They should have taken off the wings. It would have saved limbs and lives. . . . More guys are vulnerable to being hurt when they're going 17 miles an hour faster than the year before instead of three or four miles an hour faster.

"I don't think it's healthy. I think everyone feels the same way."

Dave Overpeck, writing in the *Star* for May 27, chronicled the fate of Jim Malloy and Malloy's pre-crash fears. After Malloy had taken his first ride in his Thermo-King Special, he said that "a year ago I couldn't even picture myself going 178 miles an hour, and today I warmed up at that speed." Overpeck picked up the story from that point:

The next day he ran 25 laps at better than 185 mph with a top circuit of just over 188. We talked again that night. This time I asked, "Well, can you see yourself going 190 now?" Jim just laughed . . . like the kid who'd just found the secret entrance to the candy shop. . . .

The sensation of speed wasn't that much greater, he said. In fact, static things seemed to go by in slow motion. But there were problems, he admitted. You had to concentrate more because there was less time for relaxation on the straightaways and you had to allow for cars moving much slower than you.

There were physical problems, too. The G forces in the

turns were much greater. He said he would have to wear a tighter strap from his helmet to his shoulder to keep his head upright for 500 miles. . . . Jim was looking for speed when he went out for practice on Sunday morning, May 14. He turned in a lap at 186 and was coming down into the third turn again. . . . Suddenly the . . . car Jim estimated could steer itself halfway down the backstretch turned . . . to the right. The skid marks up to the wall covered only 75 feet.

At 175 mph you cover that distance in less than three-tenths of a second.

Above Overpeck's story AP and UPI photos of the smash-up carried the legend, "Malloy rams the third turn wall head on at 195 miles an hour."

My first day at the track I walked into a conversation about Malloy. Two men in T-shirts trimmed with checkered flags, carrying stopwatches, were twisted up in binocular straps, camera straps, gadget bag straps, with side arm lightmeters on the hip.

"You there?" the first one said.

"Nah."

"How come?"

"The wife. The kids—church."

"A man can go to church June through April."

"It was a big one, I heard."

"The worst head-on in history, they're sayin'."

"That's how it goes."

"We was only fifty sixty yards from the third turn——"

"That close?"

"We was amazed to hear he lived——"

"Four days."

"You wouldn't bet nobody could live through that."

"And head-on."

"Head-on, I'm gonna tell you—it was *head-on!* Parts of that Eagle was scattered a football field away from the crash."

"Today's Prayer" in the Indianapolis *Star* for Race Day went, in part:

We pause in the midst of a busy holiday weekend, Dear God, to ask You to watch over us, wherever we go. Keep us from being so frantic for fun that we forget why this is a holiday.

In the third Race Day "Extra," this prayer appeared below a photograph of Wally Dallenbach being pulled out of his "FLAMING NO. 40 LOLA-FORD EARLY IN MARATHON."

Dallenbach's problem was a faulty fuel pump, as the *Star*'s front page story explained: "Each time the fuel hoses were disengaged from the car, the high-octane liquid would continue to flow, throwing fuel over Dallenbach and the cockpit. . . . Dallenbach suffered only singed eyelashes and a 'couple of warm hands.'" The *Star* added that Andy Granatelli's brother, Vince, crew chief for Dallenbach, "had nothing but praise for Dallenbach. 'Even though Wally was actually on fire twice, he kept worrying about the car.'" Not so lucky was a Dallenbach crewman, Dennis Tussman, who "suffered second-degree burns on both arms and a leg." Vince Granatelli I saw get so soaked with gasoline he had to throw off his clothes and service Dallenbach's car standing in his shorts.

Nobody goes into a "500" not knowing what the dangers are. Race promotion magazines go shrill at any mention of death, but car drivers don't fool themselves. The odds in favor of a serious accident shorten every time one races without a mishap. Drivers talk some but think much about too-high speeds, mechanical failure, metal fatigue, metal "wear," alloy stress. Every racing pro knows what has happened, and can happen, in the Great American Auto Racing Spectacular.

Drivers will tell you that the Indianapolis Speedway is not properly surfaced for cars going close to 200 miles an hour; nor, according to some, is it properly banked or engineered. It took the holocaust* of the 1973 "500," for instance, to mandate something so simple and obvious as putting gas tanks on the *left* side of the cars (so that contact with the wall on the driver's right doesn't turn a racing car into a gasoline bomb). After 1973 the dangerous location of pits and gas storage tanks was reviewed and altered. After 1971, when the pace car smashed into a photographers' stand and eighteen people were injured, the photo stands were relocated and new safety measures instituted. Research and foresight didn't make the changes; disaster did.

In its early days the "500" made a one-to-one connection with

* Which killed Swede Savage and badly burned Salt Walther.

car design and motor design. Cars in the 1970s, doing 190 miles per hour, and getting about 1.8 miles per gallon, however, aren't close relatives of the family automobile. The one familiar, and in 1972 still active, car name in racing was Ford—but only as an engine builder. Eagle, McLaren, Parnelli, Brabham, Antares, Brawner, among others, the important names in chassis design, are not very concerned about the family car.

Yet, no matter how intricate the "500" engine and chassis have become, a spectator can still feel that a car is a car is a car. In Louisville, only professional racing people master the genealogical intricacies of horse breeding, but in Indianapolis most veteran "500" fans know a great deal about engines, aerodynamic principles, fuels. The Speedway Museum encourages fans to view old racing cars historically. Material is provided to explain changes in engine and chassis design during the sixty years of the "500."

The horse can't be claimed as something exclusively American; the automobile, from the point of view of the "500" fan, is. The Indianapolis Speedway Museum is an American repository of technological history and social nostalgia. The "500" has always been something American, unlike the Grand Prix, whose cars and drivers have been, for the most part, foreign.

Sports car races are considered foreign, too, and worse—uppity. In the 1972 "500" a sports car racer, Sam Posey, was driving a big "500" car as an outsider and interloper. The late Peter Revson, Grand Prix in character, sports car in social class, wasn't accepted as true "500." Stock car drivers like southerner Cale Yarborough fit the Indianapolis image better than the Poseys and the Revsons, who, Middle America feels, are only slumming in Indianapolis.

"Ain't that Revson feller some kind of a millionaire?" one man said when, two days before the race, the subject of Revson's chances came up. Revson had made the first row with a lap average of 192.885, second only to Bobby Unser's 195.940.

"Don't Revson come from Noo York?" he added.

"Al Unser must be a millionaire, too," someone said, "winning them two 500s in a row."

"Not that kind of a millionaire," the first man said. "Revson is born money—society—the East—hell, Al—don't matter how many millions Al wins. Al's still one of us."

No other spectacular is so closely identified with one level of American society as the Indianapolis "500," yet Middle America does not control the big car race. Just as the Kentucky Derby higher society enclaves are sealed off from the masses, so, too, are Indianapolis's. The "Paddock" section and penthouse seats reflect one's Indianapolis social standing: there one sees few racing caps and almost no racing jackets. Indianapolis society dresses in sports clothes little different from what's worn at the Kentucky Derby several weeks earlier.

Race rituals resemble Derby rituals—"club" breakfasts, for example, which are followed by travel on buses assigned VIP traffic lanes. Club members do a lot of hard drinking in the morning, afternoon, and night of the race: Kentucky Bourbon and branch water in Indianapolis demonstrate cultural exchange.

After the 1972 "500," as I was climbing down from the press section near the Paddock and Terrace seats, I was passed by two men in a terrible rush.

"Hurry, hurry, hurry," one said, "or we'll miss the fights."

He looked as respectable as Elliot Richardson, in glasses, a gray business suit, his hair slicked back. His buddy, squirming his way through the crowd, was just a little younger, and looked a lot like a puffy afternoon game-show host. Their wives, following the sexist code, lagged behind.

"Johnny so enjoys the infield fights," one of the wives said. "Last year's fights got wild, and terribly funny."

"Grant always talks about the fights. Sometimes he almost forgets the race. Look over the side. See. People staggering. They get so drunk they *have* to fight."

"I don't like fights, Wend."

"Oh, we can't call these encounters fights. Half a dozen drunk apes just swing away. It's over in a minute."

Below us the crowd scattered, then massed at the tunnel entrances under the track as if being pulled into a huge vacuum tube. Once on the infield side, people sprinted toward their cars and buses.

"Johnny would really like to be with them," Wend said, pointing a kidgloved hand at the crowd below. "In the field. He'd love to lay out there in jeans and T-shirt all night long before the race—it's all he talks about from one Memorial Day to another."

"Oh, the dirty old man!"

"Oh, Johnny's a lamb. He'd get blind drunk immediately. He keeps saying he's going to outfit his camera with ultra violet or infra red—I never can remember which. Not the light we use in our ovens, the other one. So he can take pictures of them hugging in the dark."

Once on the ground, the Paddock people made their way back to the buses privileged to travel those designated clear lanes. Everyone quickly changed into party clothes. Post-race parties were exciting because the winners of the betting pools were declared—as the climax to the thirty-five or forty hour party that began Race eve.

For some people, though, the "500" was a five-day blow, or six, or seven. Those *outside* thought the real fun was the infield *inside,* but "500" parties, celebrations, dances, hops, gigs, funkies, formals, smoke-ins, sniff-ins, freak-outs went on all over Indianapolis. The race people—drivers, crews, owners—constituted one important "500" group, sometimes joined by the media and other "500" public relations extensions. Sponsors, equipment manufacturers, bankers, local and national financial, industrial, and business people shared the action, too.

In Louisville, though Kentuckians were prominent, the real "stars," as I've indicated, were, on the whole, outsiders. In Indianapolis, stars were rare and, for the most part, local. The "500" belongs to the city of Indianapolis and, by hospitable extension, to the rest of Indiana; the Kentucky Derby exists for Kentucky and the entire nation—and also for Louisville. The horse set establishes the Derby's tone and has no exact parallel in the Indianapolis power structure. In place of "addresses," finishing, prep, and Ivy schools, Indianapolis seems to value business affiliation. Society pages don't cater to the old-hat eastern social hierarchy. Business hierarchy is what matters. Star status is conferred by position in a firm's power structure. Locally based but nationally known firms score highest. Next come national organizations with a thriving branch or division in Indianapolis or elsewhere in Indiana. In Indianapolis society pages, board chairmen rank above presidents, presidents outrank vice-presidents, and so on right down the corporate foot-nichery, a system familiar, say, to readers of *Fortune*.

Indianapolis also seems free of upwomanship in designer clothes or gourmet cookery. Few, if any, Halstons, Norells, Diors, Coco Chanels, or even Bonnie Cashins show up. At the big Borg-Warner party, the hostess—the president's wife—was refreshingly described as wearing "a long dress of crisp white pique . . . scroll-edged with cotton plaid," no fashion-show stopper. She said her plaid "has no meaning. I don't even know the name of the tartan, but I like the dress."

The food at this same party was characteristically local: the guests "sampled breasts, beef tenderloin, smoked salom [sic], chicken wings, roast diced duck in orange sauce and imported cheeses." No cuisine starred items to invoke the great names of the "500"—Ralph DePalma *boeuf cordon bleu,* for instance, or Pete DePaolo *canard rôti,* Wilbur Shaw *petits fours,* Mauri Rose *napoléon.* Unlike Mrs. C. V. Whitney at the Derby, the star "500" hostess hadn't just rushed back from Spain or anywhere else foreign. She was from Indiana; her two sons weren't given the eastern education Fitzgerald's St. Paul considered essential. Both attended Indiana University.

Four couples married the night before the "500" rated bride pictures in the Race Day *Star*. Every college or university affiliation mentioned was local or Indiana—I.U., Purdue, Indiana Central College, Butler University, or Indiana-Purdue (the last three located right in Indianapolis). No space was assigned to describe the bride's dress. The only information beyond name, parentage, and university/college affiliation considered important was honeymoon destination. Three of the couples chose St. Louis, the Smokies, French Lick; the fourth declined to say. For all, the future home address given was Indianapolis.

Down the imaginary social scale, "foreign" intrusion became even less significant. The "500," like Mardi Gras, is, as I've already suggested, a great *local* holiday. Those who come to the "500" from all over the country and the world don't really affect the "500" 's essentially local flavor. The masses who wear the checkered-flag insignia identify totally with the "home" side.

In the infield and in the forty-acre "fun field" the usual Spectacular-followers were doing the usual Fort Lauderdale things, but the largest number of Fort Lauderdale jocks were from Indiana or attended Indiana universities. Sweatshirts and T-shirts parodied "Virginia is for lovers" into "Indiana is for lovers" or advertised certain Indiana institutions—Valparaiso Tech, West Baden College, Ball State, Hanover College, Huntington College; slightly better-known places such as Earlham College, De Pauw, Butler; nationally recognized Indiana University, Purdue, Notre Dame. The "500" provided an opportunity for one *to be* Fort Lauderdale without having to travel *to* Fort Lauderdale (or, that is, to leave Indiana).

Indianapolis departed significantly from the Kentucky Derby model: if a Hare Krishna contingent was in residence at the "500," I must have missed it. Perhaps the Hare Krishna stand-up style of delivery couldn't cope with low-flying footballs and frisbees. Loaded infield coolers were dangerous for religiously bare feet also subject to lethal beercan rings mining the grounds.

Without a computer or scientific head-count, I guessed that beer and wine drinkers outnumbered potsmokers better than 100–1 in Indianapolis—and only 10–1 in Louisville. Indianapolis drunks, in decibel competition with "500" engines, seemed to yowl much more loudly than Louisville drunks. Nonstop chugalug had its predictable consequences: almost cheerfully, infielders threw up a lot, zonked out a lot, or clung blearily to a car hood, a tree, fence, pole, or each other. From Louisville through New Orleans, people rushed to get to a spectacular in order to drink, smoke, or seconal themselves into instant oblivion. A significant portion of the "500" infield population missed the 1972 race: many in that group did not come to Indianapolis to see a race.

People attend the spectaculars to be where the action is. I don't refer to the obvious participating pickpockets, panhandlers, proselyters, palmists, policemen, politicians, plugolas, potsellers, padres, pacifists, paramours, pariahs, parsons, prostitutes, patrons, pigeons, pedants, pushers, peekers, pentecostals, pimps, prestidigitators, prophets, punks, prudes, prattlers. Louisville, or Indianapolis, or Miami Beach, or New Orleans—if not Pasadena—is "where it's happening." The attendant circuses make the Spectacular event almost secondary because the spectacular creates an instant community of festive misrule.

"You don't usually get hassled at the Derby," I was told, and heard variations on that theme for other spectaculars (again with Pasadena an exception):

"You can do what you want."

"Nobody pushes you around."

"It's our party."

"In spring you need a party," someone said about the Derby.

"At the end of the school year you need a party," someone else said about the "500."

"When winter's almost over, everybody needs a big blow-out," was the word on Mardi Gras.

Indianapolis obviously fulfills Middle America's party "needs," and also offers law-abiding Middle America a chance to participate in quasi-legal betting. The Kentucky Derby has parimutuel wagering, local or national bookies—even New York's off-track betting—to take care of the gambling urge. Side bets resist classification, and may involve owners, trainers, even jockeys. Ad hoc pools on the winning horse's number may be set up in various offices and organizations. More sophisticated pools may be based on the winning horse's time. The exact order of the first two, three, four horses to finish can be used for pools. Rare, but not unheard of, is the pool based on the exact order of finish for all the horses running.

In football Bowl games, betting is usually a short version of the weekly multigame "pool cards" college and university students play all year round. Las Vegas odds-makers, in addition, establish point-spreads—Ohio State by 3, say, or Southern California by 6—but college betting is not as systematic as weekly pro football play, or the Super Bowl.

Other versions of the football pool, to repeat, pay off on total points scored by both teams, regardless of who wins, or total points scored *and* the winning side. Which side scores first, and which scores last, is the basis of another pool, or the time of the first score, the time of the last score, the time of the first score in the second half, etc. Some go so far as to pay off on total yards scored on ground, or total yards in air, or total yards rushing and passing.

Compared with the Kentucky Derby and the football Bowls, betting in the Indianapolis "500" is homey, participatory, inventive, flexible, often spontaneous. Race car knowledge is needed for a sophisticated bet but is irrelevant to most Indianapolis "family" pool betting.

In 1972, I ran across pools ranging from a nickel to hundreds of dollars and heard that still bigger ones existed. In a World Series baseball pool or in a Bowl football pool the number of bettors is limited because baseball games rarely see more than twenty runs scored by both sides; in football, total points rarely go beyond seventy. "500" pools, on the other hand, can have an almost infinite number of participants. By requiring not only the exact order of finish for the first ten "500" cars but also, in complex pools, the time, down to 1/1000 of a second, the "500" pool invites wide participation.

Bonus points may be awarded if any of the ten cars listed finishes in the exact designated spot. For example, if the number "34" car driven by Sam Posey in the 1972 race were picked to finish among the top ten, a certain number of points were awarded; but if Posey's car was picked seventh—its position at the finish—a bonus was added.

Pools, as I've already suggested, give added purpose to post-race parties. Unofficial results—ignoring penalties, time adjustments, disqualifications—are used to decide the pool winner. In 1972, for example, the "48" car, driven by Jerry Grant, finished second but was disqualified for using fuel from the tanks of his out-of-the-race partner, Bobby Unser (fuel is restricted to 250 gallons from one's own tank only). Pools decided right after the race used Grant's second-place finish; more "official" pools waited for the 8 A.M. next-day posting, which is considered final.

"500" drivers qualify their cars in time trials over only three laps, but the race covers 200. Obviously the fastest qualifier doesn't necessarily make it over the long haul. No fuel factor exists in the time trials. In qualifying, a driver could get half-a-mile to the gallon, or less: but at that fuel-consumption rate a car would never make it to the end of the race. Two hundred fifty gallons of fuel must average out at a minimum of two miles to the gallon, or the 500 miles can't be completed.

Motor stress, chassis stress won't necessarily show up after three laps, or even thirty-three, but 100 laps might bust a car wide open. Nobody preps for the "500" by driving the Indianapolis track 200 laps under race conditions. If he did, the prep run would probably so alter his vehicle that it would have to be considered a "different" car. No one can ever be sure if an individual car has destroyed the delicate balance between speed and endurance. A driver constantly runs risks of overheating, overstraining: essential motor parts can fail, wheels fall off, transmission, steering, brakes go bad.

In an Olympics-level 100-meter race, for instance, the speed of a qualifier is recorded for the same 100 meters he'll run in the finals. Barring injury, a runner should finish roughly in the order predicted by the qualifying times—assuming everyone was pushed to the limit in the heats. Odds based on the heat times would be a fair way to prepare a tote board for those finals.

Horse races are not nearly so easy to handicap because too many variables must go into setting up a betting "line." Variations in track structure, a particular day's track conditions, race distances, allowance weights, the class of other horses in the race, the skill of the jockey and whether he is currently "hot" or not, whether a particular horse has "trained up" for a race, is bred and trained to run on turf or on dirt, as an entry or alone, is a speed horse or one who comes off the pace—these and other factors affect thoroughbred odds-making. Even so, though horses don't finish in the line's predicted order as frequently as 100-meter runners do, the favorites at most horse tracks—the "chalk"—end up winning about thirty-five percent of thoroughbred races.

In contrast, the odds against the first ten qualifiers at the Indianapolis "500" finishing 1–2–3 . . . 10 are enormous. It has never happened. Nor is it likely to, ever. Odds against the first ten qualifying cars finishing as the top ten *in any order* are almost equally large. Neophytes betting in "500" pools for the first time are cautioned by old hands against selecting their top ten finishers out of the top ten qualifiers alone. Veterans of the "500" pools have a rough formula they apply: one and perhaps two first-row cars can be expected to finish in the top ten; the question is *which* one, or ones? Though thirty-seven of the first fifty-five winners of the "500" started from pole positions 1–7 (1972 made it thirty-eight out of fifty-six), the difference, in the complex pools, between being able to pick the "500" winner and being able to list the first ten cars correctly is vast.

On the way out to the Speedway a couple days before the race I wondered how important pools were to "500" enthusiasm. I also wondered if the race meant anything to those who lived in Indianapolis but might or might not have $5 to put out for general admission (or an additional $10 for the cheapest Speedway seat).

At a local hospital, student nurses coming off a shift had just drawn their drivers for the race in the simplest kind of pool: thirty-three drivers, thirty-three nurses, and winner-take-all.

"I've got Joe Leonard," one nurse said, "is that good?"

"I had Mike Mosley last year and he near got himself killed," said another. "I picked him again this year. So I traded him to Linda for Dallenbach."

"I've got somebody called Sessions," a third nurse put in. "Is that a joke?"

"Who's got Bobby Unser?" said a fourth. "I sure would love to have Bobby Unser."

Her friends giggled.

I drove a cross-street of abandoned houses, broken windows, nailed-over doorways, peeled-paint wood structures full of sag. Wrecked cars in the back yard, collapsed mattresses leaned against an outside wall—the usual inner city slum signs. Such districts throughout America can be black or white, but are most frequently black. A couple of young black men were just standing around. I asked them if they were going to the "500."

"Car racin' is whitey's shit, man," one of them said.

"Like golf, man," said the other.

"There's one black cat hanging 'round that track. He's sick. He is no class dude. A class dude would tell them eyeglassed mothers to suck."

"That dude ain't in no position to tell nobody nothin', man. It ain't that he ain't big—hell, he ain't even *small*. He ain't nothin'. You got to be Hank [Aaron] or Kareem [Abdul-Jabbar] or

Clyde [Walt Frazier] or Mercury [Morris] or Ali [Muhammad Ali]—axe this whole town who the dude is and ain't one person knows—you don't know, am I right, man? I don't know. Maybe even this man don't know."

This man didn't, then. They were referring to Wendell Scott, a black stockcar driver, just about the only black on even that circuit. Scott had nothing to do with the "500" or big cars.

I asked the two men if they ever bet on the "500."

"You mean like money, man?"

"Sick dudes doin' that, man. Don't need more."

"I bet, man, on somethin' I expecially give one large shit about."

"The honky Olympics, man—you gonna see sick brothers and sick sisters there, but this '500,' it's just honky Olympics."

In *Autoweek* the "500"'s honky normalcy was being celebrated by one of its writers, Leon Mandel:

> The Indianapolis 500 is a midwestern phenomenon. It is loud and hokey and basic and archaic. It appeals to the simplest emotions, it does not pretend to do anything else. The race rewards Midwestern virtues: persistence, courage and willingness to come to grips with the basic elements of survival and conquer them. In this electronic age there is nothing slick and nothing sophisticated about Indianapolis. Perhaps that is why it has such enormous appeal in the heartland.

"Slick" and "sophisticated" stuff happens *not* to be foreign to the Indianapolis "500" run by its boss, Tony Hulman. The "500" is one of the smoothest and most closed-off of all American spectaculars. Somebody slick and sophisticated is in control. The formula Tony Hulman worked out is fabulously successful. Someone in the publicity office told me it was so successful that nobody was about to take the "500" apart to see why "it's doing so good." Whether Hulman consciously worked up what is now the winning combination is less important than how that combination operates. Spectators not only identify with the drivers and their cars, they somehow have a sense that they are participating in all aspects of the "500."

Indianapolis is a populist phenomenon, a spectacular which seems free of hierarchy and a ruling elite. Middle America is at home in Indianapolis 365 days a year: the "500" is a Memorial Day celebration of Middle America's being "back home." Slickness shows up in the obvious gap between what the Speedway promises—almost unlicensed fun and total misrule—and what is actually permitted: a two- or three-day party not that different from a college reunion or a fraternal order weekend. Slickness of another kind shows up, too, in the contrast between the stated racing ideals of the "500" and the actual track conditions.

One of the striking features of all spectaculars is the oneness felt by permanent residents with the unique success of the local event. That form of identification, though helped by "500" public relations and promotional policy, is probably the most important ingredient of a spectacular's uniqueness. A special energy drives the "500" and other spectaculars forward and upward, even when the gross national product wavers or dips.

5

Race Day, Indianapolis

Just before dawn I drove through heavy mist to the Speedway. It had been a hot week—humid 80s were forecast for the race, even 90s—but it was bitter cold as I drove onto Georgetown Road approaching the Speedway. Stationwagon tailgate breakfasts were in progress; everyone was warmly dressed, hunched against the wind, footstomping to keep warm.

Inside the Speedway a few parties were just getting started, some still going on from the night before. The infield—*outside* the campers, trucks, cars, sleeping bags—was fairly subdued. East sky silver light outlined a frisbee sailing silent past T-shirts, boxer shorts, a jockstrap, a cribsheet. A car aerial served as mast for a yellow bra drying.

Even in chilly semidarkness suntan rituals had begun. By sunrise every torso, female, male, would shine with oil, cardboard nose-shades would be in place, lips outlined with heavy opaque creams. Some people learn from previous spectacular experience.

The track itself was deserted, the stands empty; the garage area hid the action inside the individual shops. This was almost the Speedway I saw months later, on Christmas Eve, when, on my way to the Rose Bowl, I stopped in to see what Indianapolis and the track were like without the "500." But by sun-up everything changed. The chill was gone. Long lines formed outside the restrooms. Gasoline Alley was soon surrounded by the spectaculars fans in search of an anecdote to carry home.

This was, after all, *the* day, the promise, summer's Christmas, a communal bonus birthday. In Eastern Europe I've seen people take off for a one-day holiday or a special soccer match similarly charged-up. Socialist countries have their circuses, too. Everyone can feel that the great day is for her or him alone.

Outside the Speedway the men directing traffic in black hardhats, checkered-flag shirts, red luminescent gloves, cut the semidarkness with red-lensed flashlights. In some entering cars only the driver was awake. People from Indiana, Kentucky, Ohio, Illinois towns had started out at three or four in the morning in order to park inside the Speedway. Making it *inside* was part of the "500" ritual.

Buses dropped loads of sleepy-eyed bandmembers who staggered out with their instruments. Some kids told me they hadn't been to bed at all; others had slept only an hour or two. Even this early in the morning—Middle American ideology notwithstanding—the kid with the stash was as easily located as the Good Humor Man.

Every Spectacular has its own pace, beginning, middle, and end, but none is as serendipitously orchestrated as the Indianapolis "500." Begin its soundtrack with a spoon stirring a coffee cup, mix in ten more, then a hundred, a thousand, add the shrillness of ripping cupcake cellophane, Coleman stoves clanged by frypans, a ground bass of squinchy car tires, feet shuffling, broken into by creaking campchairs, the pop and hiss of morning beercans opening, escalate with thousands of transistor radios, the hand crunch of aluminum cans, and kids building teetery clattering beercontainer towers, as racecars are pushed noiselessly into the pits and festival bands start drumming up marches. Three or four tunes compete for air space—all in different keys. The first "500" car revs up, the second, the third, all thirty-three gunning against the band music and the girls screaming in the infield as they begin to be whirled or tossed flashily from arms to arms. Footballers leap, land, catch, or miss while the inevitable human pyramid builders climb, grunt, burp, flip, fart, and curse the impermanence of things that go up only to buckle and fall. The seemingly endless speed-past of cars, loud, then loudest, fading a microsecond, roaring back, an amplified continuous firecracker show accompanied by cheers, cries that rise with every crash or near crash, then fall back into mere loudness. Everything holds at fortissimo during the five last laps. Then it's one long loud cheer, and—suddenly—silence. Till the family stock cars start up, and bikes roar, and all campchairs snap closed. Ultimately, those thousands of feet stop shuffling; at the end, there's only the sound of one imaginary frisbee floating.

Every Spectacular has its unique images, too, mystic messengers invisible the rest of the year. At Belmont every June a woman appears in white sheeting, a combination Baby Snooks and Aimee Semple McPherson. She pats on white-flour powder for Stakes Day, adds a Marcel Marceau arch of eyebrow, two black circles for eyes, and a bright red cupid's bow. Walled away from the track by two thousand taller people, she nevertheless waves excitedly at the winning horse and its invisible jockey.

Some use the Spectacular as if it were the New York City Easter Parade. The prancing, Isadora-scarfed, putative Mick Jagger is at every big show, along with other trend tasters. The latest in eyestuff appears and the going head swoon. Canes and causes, new umbrellas and new lingo show themselves. And epiphanies of the *un*selfconscious. Those who paint their faces like Alice Cooper because those are the best faces the wearers know.

A solitary black man in the Kentucky Derby crowd, his back to the parking lot fence, wears a widebrim white panama, white patent-leather boots, white linen suit, white ruffled shirt, doublebreasted white brocade vest, one long gold watchchain, a black string tie, goatee, one gold earring, and smokes a slightly warped brown cheroot. He's the compleat stage slaveowner. In Indianapolis an enormously fat unshaved newspaper-seller in a wide black sombrero, baggy black suit, white sandals over bare feet, peddled papers in front of the Speedway. He stood on the road's double line to service traffic going in both directions while still hustling pedestrians. Inside, the "500" image was the hooded crew fuel man looking like a ghostly earthbound astronaut, a deep-sea diver, a mummy, science-fiction cocoon, hell's welder, or asbestos-wrapped firefighter.

Before the race, one could have deduced the race odds from where the press and people-with-passes clustered. Al Unser, because of his two previous successive "500" wins, stood to become the first driver to win at Indianapolis three years in a row. But Al's 183.617 qualifying speed was more than 12 mph's behind brother Bobby Unser's record average of 195.940. In addition, Al's Parnelli-Offy was not considered to be in the class occupied only by Bobby's Eagle-Offy. And Bobby was starting in the top pole first row position. Al was several rows back in a position that almost never produced a "500" winner. Racing fans wished Al well, but few expected him to make it.

Earlier in the week, the complicated "500" engines sat stripped-down in the garages, always surrounded by mechanic, owner, driver, sponsors, crew. In Al Unser's garage the Indianapolis *News* for Saturday evening, May 29, 1971, dominated a wall:

AL UNSER WINS AGAIN IN RECORD 157.735

Under that headline, a three-column caption gave 1971's bad news:

RACE CAR SMASHES PHOTO
STAND. 18 HURT

And on the wall behind the crew hung a typical car-gang joke:

CHUCK YOU, FARLIE

Decals and stencils laid claim to a share of some winner's glories soon to come. The commercial and/or business side of Indianapolis is serious. Winning, for a car sponsor, *is* everything. At stake is an advertising campaign focused on the winning car: it used x tires, y fuel, z battery. For cigarette, luggage, beer, motel, or prune juice sponsors, the free TV (and other media) coverage is the important factor. Cameras zoom in, and linger, on the "win" car only. A cigarette sponsor, with cigarette-advertising banned from television, can "buy" TV exposure by backing the champion car.

Competition affects both cars and drivers. There are always more drivers than cars, more cars than sponsors. Somebody who probably envied Joe Leonard's Viceroy cigarette sponsorship took a picture of Joe smoking another brand of cigarette, enlarged the picture to lifesize. Viceroy dropped Leonard.

Factors beyond a driver's control could affect sponsorship: Joe Leonard's main sponsor, Samsonite Luggage, claimed to have been badly hurt by the Arab oil embargo (a petroleum derivative was the base of luggage plastic). Samsonite's volume fell. Advertising became gratuitous. Joe Leonard once more was dropped.

Because of that same oil crisis, gasoline sponsors slipped away from racing—some temporarily, others permanently. One by one, all of America's carmakers quit the racing game. Television and film money became bigger factors than ever in the "500" racing balance sheet. The economics of racing are stark: it cost just under a quarter of a million dollars to back a "500" car in 1972. In 1971 only two drivers—"500" champion Al Unser and Joe Leonard—earned more than that.

Unlike the Kentucky Derby, in which individual competitors can appear only once, the Indianapolis "500" draws on the same top drivers year after year. How will Bobby Unser—or any of the other twenty or so repeaters—do *this* year? Who isn't coming? What changes will so-and-so make in his driving style? What changes were made in the first row cars? These are some of the questions raised in what is possibly the most highly competitive industry—as well as sport—in the country.

Competition between cars may be competition between drivers, mechanics, pit crews, designers, scientists, engineers. Aeronautical theory may be applied to windflow; physics and chemistry may modify fuel combustion, metal stress and fatigue, etc.

Horsebreeding is linear and irreversible: Buckpasser speed or First Landing endurance is a matter of genes. No Buckpasser genes, no Buckpasser speed. Car design and car building can go forward, then move back to an earlier concept or detail. Every engine or chassis can be duplicated, modified, improved in ways the original designer perhaps did not foresee. A good mechanic like a crafty lawyer can bend the rules and produce rather unexpected results.

In 1972, cars qualified at speeds close to 200 miles an hour, teetering on what Bobby Unser called "the ragged edge." Perhaps the limits of safety had been reached for thirty-three cars occupying a single two-and-a-half mile track. But the Indianapolis "500" is successful when it runs safely, and equally successful when it does not. There may even be goons who come to the "500" hoping their spectacular will produce the biggest crash to get into the Guinness Book of Records. Indianapolis is not without its demolition derby fans. Indianapolis drivers, however, win only when they avoid major accident. And no driver knows where or when trouble will hit.

Mike Mosley was leading the 1972 race on the fifty-seventh lap when he crashed into the outside wall coming out of the fourth and home turn. His car spun into the inside wall at the head of the straightaway, careened off, smashed into the outside wall again. Highly inflammable fuel forced up through the car's bladder shot blazing out of the cap. At more than 120 miles an hour, Mosley had to stand up like a chariot driver and fight the fire while steering his smashed car. When he jumped, or fell, out of his burning car and began to roll on the track, the firefighting crew rushed to spray foam over the car—unaware that Mosley was on fire under his asbestos suit. In 1971, on the 167th lap, Mosley had crashed into that very same outside wall, breaking a leg and an arm, getting badly burned. Because of his experience in 1971 he had insisted his 1972 car have rail holds. In 1972 those rail holds saved Mosley's life.

On its less serious festival level, the "500" has nothing to do with accidents or car trouble. The huge checkered stocking on top of the Speedway tower is filled with party balloons released just as racetime approaches on this May New Year's Eve. In the "500" parade, kids march out first, as imps, devils, woodsmen, colonials, imperialists, braided tram-conductors. Soon the morning parade inside the Speedway blends with the automotive sounds and images soon to take over. The first bands coming past the half-empty stands eyes-left just as the pit pneumatic guns rrrrrrupp in a test of essential race equipment. One after another, as the parade goes by, the "500" cars move into the pits.

The build-up to the race is a highly skilled operation. Excitement is blocked out, and suddenly escalated. The instant the almost-local Purdue University band introduced its familiar Big Ten quickmarch to the gathering crowd—"Back Home in Indiana" played at a pace for pneumatic guns—the mood changed everywhere. Older college majorettes bouncy in silver lamé perked the parade up. Even Purdue's "largest drum in the world" got a loud local roar of recognition.

By the time the Purdue band had passed out of range, pit crews had put in their protective earplugs and huddled around their revving cars. The entire area now was full of exploding starts, loud firing, backfiring, gunning as Mark Donohue, the eventual winner of this race, revved his engine. The parade continued to pass the pit area, but only the Soul Stompers of Montclair, New Jersey, could penetrate the big car roar.

By 10 A.M. the Speedway had banished its parades. The track was cleared. Now, firefighting equipment, tow trucks, ambulances realistically, unceremoniously, moved into position. Nurses hung outside the Speedway Hospital, ready to go when needed. The "500," once started, charges without intermission to its conclusion. Driver and car are existentially "seized." Yellow *slowdown* and red *stop* flags modify a race, black *come in* flags could eliminate a specific car. Otherwise blasting noise and blurring motion occupy space for three solid hours.

The "500" noise level is terrifyingly high, and relentless. For weeks after the race its characteristic roarpast remained with me. Baseball is a rather quiet sport which relaxes tensions between turns at bat. Football and basketball have their time-outs and half-times; boxing dictates three minutes of pounding, but a fourth minute of rest. The "500," however, circles loud speeding images two and a half miles 200 times—always the same four turns, always the same all-out gunning through the straightaways.

Some spectators simply cannot stand such uninterrupted assault on ear and eye. One business firm scheduled its picnic to begin at around the 150-mile mark, allowing guests to drink, eat, chat—and avoid watching about 250 or 300 miles of race. One could actually leave the Speedway for an hour. When one returned the race would still be roaring on.

In the infield during the race, amid the crush of parked cars, and the roar of the "500," football and frisbee continue. Almost as an afterthought an infielder inquires about the race, wanders to some high vantage point to check out what's happening. Many tune to the radio broadcast of the race, and never look at the cars.

The infield is a bivouac area during some old-fashioned war. Nobody bothers the "soldiers" in the bivouac, and the "soldiers" aren't that concerned about those outside.

At 10:50 A.M., with the track temperature 120°, and hundreds of balloons sailing Seurat color dots into the Indianapolis sky, the bivouacs stirred. Jim Nabors sang "Back Home in Indiana." The real "500" theme song followed—Tony Hulman's public-address system words:

"Gentlemen, start your engines."

Up rose a tribal howl similar to the Louisville cry that greeted the first notes of "My Old Kentucky Home." Two and a half banked miles of spectators roared as engines turned over, caught, and drivers held up a right forefinger in the "engine started" sign. Thirty-two cars moved at once with the pace car, and the Electro Pacer's O.K. The thirty-third, A. J. Foyt's, alas, was left standing. Quickly his crew moved it off the track. The pace car, with Jim Rathmann driving, came around on its first lap, the yellow flag out; Foyt's car still couldn't get going. Thirty-two cars hung anxiously behind Rathmann's pace car, waiting for the green flag to go up. A.J. couldn't get his car to budge. Not till the third pace lap did he make contact, and creep slowly into line. Almost immediately Starter Pat Vidan gave his flashy bent-knee, whipping "go" with the green flag. The field, led by Bobby Unser, shifted up from the pace car's final 125 mph to 160, 180, then higher.

For ten laps Bobby Unser's speed averaged over 176 mph—about 8 mph faster than the 1971 ten-lap record. In what looked like an absurd runaway Bobby lapped his first car. By lap twenty-one he had lapped all but the first ten starting. By lap twenty-three Bobby lapped his own brother, Al. Doing 185, "breathing his motor," cutting fuel consumption, Bobby suddenly stopped dead. He had broken a five-buck rotor on his distributor. His engine cut off. Bobby was out. The damage could have been repaired thirty or fifty laps later—when the car had cooled down—but Bobby preferred not.

"What the heck," he said, "I came here to race to win, not run for eighteenth place."

On lap fifty-seven I heard a terrible screaming come from the stands north of where I sat. Then I saw car "98"—Mike Mosley's—on fire, and Mosley standing up, hanging on to those outside handrails and steering to avoid hitting the wall head-on. Minutes after the crash Mosley was doused with foam, packed in ice by Speedway doctors, flown by helicopter to the special burns ward in Methodist Hospital.

Speedway Hospital, before the Mosley fire, had had to deal with the usual Spectacular freak-outs, bad-trippers, suicidal drunks, pilgrims with cut and burned feet. By ten in the morning crew members had to cover cockpits against the scorching Indiana sun which fired parked cars, infield dust, discarded beercans. Beerrings became sharp, burning foot traps in the infield obstacle course. Communal trippers, like eaters of the magic Indian mushroom, had to be comforted and reassured. One camper played a "Grateful Dead" cassette for lonely acidheads pulsating among broken squares and warped circles.

Dennis Tusman, of Wally Dallenbach's crew, was badly burned by the same spraying fuel Dallenbach escaped. Tusman, too, like Mike Mosley, was flown to Methodist Hospital's special burns ward. Just after the race began, a Speedway guard suffered a heart attack and beat Mosley and Dallenbach to Methodist, dead on arrival.

On duty at the track hospital, among white-uniformed doctors and nurses, was the seventy-four-year-old Speedway chaplain, standing by in case any Roman Catholic driver needed his rites. Fortunately, in 1972 his services were not required.

One ominous big-car word in 1972 was *turbulence*. Turbulence caught rookie Mike Hiss, spun him completely around. He hit nothing, nor was he hit. The yellow flag flashed instantly but, in less than a full lap, was replaced by the green. Peter Revson's description of the race touched on turbulence as a 1970's hazard:

> "With the turbulence out there with the wings, you have to be careful how you pass. It was about as bad as I figured with the turbulence—a lot different from last year. You can't follow a car through the turn and expect to pass him. You have to sort of hang back on one of his wheels."

When the semi-official 1972 list of mechanical and materials failures was drawn up, "turbulence" was not included. Every big car driver is as aware of turbulence as any airplane pilot. The 1972 list of failures and mishaps included Bobby Unser's already-mentioned distributor rotor, Gary Bettenhausen's ignition malfunction (at a point when Gary, too, like Bobby Unser before him, seemed to have the race cinched). Broken connecting rods on their Michner-Patrick cars knocked out teammates Johnny Rutherford and Swede Savage; Salt Walther had ignition trouble on his very first lap.

Equipment failure points up the limits of will in racing. Neither will nor skill seemed relevant to the widely differing Indianapolis destinies of Johnny Rutherford, Swede Savage, and Salt Walther: Savage and Walther were victims in those blazing crashes of 1973—Savage dying; Johnny Rutherford went on to win the race in 1974. In 1972 teammates Peter Revson and Gordon Johncock were knocked out of the "500" by minor malfunctions: Gordon Johncock won the curtailed 1973 race; Peter Revson was killed racing in 1974. And 1972's winner, Mark Donohue, was killed in Austria three years later.

Of the thirty-three cars starting the 1972 "500," only fifteen— regardless of what a driver willed—were still running at the end. After establishing a new thirty-lap average speed of 179.322—*16* miles higher than the 1971 record—Bobby Unser, to repeat, was out. Gary Bettenhausen took over the lead, held it from lap thirty-one till Mike Mosley took over. Then Mosley crashed, and Bettenhausen, only a short distance behind, swerved, avoided Mosley, and took back the lead. From lap fifty-eight, it was all Gary Bettenhausen's seemingly lucky "76"; 100 laps later still it was Bettenhausen. Even then, Bettenhausen said after the race, "I knew I wouldn't be around for the finish. Things were going too good to be true and I just had a feeling something was going to happen."

"It's the nineteenth year of the Bettenhausen jinx," said one of Bettenhausen's brothers, Merle, referring to the failure not only of Gary but of their father, Tony Bettenhausen—killed during a "500"—ever to win at Indianapolis. Those in the stands saw Gary Bettenhausen fall back, then drop out of the race; they also heard, in every section of the Speedway, the "death" sound of a "sour motor" firing out of sequence. Overheating was the result, and its consequences, useless pistons.

"My water temperature started out at 200 and it kept getting hotter and hotter," Bettenhausen said. "I was getting out of the throttle real early, then stomping on it, trying to cool things down with my fuel, but it didn't work."

By lap 177 Bettenhausen started to fall back—from second behind Jerry Grant, to third—and by lap 188, when his teammate, Mark Donohue, took over the lead from Jerry Grant (in the pit to check his left front tire), Bettenhausen was "coming back to the field"—rolling his tires, his engine not only "sour" but "sick." Every successive turn around the track was at a lower speed, continuously announcing Bettenhausen bad news with a firecracker-exploding uncelebratory farewell. The champagne set up for Gary Bettenhausen's party had to be moved one door away, to Mark Donohue's garage 76. Fruit and flower baskets, telegrams and cables of congratulations accompanied a fat winner's check, and the Borg-Warner trophy into Mark Donohue's garage 76. By the time Mark Donohue got the checkered flag, Gary Bettenhausen was just another loser being towed in the direction of Victory Lane, which only Donohue's car entered. Their two blue Sunoco-McLarens seemed exactly alike; their will-to-win commitment was undoubtedly intense—and equal. Mark Donohue was the champion. Being the champion's teammate was small consolation for Gary Bettenhausen.

Donohue, fourth, third, second for most of the race, was conservative all the way. While Bobby Unser was zooming records into the "500" books, and while Gary Bettenhausen led the field lap after lap, Donohue, without "the best and strongest car" in 1972, bided his time. As for the fastest and strongest car, "We had that last year," Donohue said later, "and it didn't work out. So this year we went for reliability." Indianapolis had the knowledgeable fans to understand the meaning of such choices. For instance, Donohue's conservative strategy in 1972 called for a "smaller blower [turbocharger]" on which he, as not only driver but engineer for Roger Penske's team, decided "to turn the boost way down. It hurt us some in the traffic. We couldn't pass very well going down the straightaways. But in the end it worked out for the best."

Donohue's "gamble" required top efficiency and speedy execution from his pit crew. In the battle with Jerry Grant, Donohue's pit was able to do his servicing—and Bettenhausen's—in under thirty seconds. Jerry Grant's took forty-three. Each thirteen-second difference translated, on the track, into one fourth of a lap. Monitoring the differences were those thousands of Indianapolis aficionados, clocking the pitwork, leaving the lap speed to the electronic timers.

"I'm just the guy who turns left and stands on it [the throttle]," Donohue said after the race. "I feel like I have the last job in a long line, and the rest don't mean much unless I do mine."

Every man in Mark Donohue's chain of assigned responsibilities was up cheering as Pat Vidan gave his gaudy double flip-flap checkered-flag victory wave. Fists shot up in the air, fingers insisted, "We're Number One!" Donohue's and Bettenhausen's men, in Sunoco gas-pumping outfits—yellow shirt, blue pants—sprinted into Victory Lane behind the shouting happy pit crew. Donohue's mother, Zilly, joined Mark in Victory Lane, Donohue wreathed in orchids, red-white-and-blue ribbons, checkered-flag bunting. Posing for victory photographs, he put on a brand-new cap with "Goodyear" printed on it clear as a billboard. The Goodyear Hermes's winged foot on a racing shoe was as prominent over Donohue's happy heart. "Sunoco," the word which had dominated Donohue's car, got only right, non-heart, billing on his racing suit.

The "500" final edition of the Indianapolis *Star* carried the headline Mark Donohue could hang on his wall in 1973:

DONOHUE CAPTURES '500' PLUM,
EXPECTED TO GET $200,000 PLUS

A picture above the headline showed Donohue's "66" getting the checkered flag; the secondary caption claimed that 1972's was the "FASTEST, SAFEST 500-MILE RACE" ever.

The race was over, but not the spectacular. Fans poured down from the stands, still restrained by the firm wire fences separating spectator from pit, Victory Lane, Gasoline Alley, and track. The end of anything attended by over a quarter million people can be scary. Everyone connected with Speedway car and pedestrian control knew about the 1968 Buenos Aires soccer disaster: lighted pieces of paper thrown into a crowd caused a panic which sent thousands charging against firmly locked gates. Seventy-one people were trampled to death in Buenos Aires. The Speedway—in response, of course—added a number of extra exit gates to relieve sudden pedestrian pressure. Even so, the rush to see the winner in Victory Lane was frightening. So was the sight of people sprinting to be first out of the Speedway. Cars, in some instances, were parked a mile or two away, which put the biggest press of pedestrians and cars not inside the Speedway, but out.

In the infield, however, people didn't hurry. An Indiana State Police lieutenant couldn't understand why "for some reason those leaving . . . dilly-dallied in the infield."

People did not want to leave the infield because they didn't want their Spectacular party to end. As long as one stayed inside, the Big Day hung on. Pedestrians rushed by, cars starting up blew huge dust clouds, tires squealed in simulated dragstrip macho display right next to infielders unconcernedly spread out on their blankets or still floating frisbees. Some people sat back in their chairs, eating, drinking, smoking, listening to the radio, dozing. Tailgates were down. New picnics were beginning.

The sun, after all, was still hot. Tomorrow was Sunday. Those who belonged in Indianapolis—and had clubs, fraternities, sororities, social groups, families, or neighbors—left quickly because their action was only beginning, and somewhere else. Once the infield people left their Spectacular their "something else" was barren highway—asphalt, cement, and motorized anonymity. Traffic jams meant one thing arriving; on the way out they were an added irritation on the road to flat time and post-party depression. Misrule was almost over. The real world broke back in with its cops, its armbanded officials, its polluting automobiles. Well-fed burghers sped to their nearby homes. In time, even the most committed revelers would have to face it: the party was over.

Outside the stadium, cars in gaggle crowded together, all traffic jams merged. Beside held-up cars, people crammed the edges of roads and streamed through ditches like refugee victims of an unexpected war.

VIPs sped off, free of cloggy traffic. In suburban upper middleclass, contractor-designed manses stimulatingly Tudor, colonial, or stonily Gothic, high-income local executives and professionals in white dinnerjackets led their career-helping wives to the champagne punch long before the last Speedway tie-up disappeared. Reluctant-to-go infielders were ultimately banished from dusty Eden; comfortable Indianapolis doctors, lawyers, Gerber scientists, Eli Lilly officials, Borg-Warner executives gathered in comfortable bowers of new bourgeois bliss and celebrated their lovely race, their lovely day, their lovely system. Black cooks, black waiters and waitresses served white hosts and white hostesses and white guests the catered side dishes of affluence.

Race Day's evening parties officially began the new racing year —fifty-some weeks leading to 1973's time trials. At Mark Donohue's victory celebration, drivers were already discussing the next week's big car race at Milwaukee and planning the USAC circuit strategies that would culminate, so everyone hoped, in a 1973 "500" championship. All night long politicians, sponsors, drivers, mechanics, designers, owners, pitmen, and assorted entertainment "stars" crowded Mark Donohue's party to congratulate him and Roger Penske, and offer condolences to Gary Bettenhausen. Dan Gurney's two great drivers, Bobby Unser and Jerry Grant, had come close, which was no consolation. Bobby and Dan would have to wait till 1975 for their Victory Lane picture and everything else exciting that followed.

Clean-up crews soon began to pick their way around the few cars still stuck in the Speedway infield. In time even the Speedway hospital was empty—of patients, and of staff. Scott Fitzgerald knew that every long bright Spectacular day is eventually followed by a darker Monday morning.

When, on December 24, 1972, I returned to Indianapolis and rode a lap over the track with Al Bloemker, the track publicity director, Indianapolis was almost deserted. In the Speedway Museum a couple of women wore diaphanous pink gauze head "bandages" over pre-Christmas rollers. A few people fingered postcards in search of yet more checkered flags. In the museum aisles a man peered at rotogravure exhibits of "500" heroes. He and a grandson wore identical racing caps. The child, about six years old, had a dozen "Purolator" crests on his nylon racing-striped snowsuit. Grandfather, for his "500" image, wore an "official" Viceroy racing team jacket. For fifteen bucks, Gramps became a teammate of Al Unser, Mario Andretti, and Joe Leonard. Though it was December, Grandfather carried his "500" stopwatch talisman. His grandson had a small Mickey Mouse stopwatch. Grandfather clutched a fistful of publicity photos—mostly of Mark Donohue in his *1970* Sunoco.

The Speedway, keyed to good news, ignored Vietnam, inflation, the threat of unemployment, and, optimistically, built posh suites, closed-in party rooms, for its 1973 Spectacular. Ticket orders poured in; many sections of the grandstand, 1973, were already sold out. Souvenirs were arriving in the shops. The 1973 "500," according to publicity man Bloemker, would naturally be bigger and better and safer than ever. The 1973 "500" turned out to be a racing disaster. It was totally successful as a car-racing spectacular. The year 1973 in Indianapolis was climaxed by the "500" that peaked time which otherwise lay flat and dull. Christmas was over Indianapolis, which meant only 150 waiting days left to the "500." In the morning the lucky opening their presents would find new stopwatches they would use for the very first time at the 1973 race.

6

The Great Miami Beach
Leap Year Spectacular

To begin with, ethnologists and ornithologists would have observed the irregularity of Miami Beach's summer migration pattern: in Miami Beach prime time (winter), vast numbers of people move from the American North to the American South. Slack season (spring), vast numbers of people leave the South for the North. Off-season (summer), Miami Beach is almost deserted, or, at best, understaffed, running on reduced ergs, ohms, decibels, pheromones. Tolstoy's simple explanation for war played down Napoleon and historical causation: "Millions of men," he wrote, "repudiating their common sense and their human feelings, were bound to move from west to east . . . just as some centuries before hordes of men had moved from east to west."

When, in the summer of 1972, political hordes disturbed the usual Miami Beach South-North migration pattern, their irregular motion was, in the case of Democrats, planned. Not so the sudden "precipitate withdrawal" and "bug-out" of the Republican Party from its originally chosen convention site, San Diego. "Precipitate" was a word Richard M. Nixon and his advisers always tacked on to "withdrawal"—from Vietnam—even after seven years of undeclared war. Tolstoy didn't go for simplistic causalities, but not even Tolstoy could have ignored the one-to-one relationship between Jack Anderson's publication of the famous Dita Beard ITT memo (on the theme of now-is-the-time-for-ITT-to-come-across-to-the-aid-of-the-Republican-Party) and the speed with which the Republicans blew San Diego town. It was almost as if a floating crapgame had been tipped off that a raid was imminent. ITT had been expected to pay off with space in its subsidiary Sheraton's San Diego hotel rooms, in gratitude, the memo seemed to say, for John Mitchell's understanding of mergers and pro-ITT and anti-antitrust niceness. Miami Beach suddenly found itself the target of not one but two summer political invasions.

Louisville and Indianapolis focus on Festival week, *the* season. The rest of a year is needed for preparation. A few days after the Kentucky Derby, the "500," the Rose Bowl, Mardi Gras, committees and crews are hard at work preparing for next year's Spectacular. Festival week is handled by first-stringers. Only the top maître d's are around to hold out their palms, and veteran hotel clerks equipped to pick up the *schmeer* of sawbucks above the roar of the crowd.

Miami Beach in summer, however, fields its scrubbiest scrub team. After working the winter trade, affluent waiters, maîtres, daters migrate North with their affluent clientele. Those left in the service trades want only to take it easy. Permanent residents, most of them retired, look forward to summer's relaxed pace. If fewer eating places stay open, fewer people are around to compete for tables. The favored hangouts don't usually shut up summers anyway.

Beaches are deserted in summer, but who living in Miami wants beaches? Big hotels usually run reduced-rate summer conventions the locals scorn as chintzy. Winter Miami Beach is on the same big-name entertainment circuit as Las Vegas:

> *In the pumprooms,*
> *Headliners come and go*
> *Direct from Vegas*
> *And the Johnny Carson Show.*

During the summer of 1972 the big name in Miami Beach entertainment wasn't Chubby Checkers, or even Tubby Chess, but somebody named Tubby Boots. The only recognizable Las Vegas marquee names were those appearing live on a Democratic Party fundraising telethon. Marlo Thomas was in Miami Beach—as a delegate. And so was Shirley MacLaine.

First-line masseuses, masseurs, among other prime-time Miami Beach featured stars, absented themselves from the summer setting. The very best pickpockets and conpersons were off to minky northern jewel farms like Saratoga. Summer's call-girls were a little shrill and anxious. The hookers in the Democratic convention hotels, looked at in the post-Watergate perspective, were possibly plants from the Committee to Re-elect the President or perhaps just nice Republican college girls donating the summer of '72 to four more years of Richard Nixon.

Every year, during Easter break, when Fort Lauderdale was being invaded, Miami Beach picked up a few lost or strayed collegians. Fort Lauderdale funsters were traditionally apolitical. The whole Pepsi Generation liked its news light and lively.

A new and different generation invaded Miami Beach in July of 1972 to set up bivouac in hotel lobbies and Flamingo Park. A few Fort Lauderdale play-people turned up in Miami Beach, and only a few familiar ahistorical apolitical hippies. For the most part, the young people who converged on Miami Beach were political and radical, last vestiges of the children's crusade and the flower generation.

On June 17, 1972, just three weeks before the Democratic Convention, the Watergate break-in made household words of James McCord, E. Howard Hunt, G. Gordon Liddy, and a group unfairly referred to only as "the Cubans." Watergate-burglar, CIA-helper, Miami Dolphin fan, and real-estate-front man Bernard Barker seemed to be their leader and spokesman. Miami Beach was full of nostalgic Cuban fascisti, ex-Batista secret police, anti-Castro suicide squads, at-the-ready private armies and marching sodalities Bernard Barker could apparently summon to service at the drop of a hat full of hundred dollar bills. The possibilities of a summer confrontation between the Cuban right and the yippying left was water in the sour cream of any Miami Beacher's blintzes.

A modern police chief, like a football coach, often studies films of the "team" he's coming up against next. Miami Beach's chief, Rocky Pomerance, figured out from the way Richard Daley's cops had played the yippies during the Chicago convention in 1968 that cool was needed in '72. Rocky was no law-and-order hard-nose. He didn't pack a Colt 45, carry a cattle prod, wear a riot helmet, plastic face shield, Wyatt Earp hat. His unspoken response to Flamingo Park pot-smokers, for example, was, "That's nice, kiddies, don't fight." Pomerance rejected the Nixon-Mitchell massive arrest strategy used in Washington a couple of years earlier. He had riot-equipped men ready behind high wire fences, not parading the streets to force a demonstrator's big hero move. Flamingo Park could have its "love-in" or "smoke-in," and Rocky Pomerance, being uninvited, would not attend. Rocky didn't play the convention for national prime-time television coverage. And *Time* wasn't likely to make him—*or* Bernard Barker—1972's *Man of the Year*.

For permanent Miami Beach residents, attending the political spectaculars was not automatic. Louisville or Indianapolis residents could participate in the Derby or "500" without being delegated by someone else. Locals almost always had the most fun. During a political convention, however, outsiders became the real insiders. One could not buy a ticket into a state caucus: the innermost political circles were far more remote than Indianapolis's Gasoline Alley garages. One had to be something official—a delegate, an alternate, a staff member, a candidate, a media representative, a big contributor—in order to be "in."

A senior citizen in Miami Beach was a person without party privileges. Here was this spectacular, here were the uninvited. One could, of course, talk with political convention gypsies like Allen Ginsberg in Flamingo Park, and perhaps join him in an *om* or his then recently discovered *ah*. Almost everything else, unhappily, was a matter of badges, tags, ribbons, passes, lapel buttons. One could perhaps make it into the public galleries on a boring day, but political pull was needed to participate further.

The Democratic Convention seemed no more democratic than the Republican: in the innermost of inner party circles sat the "givers"—sometimes, of course, particularly in the case of the Republicans, the very same people who occupied the choicest inner party seats for the Kentucky Derby or the Indianapolis "500."

The tone of the political invasion could be felt on the fringes of the convention center and headquarter hotels, in Pumpernick's Restaurant, for instance, the Miami Beach hangout that stayed open, though with a reduced staff, during off-season. At Pumpernick's, locals and badge-wearers sat table-to-table; the camaraderie began before the convention officially opened.

A retired Miami Beach couple, Pumpernick regulars, could look up at any time and see a fresh badgery of "outside" delegates.

"What kind of kweezeen is it here?" a delegate might ask, and crane forward a little to study the natives at their food.

In the set scene, repeated again and again, the waitress held her order pad close to the chest, pencil poised, face averted.

"That there is pastrami and eggs," she finally answered.

"Is it good?"

A retired resident couple raised up their insulted heads: who were these dressed-up hillbillies? Would Max and Lil eat anything that wasn't "good"?

"Pisstrami ain't seafood, is it?" whispered another delegate. "I got shellfish allergy."

"It's meat, smoked meat," the waitress said.

"Smoked—that's peppery," said the delegate with "shellfish allergy," "I get heartburn from pepper."

"So try something creemcheese."

"Creemcheese is lunch. This here is dinnertime."

"You make good hamburgers here?" the food phobias spokesperson asked.

"What's a bagel?" said the man, scanning the menu for creamcheese. "And what's a lox?"

"A bagel," a cosmopolitan woman delegate explained, "is bread with a hole in it."

"And a lox?"

"Edna," said the man who feared heartburn, "could you please make me a good hamburger, well-done, with lotsa mayonnaise, mustard, pickle, ketchup."

"Hamburger sounds real good to me," somebody else said.

The delegation voted as a bloc. Edna added nothing to her order pad. She obviously had inscribed *hamburgers well-done* the instant the delegation entered.

"Look who's gonna choose us a President," she said to the hostess as she hurried by.

Later during the convention, 4 A.M. the July night George

McGovern was nominated to lose to Richard Nixon, I dropped in on Wolfie's Restaurant, an all-night Miami Beach homing station, full of winners and losers from small-stakes poker games, salesmen attending smallwares conventions, sleepy-eyed minor Mafiosi and their double-eyelashed gold-thread-miniskirted girls.

An elderly man came in, looked around, sighed, dropped into the counter seat beside me. He leaned forward to fish a menu out of the invisible counter shelf below, carefully put on his reading glasses, held the menu close to his face as a blind for his quick inventory of the close-at-hand.

"Whatsamattah," my waitress said and slopped a glass of water in his direction, "your sleepin' pill don't work again?"

"You make me always the best sleeping pill, Mabel," the man said absently, still casing the clientele, "extra lean—an' no mustard."

"You seen me ever put mustard on a person's corn'beef?"

The man checked to see if my plate harbored a little poison mustard. He shook off Mabel's offer to relieve him of his menu, and resumed his tricky peek-a-boo casing of the customers.

Kittycorner to him is someone wearing a McGovern button on a navy see-through tanktop. This person has on bright red lipstick, matching nailpolish and toepolish, lots of black eye make-up, a single black hoop earring, a wood crucifix on a leather thong, a dozen or so rings, a pink plastic watch, a slave clasp, three bracelets, a forearm covered with wire bangles.

Mabel brings the sandwich.

"See," she says, "no mustard."

Lost in contemplation the man can't speak his lines in their nightly duet. He neglects the soporifics of corned beef, and, instead, studies Tanktop. If what he sees is a woman, his frown translates as compassion—for someone so tragically flatchested. If what he sees is a man, the frown confirms Nixon strategy. Nixon, George Wallace, Wilbur Mills, Henry Jackson, and Hubert Humphrey have been saying all along that George McGovern is the candidate of sexual deviates, the acne-faced, uppity women, poor northern whites, poorer southern blacks, Indians, Chicanos, Puerto Ricans.

"Whatsamattah," says Mabel, "the corn'beef ain't lean enough? Suddenly the man ain't hun'ry."

In July 1972 the political wisdom of enlisting Tanktop and other marginal politicals into the mainstream was a major McGovern question: the constitutional right of all to participate equally in the political process is supposedly guaranteed. After disclosures by John Dean, Jeb Magruder, Chuck Colson, James McCord, the Nixon tapes, Tanktop requires a post-Watergate double-take. Someone like Tanktop could have been hired by the Nixon team out of Central Casting and fitted with lipstick, bangles, and McGovern buttons in order to reinforce Middle America's worst fears about a "President McGovern." Tanktop could even have been "Sedan Chair III," "Roadrunner II," or "Searchlight IV," working the Democratic National Convention for the Committee to Re-elect the President. I wonder now if the lavender sweatshirts tatted "Gay Power" on the back and "McGovern" on the front might not have been manufactured by some electrified Betsy Ross treadling in the White House basement. Could anything at the national conventions be accepted as what it seemed?

To set the 1972 political Spectacular historically we must do a number of double-takes: first, for instance, on that Nixon "enemy" list. An "enemy" could fit into the total category reserved for George McGovern, or the possibly helpful category of party treasurer Robert Strauss (and, ironically, Larry O'Brien, prime target of the Watergate break-in). Strauss, O'Brien, Senator Henry Jackson, Senator Hubert Humphrey shared the *"right"* or *"moderate,* possibly helpful"* category that wittingly, or unwittingly, served Nixon's ends well during the summer conventions and ensuing election. A "total enemy" favored an immediate end to the Vietnam War; cuts in defense spending; domestic spending programs to help the poor; civil rights programs (which invariably involved what Governor George Wallace called "busin'"; membership by blacks in "white" hardhat unions; equal rights for women; clean water, clean air, an end to stripmining, offshore oil drilling, and nuclear power plants. To this left syndrome, Democratic, as well as Republican, opponents of McGovern radicals wanted to add abortion, gay rights among other goads to white middleclass and blue-collar voters.

My notes for the Democratic Convention are self-mocking, but, in the light of Watergate, almost naïve. When I thought I was being Lenny Bruce, history showed me to be, at best, Gulliver, or Candide. On closed-circuit Democratic National Committee television I watched Strauss, Jackson, Governor Jimmy Carter (of Georgia) work McGovern over, and speculated, "Who wrote this Democratic stuff—Patrick Buchanan? Charles Colson? Murray Chotiner?"

On national television I watched an anti-Pat Nixon demonstration by long hair "hippies" in workshirts and jeans: in front of them the "neat" Nixon supporters faced forward, males in David Eisenhower shirt, tie, and jacket, females in Julie's Barbie Doll dresses. The "neats" applauded Pat Nixon, the "hippies" yowled, and, I noted, "How come the Nixon faction doesn't look behind to see who's making the disturbance?" I wrote a magazine article late in August 1972, but didn't mention this incident because even after the Checkers speech, after Nixon's 1962 California gubernatorial campaign, *and* Watergate, who would suspect a man of using his wife in a phony demonstration? My notes, in fact, are full of ignored speculation: I wonder who the Nixon plants are at McGovern, Wallace, Humphrey, and Jackson headquarters? But I dismiss this kind of thing as piddling and paranoid.

My notes about the Secret Service agents assigned to "protect" Democratic candidates speculate: why *wouldn't* a Secret Service guardian-of-the-lapel-flag report Democratic Party conversations back to Nixon headquarters? The "American *apparat,*" my notes say, "makes all cops, secret agents, and soldiers brothers under the skin, and all opponents, dissenters, Vietnamese or domestic, 'enemies.'"

On July 10, 1972, in the Carillon Hotel, the National Women's Political Caucus meets the candidates. My notes read:

> Terry Sanford [former Democratic governor of North Carolina] talks to Caucus. Secret Service guy detaches himself, pretends to read newspaper, sidles over, watching the girl and boy "hippy" behind me. Now he reads a newspaper he holds in front of his face, the sly fox (What kind of labor pool does Nixon draw on?). The dangerous spies don't realize they're under a hotshot's surveillance. I hear them clearly.

The man, unfamiliar with how college kids handle boring political lectures, will need lots of luck with *A, my name is Alice* in the de-coding room.

DANGEROUS GIRL SPY   My name is Dinah, my husband's name is Daniel, we come from Dallas, and we sell diamonds.

DANGEROUS BOY SPY   My name is Edward, my wife's name is Edna, we come from Edinburgh, and we sell ermine.

A claim made at the Watergate hearings was that the Nixon Republicans had engineered the nomination of George McGovern on the Democratic ticket. This particular anti-McGovern game plan called for the new Republican majority to break the traditional Democratic Party hold on labor, Roman Catholics, Jews, the young, professional people—*at the presidential level.* Polls showed those who favored re-election of the incumbent often explained, "He's our President." Strategy thus dictated a "Re-elect your President," not a "Re-elect your Richard Nixon" campaign. Polls indicated no great love, trust, or enthusiasm for Nixon; "Re-elect the President" strategy required as Democratic candidate someone the voters would like even less—a difficult, perhaps impossible goal; or distrust even more—equally difficult but not impossible.

To use the Democratic Convention properly, the Nixon brain trust had to make sure their "loser candidate," George McGovern, was nominated. But first, other contending Democrats had to be sidelined. Number one as a winner threat was Senator Edmund Muskie. Strangely, nobody during the Watergate hearings and trials asked if the CIA had ever been requested to draw up *a psychological profile of a possible contending presidential rival for Nixon,* like, say, Senator Edmund Muskie. The successful wipeout of Senator Muskie, remember, presented *him* to the nation as a broken man—crying in public, obviously lacking the essential macho to stand up to the Soviet Union and too querulous to be entrusted with the dangerous nuclear black box.

Muskie began well ahead of Richard Nixon—47 per cent–39 per cent in the Harris Poll for May 1971. By March 7, 1972 (the date of the New Hampshire primary), Muskie was no longer a national factor. In between, the Committee to Re-elect had hired one "Fat Jack" Buckley, who, in turn, planted a Nixon man as Senator

Muskie's driver with an assignment to pick up stuff Chuck Colson and Dwight Chapin needed for their "Eliminate Muskie" plan.

If someone had told me in 1972 that Richard Nixon's personal lawyer, Herbert Kalmbach, had $250,000 available for a Segretti dirty tricks operation, I would have labeled the informant insane. Yet, somehow, the only man the Harris Poll showed capable of beating Richard Nixon in 1972 was wiped out silently and efficiently without one single doubter asking *how*.

Before the Watergate revelations, I could have looked at Tank-top at Wolfie's with passing speculation. But once accept the power of the Nixon team to orchestrate the nomination of McGovern—even if their claim is excessive—and a hideous double-take sets in. People freely favoring abortion are no longer individuals in a national debate but actors in a Committee to Re-elect scenario to win Roman Catholic votes. Women who thought they had made great political progress in 1972 were *used* in another Nixon scenario to frighten apolitical women afraid of losing their "femininity."

At the Kentucky Derby and the Indianapolis "500" I could believe what I saw: Riva Ridge won the Derby; Mark Donohue won the "500." But ever since the summer of 1972, revelation after revelation has shown that I did *not* see what I thought I saw in Miami Beach. To write about the political Spectaculars of 1972 I stand tiptoe like a painter on a swinging scaffold and try to draw straight lines on a shifting wind-blown canvas.

The people at both political conventions were real, but in the White House scenarios the "real" had roles assigned them by an old fake master scripter. Psychological profiler Iago, remember, bragged he could "turn virtue into pitch" and "out of . . . goodness make the net [to] enmesh" the innocent. Senator Muskie, like trusting Othello, thought the fake was real. He undoubtedly believed the hired staged pro-Nixon demonstrations to be genuine and spontaneous. His own driver Muskie undoubtedly considered as "honest" as he seemed. Everyone, Muskie included, knew the history of "tricky Dick" Nixon. A political and psychological profile of Richard Nixon was needed, but never drawn.

For the Miami Beach Spectaculars, history was no mere backdrop—as it had been for the Kentucky Derby and Indianapolis

"500." History *was* the Miami Beach Spectacular. Richard Nixon had created a political climate for an American Reichstag fire. One piece of door tape and many reels of sound tape changed history by ultimately bringing down Richard Nixon just when total power seemed his. Jeb Stuart Magruder—and others—were absolutely certain that success and power would win: "After all, *we* were the government." Absolute power lulled absolutely. Richard Milhous Nixon had a great fall. But the ability of absolute power to corrupt an American President and all government agencies absolutely, remains.

7

That Summer of '72

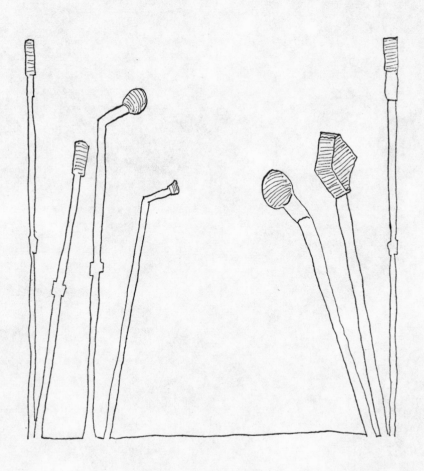

In early July as I waited in New York's La Guardia Airport for my Miami flight to be called, a girl of about eighteen slipped into the lounge-room seat beside mine. She was peddling underground papers. I didn't need a brown rice connection but bought a paper anyway. She carried a small pile in a macramé bag she also offered to sell me. The papers, the bag were produced by her commune. So were her hoop earrings, her tie-dye T-shirt beaded with askew-headed eagles and asymmetric suns; and her crocheted pale-rose wool shawl and appliquéd jeans (sunflowers, daisies, and two "I love you's"); her leather sandals, studded leather belt, studded leather watchband, matching wristband, leather neckthong, attached hemi-fired ceramic tortoise; her silver Mexican wedding rings (one on each hand), her birthstone ring (pearl), her zodiac pin (she was a Gemini); her hooked-rug shoulderbag (aswim with fish). Much like a peripatetic model who twirls past as you're trying to spoon up soup at a hotel lunch, the girl showed me the beauties, and quoted me the prices, of all her commune's creativity.

She explained that a healthy commune girl had to work a foul pollution trap like the airport because "people who fly have all the bread." *Fortune,* I think, pays out thousands annually for surveys that reach equally simple conclusions.

"Most people lead bullshit lives," the girl said, "so they buy our underground paper and pretend they're not trapped on a bummer."

The terminal door swung open and a mass of straw-hatted McGovernites charged in, which sent the girl into her hustling act. Nobody was much interested in her notes from commune underground. Undeterred, she came back to her seat.

"Politics," she said, "has never been a high for me."

The McGovernites hollered to each other from various areas of the terminal. A TV crew growled over lost equipment. A public television producer was begging for Darvon.

"They're just pretend manic," the girl explained, "part of the bullshit nostalgia trip. Get into their heads and you find fraternities, formal weddings."

A black family—man, woman, four children—came into the terminal. The girl didn't approach them.

"My high," she said, "is people."

She looked around. A drunk stretched out on a bench, his head shielded from the glare by a chewed-up *Daily News;* a Cuban couple asleep, each cradling a sleeping child; the public television gang looked terribly depressed as their producer approached hysteria.

The girl gathered up her bag of papers.

"Political convention," she made a sour face. "No heads here. No together people. You've got to be on a high your own way, no matter what, right?"

Once on the plane the McGovern people were strangely subdued, huddled in groups, studying charts, mimeographed sheets, newspaper xeroxes. That television producer tried to solicit fellow-victim understanding from Marlene Sanders, of ABC, who sat beside me. Across the aisle Tony Randall, part of the Democratic Party's fund-raising telethon, was talking nonstop with stewardesses and others. Passengers somehow lacked the pre-Spectacular excitement of those on their way to the Derby or the "500."

From Miami's International Airport I eventually drove onto Collins Avenue, Miami Beach's "Strip." If Dante had been a twentieth-century American, Hell would not have been zoned in Circles, like his Inferno, but in Strips. Las Vegas would have made The First Strip, peopled with skimmers, godfathers, shylocks, enforcers, crooners, etc. L.A.'s Sunset Strip would have made Second Strip: on such a scale Miami Beach's Collins Avenue would have barely made it as Hell's Ninth Strip. Nobody could read wickedness in obvious commercially orgiastic hotel names like "Montmartre," "Monte Carlo," "Playboy," or "Fountainebleau." A "Fountainebleau" that rhymes with "mountain doo" suggests not a wicked French king but some kind of ginrummy-playing "Looie."

In Miami Beach asphalt and cement seal out nature. A few lonely, heroic, scrubby palms push up out of poolside tile; ornamental shrubbery flashes something a little green. Once in a while a tubby pelican heaves past the watery backside of the Strip's hotels, looking disoriented, confused, lost. Birds don't nest much in ecological disaster zones. The odd gull pecks at the shore, still convinced something real exists beneath the asphalt crust of this American pie.

The people of Miami Beach, the regulars, tried to pretend life was per usual. Along both sides of Collins Avenue, elderly residents warded off the sun with flouncy parasols and old worn commuter umbrellas as bannered busloads of Democrats rolled in from the airport and nearby states.

"Soon'll come the balloons," an old woman named Becky said to me, "no matter who they pick, so long's they give out balloons, I'm happy."

Balloons and flags weren't too plentiful, but party regulars turned up with the usual whistles, horns, stetsons, straws, wedgecaps. A few elderly women wore two-piece white dresses as if this were a DAR convention. Some oldies clung to a fun formula evidently successful the year Al Smith was nominated. Democrats occupied Miami Beach like an army unaware the captured town had already been evacuated. One devilish chap in fez and goatee set off a string of tiny firecrackers to scare the silkstockinged ladies: watching, women delegates in pantsuits stared at the joker as if he were a six-year-old with his toilet-training in remission.

As a former Minnesota resident I had arranged to sit in with the state delegation and live in the Monte Carlo Hotel, Minnesota headquarters. I had friends in the Humphrey majority, the McGovern minority, knew delegates who were for Shirley Chisholm, and others who considered themselves uncommitted. Indians in the Minnesota delegation invited me to the Indian Caucus and American Indian Movement meetings. Arvonne Fraser cued me in on the deliberations of the National Women's Political Caucus.

Becky, my new Miami Beach friend, didn't much like political conventions.

"He'll make better parades," she said, nodding in the direction of President Nixon's Key Biscayne compound. "I'll tell you the truth, I'm not much for politics. Him [Nixon], who can like? Them [the Democrats] ain't overpacked with who's special [FDR]. So if it's him [Nixon], or some nother nothing?"

She beckoned me over and whispered in my ear.

"You want the truth? Him [Fischer] and the Russian [Spassky] are more interesting. I know about chess like I know about politics, but with them [Fischer-Spassky] at least something is serious."

"July August is the best time to go visit a relative somewheres," an old man, Herb, told me, "if you have. You haven't, you stay. This summer should be a little interesting, am I right? Who'll be President is a big thought."

Becky and Herb and their respective spouses lived in a highrise among the dozens of highrises, condominiums, and retirement hotels west of Collins Avenue on the Biscayne Bay side of the "Strip." Others lived south of the Strip in the older section of Miami Beach around Flamingo Park, or on the west side of Biscayne Bay. One could always tell where the old lived from the prevalence of private hospitals, private nursing homes, waiting ambulances, doctors' offices, mortuaries. These catered to the elderly; others ripped them off. Gerontologists, geriatniks lived off the old, and program directors, stand-up comedians, pinochle-hustlers, dance-instructors, heartburn-curers, film-makers, diet-crazies, stockbrokers, priests, rabbis, ministers, sociologists, shyster lawyers, quacks, bunion-parers, truss-makers, pill-pandars, matchmakers, investment-counselors, bookies, funeral home directors, cemetery-plot salesmen, writers, and makers of educational or noneducational TV documentaries.

I saw my friend Becky and her husband, at the Eden Roc

coffeehouse counter, spooning up their Sanka, blowing on it coolly, oblivious of the swirling delegates, cameramen, headphoned media women, staffpeople with walkie-talkies and clipboards, poll results and advertising mock-ups. Sunday, one day before the convention formally opened, the key hotels were full. People massed in front of the Doral waiting to see "President" McGovern, lined up at the Deauville for a glimpse of Shirley Chisholm or Wilbur Mills. Muskie and Eugene McCarthy were at the Americana, Jackson at the Montmartre, and Humphrey at the Carillon. George Wallace had put a lot of distance between himself and McGovern by settling in the Four Ambassadors Hotel on the far side of downtown Miami.

Becky watched, Becky waited, and, right behind her back, the great political Spectacular began. Outside Convention Hall troops and police made one quick display, then retired behind high wire fences. On side streets between the Convention Center and Flamingo Park kids halfheartedly hustled a few cars into private driveways. Rooms-to-let went fast but, unlike Indianapolis and Louisville, Miami Beach unofficially encouraged people to camp out, in Flamingo Park. Tents went up at night, disappeared early in the morning. Packed campers sat out on Park area streets. Miami Beach's summer transformation had begun.

All the big-name anchormen were in Miami Beach—something none of the other Spectaculars could accomplish. Above the convention floor CBS News hung its cyclopean orange eye. ABC News glared its three-letter logo in red, blue, and green. NBC News, in contrast, muted its presence, coming on in black and white.

Becky in the Eden Roc didn't seem impressed. She sipped her Sanka and off-handedly prodded the counter poundcake to see if it was fresh. When she spotted me, she had only one question.

"Say, maybe you know Walter Cronkite?"

I didn't.

"It maybe ain't too late to talk him in to run?"

In the Eden Roc, and elsewhere, one fell—unconsciously at first —into a recognition game. From someone's stance, thrust of jaw, a woman's skirt length, the fullness of a man's sideburns, the prevalence of hair spray, enamel flags, clip-on earrings, one guessed whom the delegate was supporting. The Wallace and Mills syndrome was hard to miss—stern face, military posture—though one frequently mistook a Wallace for a Mills, and vice versa. Senator McGovern's delegates were rarely confused with anybody else's.

Among the McGovern volunteers were people brought into American politics by Jack Kennedy. Some had worked with Bobby and Ethel Kennedy. Before joining up with McGovern, some had been part of the Eugene McCarthy "Children's Crusade." The very young were here, and another group made up of the lame and the halt. Stammerers, the spastic, the paraplegic found once again, in the McGovern campaign, the Kennedy welcome. Children of the liberal upper middleclass were a source of much McGovern pre-convention strength. In August, when the Nixon convention took over Miami Beach, these people, and others like them, disappeared from the convention hotels.

The "different," the "unusual," the "powerless" believed that this, their convention, would not only nominate George McGovern but turn America around. These were the naïve. To assure doubters that hardheaded professionals rather than kids or amateurs would be running the McGovern show, McGovern's strategists started to refer to his key people as "hard" and "tough." The amateurs McGovern's primary opponents had once mocked were now celebrated as the new tough political tacticians. Their success in primaries was matched by their tough handling of certain state nominating conventions.

Some minority delegates believed they were an advance guard of the quietest American revolution, the one that had brought participatory democracy to a political convention. One person, one vote was the ultimate meaning of the formula the McGovern-Fraser Commission had decreed for 1972. But non-McGovern, and anti-McGovern, delegates believed that formula was a minorities scheme to steal the nomination for George McGovern.

A Texas Chicano told me that just being at a political convention in Miami Beach was a dream—and he was a *voting* delegate. For the first time in his life, the man felt he was being courted. Politicians wanted to have lunch with him. He met with delegates from other states in late-night conversations about the southwestern political situation and Chicano expectations.

"Senior Citizen Power," too, felt strong in July, along with "Youth Power" and "Poverty Power." In July, some Democrats could imagine righteous McGovern power overcoming malignant Nixon power. Majoritarian rule and exclusion would be vanquished forever.

Richard Nixon's Committee to Re-elect wasn't flustered because it well knew that no President had ever been elected by the "minority."

"What's the matter with those guys, can't they count?" was the standard Nixon-team response to any idealistic McGovern pitch aimed at only a certain minority.

The consequences of the McGovern-Fraser formula were exciting for those brought in, a personal judgment against those left out. In almost every case—again, as Nixon's men knew—the person excluded was part of the traditional Democratic majority, overwhelmingly male, overwhelmingly white, farmers or trade unionists or smallbusiness people or party workers who considered the nominating convention Spectacular a right and reward earned by hard work, much of it voluntary or unpaid. In Minnesota, a self-imposed tithe supported the Democratic-Farm-Labor Party. People who had joined with Hubert Humphrey and others in the 1940s to win control of the Democratic Party remained involved through a regular monthly contribution to the DFL. That donation bought a share in political democracy *and* convention sweepstakes.

The immediate effect of the McGovern-Fraser formula in Minnesota was that between a fifth to a third of the regulars objecting to the new distribution dropped out of the contributing roster. Nor would any of these people work for George McGovern—were he, by defeating their own Hubert Humphrey, to get the Democratic nomination. Few, as it turned out, voted for McGovern in November. The French have a word for the feelings McGovern awoke in the party regulars—*ressentiment* (which "resentment" doesn't quite translate), a word implying jealousy, even hatred, of those with special privileges, a hatred much magnified when those privileges are considered rightfully your own.

"The kids got to learn," a Humphrey delegate said just one day before the convention opened—loudly, within hearing of lots of young people wearing McGovern buttons. "Why not do it for them in the year you can't win anyway?"

This woman was standing on the wide green lawn behind the home of Joe Robbie, owner of the Miami Dolphins, a dedicated friend of Hubert Humphrey and the Democratic Party. Joe Robbie's garden party was a big pre-convention social event. Listed high among Robbie's guests were Hubert and Muriel Humphrey. Everyone in the Minnesota delegation had been invited, and almost everybody came.

Robbie, to be fair, had also invited the McGoverns. This was no casual affair: men wore ties and jackets, women their best dresses. Booze was available in a scatter of bars, and a cater of hors d'oeuvres. Robbie's Miami Dolphins were expected to win the Super Bowl in January: Robbie, as team owner, got almost as much media exposure as Coach Don Shula, if not quite as much as the actual players—Larry Csonka, Bob Griese, Paul Warfield.

In the Edenlike setting of Joe Robbie's garden I discovered for the first time that massive hatred of George McGovern which would be a large factor in his eventual defeat. That same woman delegate anxious to teach "the kids" a lesson—I'll call her "Mary" —was redfaced with sun, cocktails, fear, anger, and hate.

"Couldn't they let Hubert be our favorite son, *our* choice—on the first ballot? We could have come to this convention unified behind Hubert. Those kids," she said, pointing to an eighteen-year-old Indian girl named Dulcie, "never worked for the DFL one day in their entire lives. I've got friends who put in twenty years doing the real hard nuts and bolts slavery, and because *she's* a minority and a first-time voter, she comes, they don't. McGovern must be real crazy if he thinks he's going to win with *her*."

At the Robbie party I met otherwise compassionate people who ordinarily would have approved any extension of political representation, but who, instead, hated McGovern for forcing the effects of that extension on them and their friends. Wives used to attending conventions with their husbands, husbands who had always come with their wives, turned up alone, and angry. In every case a minority delegate denied the Spectacular's fun to a party worker. People normally not yahoos hated the McGovern kids as just another batch of "McCarthy kids," the kind that did in Hubert Humphrey in 1968. These once compassionate DFL regulars sneered at the lame and the halt as nothing but proofs that McGovern was the candidate of freaks. Richard Nixon's people, all of a sudden, weren't all that wrong: McGovern *was* for fags, lesbians, radicals, and didn't care about ordinary decent people. Richard Nixon was right, George Wallace was right, Henry Jackson was right. As for Hubert Humphrey, he had always been right.

McGovern has probably never realized that, to differentiate themselves from him, pacifists turned themselves into Vietnam hawks; ecologists became staunch defenders of nuclear power plants, offshore drilling, strip-mining. People who abhorred the Pentagon suddenly opposed any McGovern cut in defense spending—even the piddly nicks Humphrey himself approved. *Ressentiment* was a powerful stimulus to hatred. It wasn't lessened by what was happening inside Joe Robbie's house.

A bus stopped in Robbie's driveway to unload twenty-five South Dakota "kids," who, somehow, had traveled nonstop forty-four hours to get to this party honoring Hubert and Muriel Humphrey. The kids hurried into the house, displaying flagrantly large McGovern buttons. In Joe Robbie's garden, Mary's hate orbs found them out. To others they might have seemed nice ordinary, familiar small town or farm kids. Mary glared at them as if they were child monsters recently released from the "Village of the Damned" to do a gleamy-eyed confront on behalf of wicked George McGovern.

A young boy and young girl approached Mary. She tried to turn her broad back: one fronted her swivel, the other stood guard behind.

"I see you're for Senator Humphrey," the girl said.

"You damn straight," said Mary, and lit a cigarette.

Cigarettes and alcohol, oldfashioned vices inimical to the McGovernite "lifestyle," were believed to have exorcistic power over pot-wise preachments.

"We're for him, too," said the McGovern boy. "He's a good South Dakotan, just like George McGovern."

"He sure is a good South Dakotan," Mary said menacingly, "but he ain't at all like George McGovern."

"They vote together," said the girl, "more often than not, as I'm sure you know."

"They're neighbors—I'm sure you know that, too," the boy recited. "Muriel and Eleanor McGovern are very close, like our two states."

"Neighbors," Mary countered, "ain't always close."

"The ADA rating for the two senators——" the boy began.

"We were talking about the women," said Mary.

"Well," the girl said, "would you rather talk about the women?"

"Get this straight," Mary said, "I would rather talk about nothing."

"Excuse me," said the boy, "not even our one mutual goal? I mean we all are working to beat Richard Nixon."

"That's only one of my goals," Mary said, trying to walk away.

"We have different *ultimate* goals," said the girl. "Our one immediate goal is to defeat Nixon, right?"

Her tone was medium snappish, controlled, reasonable, a nursery-school teacher trying to prevent someone from slopping over the pastepot for the fifth time that day.

"*Partially* right," said Mary. "Beating Nixon will be my goal when I'm damn good and ready."

"Do you want the war in Vietnam to continue?" the boy asked politely.

His tone wasn't snappish at all. With each parry, he simply cut Mary's assumed I.Q. by about fifteen points. Proselyting, he was unaware of Mary's deep throat gurgles and violent breathing.

"Vietnam," said his partner with a wonderfully tolerant smile, "unifies us all. Democrats of all persuasions agree the war must end immediately."

At that moment people on the lawn turned to the rear of the Robbie house where Florida's Governor Reubin Askew appeared suddenly. He was spotless in a creamy white jacket; his sunburnt face was newly shaved. In front of him was a tiny woman, Eleanor McGovern, her hair frosted white. She wore lots of eye make-up and dressed "now" as Jackie Kennedy Onassis, not "then" as Pat Nixon and Muriel Humphrey. White blouse, long white-dotted black pleated skirt, American Indian silver neckpiece with turquoise almost the color of her eyes, the total image was cool and measured as tall courtly Reubin Askew bowed making introductions.

If Mary, still clamped between the McGovernite girl and boy, thought the entrance of Eleanor McGovern would free her, she was wrong. They ignored Eleanor. Their eyes remained fixed on Mary and her possible redemption.

Governor Askew stood fidgeting, in conversation with Joe Robbie and the Robbie family as Eleanor McGovern carefully, graciously, engaged every exposed Humphrey button in some kind of talk. How a busload of South Dakota kids picked up in a dozen stops across that state was programmed to head straight for Joe Robbie's house and arrive coincidental with Eleanor McGovern was a question Mary would have liked someone to answer. Mary fumed, Mary cursed, but the Robbie "Humphrey" party, nevertheless, became a McGovern affair.

Mrs. McGovern didn't blink as Minnesota and South Dakota Instamatics clicked; she spoke quietly and confidently for all proffered tape-recorders. Mary was about three Eleanor McGoverns-wide, and, in the hot sun, felt, perhaps, six. Mary did not approve of the Eleanor *gestalt*.

"I been to Woonsocket [S.D., Eleanor McGovern's hometown]," she said, "and nobody there—I mean nobody—dresses like that."

Even wearing a Sears catalogue Mother Hubbard, Eleanor McGovern couldn't have won Mary over. Mary was in her late fifties, but her disaffection was not a function only of her age. Younger Humphreyites disliked the "beautiful people" Kennedy image the McGoverns were projecting. The romantic Kennedy thing picked up only a little sympathy in the Midwest during the 1960s. Humphrey people barely forgave Jack Kennedy for humiliating Hubert in the 1960 West Virginia and Wisconsin primaries. George McGovern was doing a familiar Kennedy number on Humphrey. From Mary's point of view, these new South Dakota swingers were nothing but oldfashioned social climbers.

In time Governor Askew and Eleanor McGovern left the Robbie party. Eleanor had stayed just long enough for someone to send Hubert and Muriel Humphrey a message—they never did turn up at Robbie's for "their" party.

After Mrs. McGovern left, most of the Minnesota people took off, too. Even those two McGovern workers eventually gave up on Mary.

A pretty woman in her early thirties, an important Humphrey worker, was among those who lingered.

"I don't know," she said as Eleanor McGovern was leaving, "if anything the McGoverns do is going to make a difference. He's probably got it sewed up already, old Nixon."

She filled her glass with ice, scotch, and a perfunctory drip of water.

"I'm that oldfashioned hard drinking type," she said, laughing. "Smoke like a chimney, cough like hell—do whatever comes naturally. What I don't do is talk and talk and talk. Did you see that teenager go after me? She wanted to teach me how to pee—I swear. Talk talk talk, about Vietnam, about Humphrey's Vietnam stand when he was Vice-President. Jesus, I've been bleeding with Hubert since 1960. I don't need the consciousness-raising thing done on *me*. And I've worked my ass off for women's rights. No skinny flatchested grump is going to chat me up on masturbation."

She pointed me to a rather depressed young man sagged on the lawn behind Robbie's house.

"That guy," she said, "was for Humphrey. He was a heavy brew-drinker—you better believe it—heavy, till McGovern's gang got to him. He turned mod, and became a swinger, right? Beards didn't work for him somehow. So he gave up beer, and cigarettes— lowbrow, no class, get it? Now he carries his little stash in a pouch, turns on with kids half his age, and talks a lot."

Five of us drove back to the Monte Carlo Hotel after the Robbie party, one a DFL worker who characterized herself neutral, the others for Humphrey, including the young woman I had just listened to.

"The hardest thing in politics," she said, "is to win the infights without making wounds. The primary system is a killer. You murder your opponent and a month later beg for his support. In the convention, you beg his people to work for you. It won't work at all this year. Georgie gets the nomination, Minnesota people go fishing."

"Even when it's Nixon who'll be the winner?" said the party worker.

"Even if it's Genghis Khan."

Class and style were as important in Miami Beach as they had been at other spectaculars. When Mrs. C. V. Whitney gave her Lexington pre-Derby party, its political implications weren't immediately significant. Nor were the upper middleclass implications of the post-"500" parties. Style and "class" structure at the Democratic Convention, however, had instant reverberations. At the exclusive upperclass contributor parties one could ostensibly meet, and talk to, Marlo Thomas, Shirley MacLaine, Warren Beatty, Paul Newman, Dustin Hoffman, Barbra Streisand. McGovern's "beautiful people" were part of a "post-Chappaquiddick holding pattern," a large contributor told me, and *really* belonged to Teddy Kennedy: "But farewell McGovern if Teddy ever says 'yes.'"

Democrats had grown used to the Kennedy "beautiful people" combo, but few really approved the jet set's circuses on unearned income. By 1972, Democrats had even become resigned to Eugene McCarthy's transmogrification. Social St. Paul was after all Gene's as well as Scott Fitzgerald's hometown, and, as I pointed out earlier, a close relative of Kennedy's hometown, Boston. The George McGovern of the 1960s could not make it in such a social league. Flared trousers somehow did not go with a plain body from South Dakota. The 1960s George never was chummy with rich easterners full of liberal Ivy League talk and Wall Street connections. The 1972 McGovern could try to be eastern, knowing that a "populist" couldn't have it both ways. By enlisting the "beautiful people," McGovern gave up the claim that he was truly a grass roots candidate. Richard Nixon, later, would cry public populist crocodile tears over the theft of the Democratic Party from those grass roots folk who had always worked to support it— whites, Southerners, trade unionists, farmers, small-business people. George Wallace excoriated that elite, and so did George Meany, Scoop Jackson, Hubert Humphrey. To show their independence of the arrogant elite, and its blacks, its poor, its welfare chiselers, its dope addicts, its bomb throwers, etc., hardworking, taxpaying, flagsaluting, churchgoing, sportsloving Democrats should vote for—not a Republican—but a President who was every patriotic American's Commander-in-Chief.

The doubleness of McGovern's victories must have amused the Nixon side. Take McGovern's winning the battle to seat his preferred Mississippi delegation. Mississippi divided twenty-two of its twenty-five votes between George McGovern and Shirley Chisholm—with *none* going to George Wallace. This fantasy McGovern victory became, in reality, a staggering election disaster.

From the Republican perspective, then, the Great American Democratic Convention was a remote-controlled puppet show. But sometimes the puppets, without manipulation, served the Nixon cause: the Welfare Rights movement, for example, with its prime time TV slogan "$6,500 Now!"

On Collins Avenue, in the Deauville Hotel, the Democratic telethon which tried to do without privileged big-money contributors must have looked pathetic to Richard Nixon's men. After much labor, the stars had gathered a pledged equivalent of what Nixon associates Herbert Kalmbach or Bebe Rebozo could collect in a medium-sized shoebox on a middling afternoon.

Autograph collectors didn't care about political implications. They huddled in Pumpernick's on a coffee break, watching the Deauville, saw a star, dashed across the street to make a signature score. Delegates collected autographs, but the majority seeking scrawls were local highschool kids. For the serious young the telethon provided Robert Klein, not nearly as bitter as Lenny Bruce, not nearly as political as Mort Sahl. Klein, however, was familiar with the pop scene, and more city than George Carlin, less cute than David Steinberg. For middlebrows who believe culture is talk, there was Tony Randall, a chatty operalover. Straight hard political pitches were left to Jackie Cooper, who every hour would spell out what Nixon meant by "Four More Years."

Political groupies at the telethon wanted only Warren Beatty, or Shirley MacLaine, or Marlo Thomas. Hollywood, Broadway, and TV people in general weren't the usual show-and-blow guests who appear at telethons. Warren Beatty, for instance, ignored the show-biz interview game. Instead he urged other "celebrities" to join McGovern in his big campaign, to end the Vietnam War.

By Sunday evening, when the telethon was over, "hippies" had set up in Flamingo Park. If Rocky Pomerance wasn't going to be a Daley Chicago cop, radicals in Miami Beach weren't going to play at Abbie Hoffman. 1972's radicals talked about educating the people. Love was their theme, strategy, and action. Senior citizens would be taught not to fear hippies. Allen Ginsberg's tuneless chanting was supposed somehow to help love, too.

A marriage-between-the-generations to bridge the age and life-style gap began with eating a communal watermelon "sculpture" of Richard Nixon. Both old and young celebrated secular communion in this symbolic cannibal act. The "love-in" was followed by an initiatory gap-closing "smoke-in."

Over the street, banners stretched the July Collins Avenue message, MIAMI BEACH LOVES DEMOCRATS; in August, the signs would say MIAMI BEACH LOVES REPUBLICANS. The exact number of donkeys Miami Beach displayed in July was matched by the elephants of August. Buses carried the posters; supermarkets showed the slogans in all display windows.

How much of that hippy population camped out in Flamingo Park was wired for the CIA or the FBI I don't know. I can't swear to the number of CIA Good Humor men or FBI Southern Bell Telephone vans on the scene. Army, navy, air force, coast guard, merchant marine, ITT, ROTC, GE, GM intelligence, I take it, were all represented. How many of McGovern's people in the Doral or in the Park were provocateur "Tommy the Travelers" we'll never know either.

Between 1968 and 1972 "the movement" had undergone a revolution of its own. Unlike Chicago yippies, Miami Beach hippies did not advertise "free dope, free music, free women" in leaflets and underground papers. Four years had made a great change in the women's movement. Movement women had been so revolted by the sexist attitudes of the male left that they took over *Rat,* one of the best radical underground newspapers, and began to attack Abbie Hoffman, Jerry Rubin, etc.

Late Sunday night the hoopla mood in Miami Beach suddenly changed. The serious big-time anchormen hit town. CBS's Walter

Cronkite came to lay everything out straight. Eric Severeid was there to exhale seriousness, bare his lower teeth a little, and unload sentences all of a length, like railroad ties. ABC's Howard K. Smith offered a slightly querulous conservative point of view in contrast to his confident partner, Harry Reasoner, the only nightly news star able to relax both sides of his mouth at once. NBC's John Chancellor, possessed of an especially eloquent forehead, shared time with David Brinkley, whose thing was ironic fatigue.

The convention didn't open formally till Monday night—July 10 —though action was already underway earlier that day. The National Women's Political Caucus (with Betty Friedan and Gloria Steinem seated symbolically on opposite sides of a lectern) heard from the presidential candidates who wished to speak—all had been invited. Bella Abzug sat at the power table wearing a red picture hat which bobbed a "yes" or "no" as speakers asked for support from political women.

As the women knew, 40 per cent of the bodies, but not the convention's voting strength, were female—a direct result of the McGovern-Fraser guidelines. A candidate for the presidency was thus going to be judged by NWPC on her or his reaction to those guidelines.

Before Terry Sanford came on, Betty Friedan gave an old political rouser, pre-TV game show warm-up, which several New England and southern state women at the table next to mine found amusing.

"O dear," a young white Tennessee delegate said—she wore a large "Shirley Chisholm for President" button—"I do b'lieve Betty's gonna give that li'l ol' Vassar speech agin."

While Terry Sanford spoke, the ABC crew under a woman, Marlene Sanders, started filming, and the next speaker, Senator Hubert Humphrey, made his appearance, completely surrounded by Secret Service agents. Humphrey had always been for women's rights, but now political reality put him on the wrong side, against the McGovern-Fraser formula. As he entered the hall, women began to hiss. They stopped only after Betty Friedan and Liz Carpenter shushed for quiet. The moment Terry Sanford stopped speaking, women wearing "Mis Chis for Pres" buttons began shouting, "We want Shirley!" The "Chisholm" buttons were displayed next to "McGovern" buttons by these tanned white upper middleclass women giving Shirley the clenched-fist salute, forgetting for the moment that Shirley Chisholm wasn't Angela Davis.

Representative Chisholm entered briskly, like a no-nonsense schoolteacher. She waited for the spirited "girls" to get down off the tables and back into their seats. The Secret Service must have confused the Shirley Chisholm demonstrators with Angela Davis, too, I think. Their quick-draw specialists moved into position, the Number One gun this day, fittingly, a woman agent playing photographer. Her camera hung from the neck like an afterthought as she joined a male agent wearing 1972's long hair and Fu Manchu moustache.

Candidate Chisholm's speech demonstrated that she wasn't Angela Davis. If Betty Friedan made women think of the sixties, Shirley Chisholm brought back the fifties. When she was through, nobody climbed back up on the tables to shout, "We want Shirley!" The women who jumped up were shouting, instead, for George McGovern. Bella Abzug stood to applaud; Gloria Steinem's cool blue-tinted aviator glasses topped a smile. Photographers charged forward; tape-recorder and radio microphones fenced over ducking heads to catch a McGovern word.

McGovern looked leaner than on television—just as Bella Abzug looked younger. He wore a blue-gray glenplaid business suit moderately mod but little affecting his generally sad craggy face.

McGovern immediately demonstrated that he was not to the role of women's champion born. Liz Carpenter's generous introduction said what most women were thinking:

"We know we wouldn't be here if it hadn't been for you."

McGovern, properly modest but politically fuckyknuckled, responded:

"To give proper credit, you have to go all the way back to Adam."

To which the women shouted as one:

"Eve!"

The women then sat back to shout, "Right on," to almost everything McGovern said. If one placed a Nixonian grid over this McGovern-women love-match, something menacing showed through: the National Women's Political Caucus was energetic and articulate, had power proportionately greater than its numbers. Any Nixon scorekeeper would only say, again, "What's the matter with those women, can't they count?" Slightly more than 10 per cent of the one thousand female "bodies" made eligible by the McGovern guidelines chose to be aligned with the National Women's Political Caucus; about 90 per cent wanted no part of it —or any other militant women's organization. Smarmy cheap-shot bar-car jokes about liberated women and lesbians were not without their political effect in 1972.

Even before McGovern started to speak, it was obvious that someone in his organization *had* been counting. The American political consensus is a kind of blanket lengthened at one end by cutting off at the other. Only 17 per cent of the American people favored unilateral and/or complete withdrawal from Vietnam; therefore, George McGovern could count on no more than that 17 per cent by taking an entirely unequivocal withdrawal stand. His eventual position—end the fighting, slowly withdraw, yet leave a small residual force in Southeast Asia—killed off most in the 17 per cent "total withdrawal" category without greatly attracting those in the 83 per cent majority. McGovern's political blanket turned into a small mean, thin scarf.

For example, George Meany's AFL-CIO anti-communism could be triggered by the standard Kissinger "bug-out" or "precipitate withdrawal" speech. By forcing Meany to play Vietnam roulette, the Nixon team could get him into a golf game with Labor Secretary Brennan and thus cancel out his earlier peeved public slash at Richard Nixon as a liar, big business stooge, and enemy of labor.

McGovern, adjusting his unequivocal Vietnam stand to where it could meet the majority positions revealed in the polls, immediately changed the attitudes of those unequivocally committed to him. A white, urban, University of Minnesota freshman and eighteen-year-old first voter who had worked for McGovern in several primaries told me, "No way I'm going with McGovern's waffling from here on in, man. I pushed unilateral withdrawal on a thousand New Hampshire doorbells. From now on I'm for Dick Gregory."

In his National Women's Political Caucus speech McGovern fell back on an aria from his spring primary repertoire only once: "Never again will we spend the precious young blood of this country trying to bail out a crooked dictator."

The women dutifully, and politely, applauded.

Again, in recognition of the polls, McGovern adjusted his abortion stand by a simple political device—omission. As his speech was ending, however, shouts of "What about abortion?" sounded all over the hall. When McGovern's strongest partisans tried to get a new louder "We want George!" chant going, the cry of "What about abortion, George?" rose in volume. Fists were shaken at his retreating back. His 17 per cent "Vietnam withdrawal" support base was being further eroded by his refusal to take a stand on abortion.

McGovern left, speeches continued, but the hall thinned out. Marlene Sanders and her ABC crew temporarily stopped shooting till Bella Abzug rose to pep the women up again. "Women," she said pointedly, "will not waffle" on any issue—Vietnam, abortion, or the seating of controversial delegations. "The real candidate against Richard Nixon," insisted Representative Abzug, again not doing George McGovern much good, "is the people."

If the Committee to Re-elect strategy was to hide Nixon, Representative Abzug, and other Democrats, wanted to counter by cuing on Nixon and hiding George McGovern.

"I hate speeches," a South Carolina woman said to me as we left the Carillon Hotel. "In this day and age, why have them?"

From the NWPC meeting I went to a press conference called at the Monte Carlo by the Indian Caucus. The hall was almost empty. I thought of Glendower's boast to Hotspur—"I can call spirits from the vasty deep"—and Hotspur's reply, "But will they come . . . ?" One *Time-Life* woman was obviously insulted by the small turn-out, so left. One Associated Press woman covered the conference, a local TV station woman, and four TV crewmen from Germany. If one assumed the FBI had to have at least one agent present, not to mention Indian Affairs and the Nixon apparat generally, the press conference had a minus attendance reading. Senator Mike Gravel of Alaska, running for Vice-President, was the only candidate to make an appearance. While he spoke, the German TV cameramen matched lightmeter readings as if playing "high-card cut." Then they ducked under black-hoods like falcons.

The Indian delegates in the empty hall were clearly down. A few older men tried on the white racist Indian stereotype by showing up drunk and muttering. Mike Gravel, the only "Establishment" white around, became sole recipient of legitimate complaints and broad-spectrum bitching. Gravel had expected a large press turnout and had a fairly long speech prepared. The hall was abandoned for a small hotel bedroom. Even then the press conference looked silly. The drunks stretched out on the floor, belching and sullen as Gravel began to speak.

"How you stand on Menominee Restoration?" one man called up from his prone position.

Lee Cook, an Indian leader from Minnesota, explained that Gravel had sponsored most of the Indian legislation the Caucus wanted to see pass.

Senator Gravel offered himself as a bridge between native peoples and Congress. Native peoples were represented by thirty-one delegates at the convention, not all of them with full votes. They came from sixteen states, represented twenty tribes, but New Mexico, with a large Indian population, had no Indian delegates at all. Oklahoma, with an even larger population, had two Indian delegates, each with half a vote. Arizona, with its more than 150,000 Indians, had no Indian delegate—in spite of the McGovern-Fraser formula. The host state, Florida, with its significant Seminole population, had no Indians among its eighty-one delegates (seventy-five of whom were pledged to George Wallace). Of the thirty-one voting delegates (whose actual voting weight was around ten), twenty-four were for McGovern—who didn't even send a representative to the meeting—one was for Shirley Chisholm, six were uncommitted.

"We should start to make coalitions," a young woman said as soon as Gravel stopped speaking. "With Cajuns, Chicanos, blacks, the poor, anybody minority."

"Those ain't native peoples," an older man countered. "Blacks are Africans, that ain't native peoples. Poor whites are just Europeans."

From the sparse AIM meeting I went to George Wallace's packed press conference at the Four Ambassador's Hotel. Governor Wallace looked very thin, sounded subdued, but the Wallace political stance had neither changed nor weakened. He began by affirming his credo:

"My positions are the majority positions of the country."

The conference had been called to show the governor was substantially recovered, but also to make the point that the governor's majority positions did not need a third party: "I don't have any plans other than the pursuit of the nomination of the national Democratic Party."

Wallace didn't mention McGovern, though he obviously considered himself an important member of the stop-McGovern movement.

"The Democratic Party," he said, "has always been the party of the average citizen," but "If I hadn't won the primary in Florida and the one in Michigan, and had to rely on state conventions, I wouldn't have been able to get one single delegate [in those states]."

Questions about the state of Wallace's health got answers which referred to Wallace's "accident in Maryland."

"I have been discharged medically," he said. "I'm gonna learn to wheel this wheelchair around just as fast as I could walk."

With four hundred pledged first-ballot votes, "We're gonna put the hay down where the goats can get it best," Wallace said. His majority positions would attract uncommitted delegates from every state in the union, he was certain.

After Wallace's press conference, I drove to Flamingo Park just in time to hear a local rabbi offer an invocation to a newly formed senior citizens' lobby enjoying the political spectacular.

"We are practically on our backs," the rabbi prayed, "with our faces turned heavenward. May we grow ever closer to Thee, and nearer to Thy heartbeat."

8

The Circus
Whose Subject Is Bread

Late Monday afternoon, July 10, 1972, the political spectacular broke prepackaged patriotism over Miami Beach—honor guards, flag squads, huge choruses all in red-white-and-blue to sing the happy family, farm plenty, technological progress, military winning. In this 1972, a Democratic fight song was socked out by Johnny Mann-like singers programmed to smile, wiggle a hip, salute hand-to-brow. The true spectacular had begun. The franchised Democratic show wouldn't differ from the Nixon production scheduled to replace it in August.

At 6:50 P.M. Bella Abzug, easily spotted in a red straw hat, sat in her New York delegation seat completely surrounded by "MEDIA." Everyone—TV, radio, magazine, newspaper—wore a "MEDIA" tag hanging from the neck like a "BLIND" sign. Backpacks, rolling dollies, "minicams," moon rigs, life-support systems passed a science-fiction movie-in-progress into the convention aisles. German crews were joined on the floor by Japanese, Dutch, French, Italians.

The 1972 convention turned into a small literary congress. *Life,* at its final convention, as it turned out, chose Norman Mailer to report its last political show. Mailer wore his usual three-piece dark-blue New York Central conductor's suit and new spectacles. He sat in the *Time-Life* box behind the speaker's platform, looking like a chubby, squat, curlier, sadder Daniel Ellsberg.

Mailer didn't seem weighed down by the third-person (called Hemingway) he had begun carrying around several years earlier. What made it easier, perhaps, was that in Miami Mailer was a small conglomerate, a wholly leased subsidiary of *Time-Life.* To do Miami Beach for *Life,* Mailer put aside his ongoing biography of Marilyn Monroe, whom he had never met but was anxious to explain. Marilyn Monroe's ex-husband, Arthur Miller, was also covering the convention, applying his 30s–30s vision to these '70s.

Betty Friedan settled in the press section of Convention Hall early, almost joined, later, by Germaine Greer, who, in a pale flowered ankle-length sheer, looked like Faye Dunaway or Vanessa Redgrave playing journalist in a serious political movie. Ms. Greer may have intended to observe, but what she saw turned her advocacy journalism into active participation. She discovered that Miami was loaded with hookers shamelessly hustling the great American political spectacular. Ms. Greer confronted the workers and told them their behavior was demeaning. They told her to fuck off. A few of the nervier women mistook Ms. Greer for out-of-town competition trying to make it with educated Democrats by faking an English accent. In any event, the women wouldn't get out of the hotel pools or stop walking the sauna-approach beat.

With all the press representatives settled in their seats, Lawrence O'Brien, the Democratic Party chairman, called for order—late. In what might have been another omen, O'Brien mis-pronounced "Democratic." O'Brien himself was in a way an omen, a colorless concession that 1972 was Richard Nixon's year. The Democrats, to call attention to the party's traditional role, chose a Roman Catholic cleric to back up O'Brien and give the opening invocation. After two familiar ploys, the party followed with one of its few new political figures, Florida's recently elected senator, Lawton Chiles. In the 1970 off-year election Chiles had knocked off none other than Richard Nixon's rejected Supreme Court nominee, Harold Carswell (whose mediocrity, Nebraska's Senator Roman Hruska had argued, would democratically repre-sent mediocre Americans on the Court).

Down on the floor, delegates were already caucusing when O'Brien and then Chiles began speaking. It was a time of reunion, getting acquainted, everyone crowding the aisles around section leaders, delegation chairs empty. People popped up, ran out, then ran in again to grab an armful of fellow delegates. Excitement was everywhere and building. New York and Massachusetts seemed most active, almost always surrounded by important network TV reporters, who, headsets on, stared alternately into the floor cameras or up at the glassed-in network booths. Reporters favored Father Drinan and Kenneth Galbraith of the Massachusetts delegation, Bella Abzug and Arthur Schlesinger, Jr., of New York. McGovern people scurried through key delegations like odd-lot couriers at the Stock Exchange.

What the McGovern side wanted was indeed happening. McGovern runners got and gave the promises that hourly added to McGovern's first-vote totals. Meanwhile, stop-McGovern workers came up with arguments Richard Nixon's committees soon would adopt as their own.

Most amazing—and largely unreported by the "media"—was the steady anti-McGovern line on the Democratic National Committee's own closed circuit television channel. A Humphrey interview followed by a George Wallace or Jimmy Carter interview, an interview with Senator Russell Long of Louisiana or Senator Robert C. Byrd of West Virginia would sound all the anti-McGovern themes. McGovern's designated detractor, Senator Henry Jackson of Washington, would appear with or without his union supporters, George Meany and I. W. Abels (of the United Steelworkers), and pick up the theme again. In September 1971, when McGovern registered 6 per cent in presidential preference polls, Jackson and Meany had begun the "McGovern can't win" line. In July 1972 they were doing everything possible to prove their prophesies accurate. Jackson argued that McGovern, in spite of primary successes, was a born loser. Primary statistics "proved" that though McGovern came out of the primaries with most *delegates,* Wallace, or Humphrey, or any combination of anti-McGovern candidates, had the most *votes.* In one form or another all anti-McGovern candidates repeated Governor Wallace's argument that McGovern did *not* represent the majority positions of the American people. The McGovern guidelines sneaked into conversations: his opponents predicted that only "minority" Democrats would work or vote for McGovern in November. Labor, Democrats on closed circuit TV were told, wouldn't work for McGovern, nor would the middleclass opposed to school busing or in favor of a militarily strong America and a domestic policy of "law and order."

The "no win" argument sometimes included references to McGovern's "gay" and "lesbian" following, his "radical" connection with "campus unrest." Even as the anti-McGovern Democrats kept up their closed-circuit TV assault on McGovern, one of their number, Senator Humphrey, announced at a press conference that because of weak first-ballot support, he was withdrawing from the race. It was not a gracious stepping-aside by Hubert, "the happy warrior." Humphrey's people complained that McGovern, by concealing his strength, particularly in California, had faked them out completely.

Humphrey's withdrawal was not intended as a concession speech. It didn't mention George McGovern at all. Humphrey began, "After consultation with my closest friends and supporters . . . I am . . . now releasing my delegates *to vote as they wish.*" There was, of course, no other way for Humphrey to withdraw since his violently anti-McGovern supporters would never go over to the McGovern side.

On quite another level, Hubert Humphrey once more was the archetype beaten political man. Thumped by Jack Kennedy in 1960, dressed up as a vice-presidential Texas Cowboy "Ken" doll by Lyndon Johnson in 1964, chosen only after Bobby Kennedy's assassination to be the Democratic candidate against the Big Loser, Richard Nixon, in 1968—Humphrey himself became the Bigger Loser in that contest. Only because Eugene McCarthy, Humphrey's old enemy, pulled out of the Senate could Humphrey get back into federal politics in 1970. Now he was being badly beaten once more, and by whom? George McGovern.

I well remembered a Jefferson-Jackson Day dinner in Minneapolis, just after Jack Kennedy had defeated Humphrey in the West Virginia primary. As Minnesota's senior senator, Humphrey had to introduce his Massachusetts colleague. Looking sandbagged, but trying to put on the style, Humphrey passed into the hall, thinking Kennedy was immediately in back of him. He stood at the head table mike, turned to see Kennedy still far across the room, mobbed by Minnesota admirers of Kennedy charisma, Kennedy winning. For more than ten minutes while Jack Kennedy was being applauded, cheered, and gladhanded, Humphrey stood alone, smiling a fixed, grim, trapped, exposed smile.

The man withdrawing in Miami Beach in 1972 was twelve years older, equally crushed, and crying.

"We've always been good Democrats," he said, "and, hopefully, good citizens, and a good family."

The night Humphrey dropped out, his supporters continued to wear "Humphrey" hats and buttons on the convention floor. By next morning, Wednesday, July 12, when George McGovern's nomination seemed certain, the Carillon Hotel began removing all signs of Humphrey. A CBS-TV crew filmed Humphrey banners coming down, and caught the loud ugly ripping of his posters off the hotel pillars. By noon Humphrey's name had disappeared from the hotel marquee as if he were a departed pharmaceutical convention. Humphrey's depressed supporters eventually put away their hats and buttons, but not their hatred of George McGovern.

By noon Miami Beach was well into its spectacular. Streets flowed with people. Cars, buses, trucks, loudspeakers passed through lines of police, national guardsmen, army reserves being briefed for nomination night. Helicopters flew a continuous patrol over the headquarters of all candidates—including the silent Humphrey suites in the Carillon Hotel. By Wednesday, July 12, Miami Beach was the place to be for the country. The Great American Spectacular Derby run, Speedway, Rose Bowl was Convention Center. The action spilled out into the adjoining streets. There anti-Castro Cubans began fresh oinking for another Bay of Pigs.

That special Spectacular rhythm took over Miami Beach, more intense than Louisville's before the Derby, much more charged than Indianapolis's on the eve of the "500." In Miami Beach crowds massed in a solid shuttle between the Convention Center and McGovern's Doral Hotel headquarters. Big names, big money, and media power packed the upper reaches of the Doral Hotel, where, in a closed-off penthouse one got to by passing through smaller and narrower entrances, the McGovern side contemplated the coming big win.

By Wednesday, social, political, financial, cultural hierarchies showed themselves in Miami Beach, part of the Democratic process. The Doral lobby was constantly jammed with the young and the casual commuting between McGovern headquarters and Flamingo Park. New groups showed up, one calling itself "Bicycle Riders for McGovern." The lobby looked like pre-exam reading week in an Ivy League dorm.

The press quarters were papered with apolitical blue seahorses, sea anemones, starfish, barebreasted mermaids nipple-denied with stylish classical pasties. A young McGovern worker was nursing her six-week-old baby, debating the advantages of Hubert Humphrey's withdrawal. In the next few days she and her associates would become winners and josh each other with the "We've come a long way, baby" line. Richard Nixon and post-Nixon Republicans who wondered why Republican Party membership was drastically down should have asked this young woman and other McGovern workers in the Doral Hotel. At least half of the ones I spoke to said their families—on both sides—were solidly Republican. Socially and culturally, Richard Nixon was more than the upper classes could take.

One illusion prevailed in the Doral, that getting the nomination and winning the election were synonymous. This illusion led to changes in style. Since McGovern was already in, pot was obviously legal. One could now smoke openly, and never fear a bust.

Outside the Convention Center and on Collins Avenue, correctives to these illusions patrolled the approaches: pre-McGovern police and army people. I sat in a small grass police hut outside the auditorium while undercover men checked out rookie cops and told them what to expect. On the other side of the high Convention Center fence, a few stoned or drunk highschool kids were hollering at the police. A boy who swore at a cop neglected to pull his vulnerable fingers out of retaliatory range. After the cop had cracked him smartly on the knuckles, the hurt kid, crying, yelled at the cop to take off his equipment and fight like a man. To comply, the policeman would have had to remove:

his plastic face-shield
his riot helmet
his riot stick

his gas mask
his mace can
his revolver
his boots

Security around the Convention Center was as careful as at a large airport. Handbags and briefcases, cameras, camerabags had to be opened, checked over, and okayed (with an oval two-color label "AAAAA" the first night, a different colored "BBBBB" the second night, etc.). Security on the convention floor was obtained largely by controlling access. Ramps were guarded, aisles patrolled, galleries scanned, passes constantly asked for, constantly inspected. Entrances and exits were rhythmically ordered. Busloads of people filed into the visitors' gallery, were seated for a fixed time, then smartly hustled out to make room for the next busload.

Demonstrations formed up, orderly, patrolled by armbanded marshalls and higher-ranked program directors. For the most part, demonstrations were for demonstrators. From the convention floor, gallery demonstrations could hardly be seen. Most demonstrations went off privately, a card-section stunt rehearsed a day before the Rose Bowl.

Most speakers who came to the rostrum were similarly ignored. Cadences programmed for applause appealed to a few from the speaker's own state. Of the several thousand people on the convention floor, only a hundred faces would be turned in the direction of a speaker. At most, fifty hand-clappers, whistlers, footstompers would throw a few hurrahs the speaker's way.

In the year 1972, the political "spellbinder" became a dodobird. Farewell the sweat-layered lovable political hack who could get the delegates up and cheering during pauses spaced through a speech like coffee breaks. Delegates seemed to pay more attention to the VIP boxes left of the rostrum. A candidate might appear, a celebrity like Colonel Sanders, or a real star like "Jimmy the Greek" Snyder (whose Las Vegas futures quotations made Richard Nixon an overwhelming favorite over George McGovern).

Media monitoring of those VIP boxes was shamelessly trendy: if Muriel Humphrey appeared, the mikes and cameras instantly followed, till, say, Eleanor McGovern turned up. She would be swarmed around by the same reporters who had been putting in time with Mrs. Humphrey. A bubblegum-card hierarchy governed the convention: one Kennedy was worth about twenty of anybody else. Yet the most dramatic moment of the Miami Beach Spectacular wasn't provided by Senator Edward Kennedy.

What happened transfixed the media, stopped delegates in the midst of their state-hopping: Governor George Wallace came out on stage. For a short hour, oldfashioned rhetoric re-entered the convention. The George McGovern one-man magic show was temporarily suspended. In the VIP section Colonel Sanders smiled a glassy, goateed, string-tie imitation of his waxed chicken-bucket image. The media stampeded for the rostrum, delegates stood up. Colonel Sanders understandably mistook the excitement as gratitude for the free fried chicken he had distributed. But what roused the hall and the VIP section was the sudden appearance of Cornelia Wallace, the governor's wife. The hour for Governor Wallace's promised speech was come around at last.

As if, right before the convention's collective eyes, an updated version of *All the King's Men* were being filmed, two huge bodyguards slammed a ramp against the rostrum, whirled to grab up a shrunken collapsed Governor George Wallace, chair and all. They strapped chair and governor into place firmly, checked to see he was secure, then stepped back, casing the convention floor and spectator galleries in concert with the dead-look, ear-plugged Secret Service. It was exactly the eleventh hour—11 P.M., just before presidential balloting was to begin. Wallace had timed his appearance as a reminder to anti-McGovern delegates that their fight wasn't over. As that ramp slammed into place, the Wallace demonstration began. His followers tried grasping reluctant state banners, to charge uncommitted conservatives into a last-minute surge against George McGovern.

Alabama, Texas, South Carolina, Florida, Maryland—pre-primary, anticipated Wallace states—were joined by the Michigan primary's victorious Wallace delegates, and Indiana's, New Mexico's. A single Wallace enthusiast showed from North Dakota, George McGovern's neighbor state. None of the committed delegates responded to Wallace's invitation to join the "victory" dance, though almost all the delegates stood up to applaud Wallace's survival.

Wallace's image on the podium contrasted with the bushy-browed, chesty posse-leader Arthur Bremer had almost killed. Here was a shrunken man scrunched down in a wheelchair, his scrawny neck exposed by a shirtcollar that gaped far below his thin chin. Cornelia Wallace, cool now, hair combed, face set in a smile, contrasted, too, with the image of her moments after the shooting, hair scattered over her face, her body shielding the governor just as, earlier, the nation had been imprinted by the image of Jacqueline Kennedy throwing herself across the body of her dying husband.

Without such images, Wallace was an abstraction, a sum of his racist, rightist, and confusingly populist political positions. His survival, though, demanded, and got, a human response.

Once Wallace began to speak political realities reasserted themselves. A shrunken man in a wheelchair repeated—almost parodied—the familiar Wallace tag-lines celebrating "folks who work," excoriating "those" on "welfare." A few boos broke from the floor, to be lost in louder booing from the galleries. But when Wallace sounded his "busin'" theme, the boos and hisses were absorbed by conservative delegate applause and Rebel yipping. That McGovern partisan I had seen nursing her baby at the Doral cradled her child and shook a vigorous "no" at what Wallace was saying. Wallace attacked the "elite pseudo-intellectual snobbery [which] has controlled [the Democratic Party] for so many years," bringing on more boos. Yet, when Wallace finished speaking, and those bodyguards sprang to release him and his strapped-in throne, McGovern delegates were among those who stood up to applaud. The wheelchair sank out of sight, the ramp disappeared, Cornelia Wallace slipped away, leaving Colonel Sanders to preside over the now-empty VIP stalls.

Wallace's dramatic show closed the convention's last anti-McGovern stand. Nominating began, and, soon after, balloting. California delivered its winner-take-all total of 271 votes to McGovern before any other candidate's tally-sheet was marked. Soon after, Ohio added 77, New York its significant 263. McGovern's opposition had no real focus. "Scoop" Jackson was not the man to inspire a countermovement. Nor was George Wallace. For all his talk about majorities, Wallace had less than 20 per cent of the first ballots being called out from the convention floor.

Wallace's defeat inspired the "We Want Welfare" signs to wig-wag victoriously in the gallery. Posters reappeared to urge "$6,500 NOW!" and "Welfare Now!" Welfare Rights and Poverty Rights groups raised their clenched fists and chanted the slogans Nixon people loved to hear. The poverty group was soon joined by National Women's Political Caucus demonstrators noticeably whiter than those chanting "Welfare Now!" Noticeably trimmer, too, and noticeably older, though youthfully blue-jeaned. Down on the floor, younger NWPC members from the South—known to the media as the "Magnolia Mafia"—were dancing in the aisles for George McGovern.

Delegations huddled, tallied, checked, rechecked, asked to be passed, then passed again, making new counts that invariably moved totals closer to the 1509 votes George McGovern needed to win. Virginia, for example, came up with seven more first ballot votes than McGovern was originally pledged; twenty-six Humphrey first-ballot Indiana votes turned up in McGovern's column. Arizona, where McGovern once expected only six, delivered twenty-one, most of them once pledged to the all-but-forgotten Senator Muskie; Mayor Richard Daley's lack of enthusiasm for McGovern didn't prevent Illinois from adding 119 crucial votes to McGovern's total. As the counting continued, every switch spoke of a political realignment. First Muskie, then Humphrey faced the ultimate either/or of liberals taking a stand against conservatives like George Wallace and Henry Jackson.

Those politically born under the McGovern guidelines read each tally as a winning cash register ring. Big numbers signified big power.

In Louisville and Indianapolis, and later in Pasadena after the Rose Bowl, those who backed a loser were understandably less happy than those who backed a winner, but just being at the Spectacular was the important thing. In Miami Beach, however, that McGovern tally, to many, sounded a Democratic Party death knell. Some delegates left rather than stick around for a

McGovern celebration. The galleries looked down on what seemed unified Democratic joy and happiness: TV screens flashed unanimity having itself a wild New Year's Eve ball. Kenneth Galbraith held his 6'8" happy totem high above the dancing Massachusetts delegation, which was soon joined by happy New Yorkers from across the aisle. When the 1509 total was reached, Galbraith joined in a wild kicking hora to "Happy Days Are Here Again." I saw no Wallace, Jackson, or Humphrey people in that illusorily triumphant circle.

Late that night, after McGovern had won, I met members of the Minnesota delegation out walking, and terribly down. Back at the Monte Carlo, victorious McGovern delegates were feeling sorry for the Humphrey people or scorning them as bad losers. Some actually believed that the Democratic Party would hold together in any fight against someone so corrupt as Richard Nixon. The bar stayed open late into the night; happy and not-so-happy people splashed in the hotel pool; a few of us waded out to swim in the calm dark ocean. From where we were we could see the Doral, all lit up, including that secluded penthouse in which McGovern folk stayed awake till morning congratulating each other.

By sunrise, Democratic defectors to the Richard Nixon side became known. Others were rumored to be going over—old Democratic blocs: unionists, professional men and women, Jews. Mayors like Rizzo of Philadelphia, and the wife of Milwaukee's Democratic mayor, Henry Maier, would be campaigning for Richard Nixon.

The nomination of George McGovern meant "go" for President Nixon's men and women. All the anti-McGovern themes of the Democratic National Committee's DEMO 5 closed circuit television channel now could be unleashed.

The Minnesota split, for example, went so deep that Governor Wendell Anderson and Senator Walter Mondale scheduled pep talks and unity meetings to underline the danger of the DFL not holding together.

Noon the day after George McGovern was nominated I attended an Indian celebration, which was two carloads of American Indian Movement people light. Both AIM cars had started out, one day apart, for Miami Beach: both had used the same route south from the Dakotas and Wisconsin. On the way through some small town the first group came across a strip joint featuring a "real genuine Indian Princess" who shakes "free of her feathers and gets down to her buff." With a Hollywood war whoop the AIM members slammed on the brakes, piled out of the car, tore down the offending signs. Cops arrived in time to arrest all the Indians and throw them bail-less into jail. Less than twenty-four hours later, the second AIM contingent, ignorant over what had happened, passing through the same town, saw that same stripper sign newly and patchily repaired. Their ideologies suffered as much as the first group's: they tore up the joint, and were of course arrested, *and* jailed. Because they were after all only imitators, and not innovators, they got ten days in jail to the first group's prestigious twenty.

July 13—the eve of Bastille Day—everybody Democratic was a big winner. Women Democrats were obviously winners—so Texas's Sissy Farenthold would be nominated for the vice-presidency (by Gloria Steinem and Allard Lowenstein, winners in every category but politics). While Gloria Steinem was nominating Sissy Farenthold, Hubert Humphrey left his VIP box to be George McGovern's escort to the rostrum for the nominee's ritual acceptance speech. Bella Abzug, in a huge off-white picture hat, was busy trying to organize reluctant delegates for Sissy. The vice-presidential fix was already in—for Senator Thomas Eagleton of Missouri (the less-than-famous "Tom Who?").

Hodding Carter III, of Georgia, withdrew his name from vice-presidential consideration with a speech. Nobody was listening. Hodding Carter's "changing South" was a counter-Wallace political force. Carter's language was anti-populist and tried to establish a new "here we stand" for the South. "We are in the process of recreation," said Carter; "we are home [in the Democratic Party] and we are going to stay here," words strikingly similar to George Wallace's, though their political meaning was quite different.

If, on July 13, 1972, Hodding Carter III's South was a winner, so were blacks, and Indians, the old, and the young. Yet of the delegates waiting to confirm George McGovern's choice of a vice-presidential running mate, as many as 30 per cent would either *not* vote for George McGovern in November, or not vote at all!

When Thomas Eagleton was finally nominated, and cheered, and applauded, he made his appearance, his face covered with heavy perspiration. It was warm in the hall and around the platform, but warmer still in the VIP boxes and on the convention floor where people heavier than Senator Eagleton, and dressed more warmly, weren't perspiring at all. Senator Eagleton stood his daughter on a table, and the little girl pulled a handkerchief out of his breast pocket and began mopping his wet brow. Something about the way she dabbed at Eagleton's forehead suggested that she had done this same thing many times before. I wondered—in my notes—whether Senator Eagleton were suffering from some kidney ailment, or perhaps under medication for the flu or a bad summer cold.

Here was someone who looked like Jack Lemmon and talked like Jack Lemmon, frowning with the perplexity of Jack Lemmon. The second-lead in the movie boy-girl game, a marked loser, had surprisingly turned winner. Eagleton had been called at the last minute, and in the last minute chosen. Then why did the gaiety and delight of his children contrast so with his own doomed expression, and his wife's? At the time I put Mrs. Eagleton's reaction down to her realistic reading of the Missouri presidential polls. Or maybe she was concerned that her children would be upset by the late hour and confused excitement.

Every Spectacular is, at its heart, a huge party, a political Spectacular no less so than others. The celebration of Thomas Eagleton's sudden political rise overwhelmed my questions about the strange Eagleton family tableau. During Spectacular days of misrule, meanings and consequences are frequently missed the first time around. Images are accepted for what they are programmed to show. McGovern and Eagleton with arms linked, and family-surrounded, made a winner pose. Then Senator Edward Kennedy enlarged the traditional picture (getting the night's loudest cheer). Then came Senator Humphrey, and Senator Muskie. Everyone took a turn at raising McGovern's and Eagleton's hands in victory. Finally Senator Henry Jackson, sweating almost as heavily as

Eagleton, broke into the family picture, welcome as Simon Legree or Uriah Heep.

Delegates did a dance in the aisles as general rejoicing started up in the Great Spectacular's streets. Outside the Convention Center and the Doral Hotel kids turned on, once again, for George. Blacks and whites unselfconsciously hugged each other. Hippies and senior citizens saluted the new McGovern day. TV cameras swept the hall to zoom in on confident smiles, V for victory signs, the semaphores of momentum.

Thomas Eagleton, an unknown at midnight, by 5 A.M. was the best thing that had ever happened to the Democratic Party; he was suddenly the right kind of liberal—i.e., a conservative. Just as suddenly not too old—i.e., early middle-aged. Not power hungry—i.e., powerless. Not too southern, not too midwestern, not too northern, Eagleton was unhappily not too unknown.

The rest of the Spectacular is a slow dance in reversed reels, a shocker filmed by Fellini or by Buñuel. Smiles freeze, are soon replaced with blank staring. The news is out about Thomas Eagleton's past depressions, his "breakdowns," his shock treatment. Early explanations try to pass everything off as only alcoholic. Faces stay fixed in shock as George McGovern lets days pass without deciding whether to dump Eagleton or to let him hang on. His words, "I'm one thousand per cent behind Thomas Eagleton," perplex everyone.

In the severely edited scenario, the same people McGovern had thumped in primaries or outmaneuvered on the convention floor return, now as members of the Democratic National Committee. Larry O'Brien, a bad-mouther on the DEMO 5 closed-circuit show, comes back as star of the second vice-presidential go-round. The McGovern team once built up as brilliant and inventive is changed into a klotzy crew not careful enough with the obviously incriminating Eagleton data. The McGovern team is now called "amateur," "indecisive," "poorly organized," and "poorly led." Inside the Democratic Party, and outside, at Nixon headquarters, the bumbling rap was laid on George McGovern.

In the new scenario the Democratic National Committee, not being subject to the McGovern-Fraser guidelines, was pre-formula —whiter, older, male-er. Few were gung ho over McGovern. And

Donald Segretti's complete success was underlined by the Eagleton disaster. Had Senator Muskie been left even wobbly he would have been an automatic instant compromise, and McGovern would have avoided the floppy swim in the national goldfish bowl which ended with him displayed for everyone to see belly-up.

Democratic fission contrasted with programmed Republican togetherness. The GOP August Spectacular, packaged by *The Dating Game* TV team, was obviously dedicated to Senator Roman Hruska's reigning mediocrity party. A *This Is Your Life, Dick Nixon* introduction presented the country as strong, busy, and happy as a Coca-Cola commercial. Everybody Republican dressed neat, pressed, and clean as in those urban TV fun shows beamed at detergent freaks and aspirin junkies. *Dick and Pat and the Girls* starred in a Miss Teenage America package-dream of romps through Disneyland in Barbie and Ken cruise clothes. Flashes of mushrooming nuclear explosions in the midst of Miami Beach vacation and sunniness reminded conservative hawks that Richard Nixon meant business bombing Hanoi and mining Haiphong Harbor. Several days before the Republican convention opened—on July 27, 1972—Richard Nixon announced, "We are not using the great power that could finish off North Vietnam in an afternoon," and added, "and we will not" in a tone Americans two years later connected with his tape transcript message that buying the silence of Watergate burglars "would be wrong."

By that time in July, George McGovern had been changed from a seemingly easy mark to an absolutely certain knock-over—a bad prelim fighter standing in for the indisposed post-Chappaquiddick Edward Kennedy, and the disposed post-New Hampshire Edmund Muskie.

In August when the anchormen and the commentators came back to town and the political Spectacular started again, the tone had changed. The media referred to the Nixon renomination as a coronation, a spectacular *Queen for a Day* with ominous commentary by an old *March of Time* voice. The delegates were actually a Monty Hall studio audience fitted out with little flags and funny hats they waved like space engineers whose payload has just landed safely in the clear blue Oh Golly. People on the convention floor were taught to chant *Nixon Now* instead of the Democratic

Peace Now—just in case anybody still didn't understand the Vietnam alternatives. The GOP rostrum was transformed into a looming slatted ark featuring all fifty state seals. Without the GOP elephants and "Nixon" signs, Miami Beach could have been hosting a massed convention of Elks, Lions, Rotarians, Legionnaires, which, given the make-up of the GOP, it was.

Interviews with Republicans and rostrum speeches mentioned "game plans," "guesstimates," "getting back to the drawing board," "the name of the game," "it's in the ballpark." Shakespeare, I concluded after listening to Ron Ziegler, Bob Haldeman, John Erlichman, and Herb Klein, was quite wrong—all the world *wasn't* a stage but a ball park, and we but poor concessionaires trying to hustle a hard bottom-line buck by peddling perishable peanuts in its stands.

The two conventions came off as allegorical contrasts. A tattered Flamingo Park-Resurrection City crew broke in on George McGovern's Doral headquarters during July to accuse him of using the poor, using the aged, using the young. McGovern came down in his shirtsleeves to confront the noisy, disorganized demonstration, and, in doing so, of course demonstrated what the Nixon side could call his "weakness," his "gutlessness," his "permissiveness." In Republican August when nobody went tieless, wore jeans, or tried to pass barefoot through Convention Hall security, Allen Ginsberg, who made his peace moan all through the Democratic days of July, was busted, but let out on $150 bail. Not even Rocky Pomerance could prevail when John Mitchell's massive arrest and massive detainment police peer pressure was applied to Miami Beach: the night President Richard Nixon gave his acceptance speech, 805 demonstrators were arrested.

On television, however, the show went off unruffled. Jeb Stuart Magruder indicated why:

> Under Dwight Chapin's direction, a minute-by-minute scenario was prepared, and it was followed. Speeches were written in advance, approved, and timed so they would not run over. The less interesting parliamentary aspects of the convention were held during the day, so the prime-time hours could be used for dramatic events—the films of the President's

trip to Russia and China, demonstrations by several thousand enthusiastic young people, and finally the President's acceptance speech. An estimated sixty million Americans watched some part of our convention, and while they may have occasionally been bored . . . they could not help but contrast the efficiency and unity of our convention with the confusion and conflict of the Democratic Convention a month earlier.

No blacks demonstrated in the galleries during the GOP Convention, no Welfare groups, no Poverty groups, nobody holding up signs of "$6,500 NOW!" During the Republican Miami Beach Spectacular all demonstrations had to be *outside* Convention Hall. On the night of President Nixon's acceptance speech tear gas fired at a build-up of demonstrators was blown by the wind into the Convention Center's airconditioning, sucked into the hall, choking delegates and guests. The tear gas even reached the houses and yards of Nixon's Cuban partisans in the Convention Center area; some tear gas wafted into the pot smoke senior citizen converts still inhaled as their extended summer political spectacular drew to its end.

Dwight Chapin's scenario was in fact a programmed play for non-persons. They would take poll-chosen positions in tones and expressions indicated as preferential in sweepingly thorough voter research. The Number Two man in America, Bob Haldeman—ex-ad agency star—oversaw the Chapin script and other important convention details. Public relations men worked every touch in the Nixon show. Haldeman as the inventor of "uncola" knew how to present unattractive Richard Nixon as a preferred "un-McGovern." The America worker could be placed in Nixon's pocket with proper pitches about Vietnam, the flag, and "busin'." Once neutralized in the class struggle, workers obviously didn't resent the golden yacht flotilla in Biscayne Bay, each worth a hundred thou and up, each owned by big-business Nixon contributors wearing what Charlotte Curtis of the *Times* described as "dinner jackets [and] a little diamonds."

Throughout July and August other Spectaculars images took on a literal meaning—the color guards, the honor guards, the pledges of allegiance, the patriotic windblown, spotlighted flags. In August nothing was merely symbolic. Every uniform could be ordered into action by the Commander-in-Chief, Richard Nixon; nobody could be mobilized by his powerless opponent, George McGovern. The IRS, the FBI, CIA, FAA, CAB, FDA, SEC, etc., were similarly at Nixon's disposal—just how completely we are still finding out. If people who dealt with the government still did not understand the meaning of power, John Mitchell and Maurice Stans spelled it out. Under Stans the Committee to Re-elect put on a highly organized political United Fund appeal. "Giving" was based not on the donor's rough estimate of what his firm or its officers should come up with. Hard numbers, IRS figures, existed for the Finance Committee to use. *Ask not what we can do for you in the future,* was the clear Stans message, *unless you have shown proper understanding of what was done for you in the past.* The Nixon administration knew precisely how much a certain industry, firm, or individual had gained through preferred legislation or the nonenforcement of laws on the books. Thus the "golden flotilla," secure in its relationship with absolute power, didn't hide its affluence but flaunted it. To do less might have been interpreted as a show of nonconfidence, or ingratitude.

Miami Beach's Spectacular unfolded allegorically, first with the powerless displaying the aspirations of traditional have-nots. In August the powerful displayed the fruits of political pay-off. Throughout the summer Miami Beach's residents watched it all, trying to participate, trying to understand, clearly a third force, more useful to the powerful Nixon than to the powerless Democrats.

In August Julie and David Eisenhower projected the neat Nixon images of youth power with Pam Powell, daughter of waned film stars June Allyson and Dick Powell. Pam, like Julie and Tricia, was Hollywood's own Miss Voting Teenage America provided with an oversize Hollywood gavel to call the convention to order. Jaw-tense grinner Glenn Ford showed up with a flag in his lapel. Flag-pin local Cubans gave a Spanish-language pledge of allegiance to a somewhat larger American flag. The official Republican Party film mixed together images of "Ike" with images of John L. Lewis, Vince Lombardi, John Steinbeck, Cardinal Spellman, Cardinal Cushing, Louis Armstrong, Marianne Moore, and J. Edgar Hoover in an obvious pitch to "un-McGovern" Democrats. A "tribute to Harry Truman and Lyndon Johnson" was included; Ronald Reagan came on to complain about the McGovern, leftist, and radical treatment of a *"good* Democrat," Hubert Humphrey. Mrs. Anne L. Armstrong, of Texas, Vassar—and a friend of Democrat Sissy Farenthold, she added—made her pitch to Democrats by praising "this man," Richard Nixon, as "warm and thoughtful," and a "peace president." Mrs. Armstrong's testimonial was sworn to by Shirley Temple Black before James Stewart came on to praise the "gracious" Pat. During the election, Mrs. Nixon was always referred to as "the gracious." When Mrs. Nixon popped up like a surprise guest star on a Doris Day Show, Stewart referred to "her ready warmth [that] extends across the nation." Pat Nixon, he said, was "elegant but never aloof," a tag line good enough to be in a perfume commercial.

On August 22 a second film salute to Nixon had John Erlichman saying, "Education is the name of the game." This put education in a "name of the game" league with "winning," "production," "profits," "higher GNP," "politics," "business," etc. Patrick A. Buchanan, Nixon's speechwriter, characterized his boss as a "political realist." Henry A. Kissinger came on modestly to say he could "only judge foreign policy [pronounced *vorin bolizy*], [where] his [Nixon's] impact . . . will be enormous." Nixon seconding speeches were given by a nineteen-year-old Iowan who called Vietnam "the war for all Americans"; Senator Buckley praised Nixon for that same strong national defense posture and his Supreme Court appointments which have "regained the confidence of America." A United Automobile Workers official announced that the people of "Pittsburgh have asked me to come here to speak to you tonight" on behalf of Richard Nixon; Mrs. Anne Bedsole of Alabama, ostensibly speaking for all Wallace voters, and the Democratic South, said, "We cannot take George McGovern."

During all the talk, President Nixon slipped into a youth concert being presided over by middle-aged Sammy Davis, Jr., a notorious hugger and habitual convert. Sammy, used to hugging the likes of "Dean," "Frankie," "Peter" [Lawford], didn't see why he should stop at "Dick"; he sneaked up behind the President, gave him an approving public hug which Nixon reacted to with a brave, smiling flinch that soon broke down into a cringe. Sammy, shortly after, began appearing in General Electric TV commercials, GE a flamboyantly pro-Nixon defense operation. Chuck Connors, John Wayne, and other Nixon supporters appeared in TV commercials sponsored by pro-Nixon corporations prohibited from making direct contributions to political campaigns.

Next day, another winner, Spiro Agnew, was renominated, and Richard Nixon finally made his reappearance as the "partisan of principles that can unite us." Nixon boasted, though not as ominously as post-Watergate connotations implied, "We have changed America and America has changed the world." In the final fade-out Nixon and Agnew, intertwined, were singing "God Bless America" beside Roman Catholic Cardinal Krol of Philadelphia.

The millionaires' yachts floated out of the harbor. Planes took delegates out of town. Cars and buses left the Strip. Labor Day was at hand. Another winter season for Miami Beach lay not far ahead.

The old folks didn't stay on pot much after their Spectacular sources left town. A few hippies stuck around when Nixon's "Cubans" reinherited Miami Beach. Summer finally arrived two months late. Complainers could now complain Miami Beach was "real dead." Once the last elephant banners and posters disappeared, cops put away their riot equipment, the national guard left, so did the army. Senior citizens could get into the Doral. Pelicans flew solitary sorties, unmenaced by hovering helicopters. Traffic thinned. Hookers, without Germaine Greer to hassle them, returned to monitoring salesman Johns and chintzy summer-conventioneers. Rental cars piled up in the airport lot.

Only in Key Biscayne, the Republican cats who had swallowed the Democratic canaries held a great big party to celebrate the coming "Four More Years." The guest of honor would soon announce to the world, "I am not a crook."

The Political Spectacular, begun in Miami Beach, ended there, too. To show the party was indeed over, triumphant Richard Nixon left Key Biscayne and went West, to a temporary San Clemente seclusion he could not possibly imagine, during that 1972 summer, would soon serve him as a permanent retreat.

9

The Little Old Lady's Block Party

The Huntington (now the Huntington Sheraton) Hotel in Pasadena is a Fitzgerald dream. For most of the year it just sits there, in a settled green setting; chauffeured limousines drive up, drive away, their passengers either aged residents of the hotel or regular dining patrons—their relatives, their visitors, their paid companions. The cars, even when forty years old, are always in what auctioneers call mint condition. So are the mink coats and mink collars the little old ladies and little old gentlemen of Pasadena wear mornings and evenings, even on the warmest summer days. A 1972 octogenarian could have been a 1920s flapper, Hollywood party-goer, or Parisian dude. Some of the Huntington's residents are almost the exact age Fitzgerald would have been, had he been one of the very rich and lived to a pampered ripeness.

The shops in the hotel are expensive, usually the branch of something bigger and posher in some other part of the country or Europe, the merchandise invariably marked "imported." The Huntington Hotel is related to those torn-down grand hotels of Saratoga. It's an ideal place to clip a coupon, check the *Wall Street Journal,* stretch out in a lawn chair; it's good for rest, good for diet, good for short views. Wheelchairs coast through its corridors and lobbies. Canes are stylish, antique, not the usual invalid stuff from Abbey Rents. More often than not, the proffered arm of an attendant is ununiformed. The Huntington Hotel, for genteel old folks, is home.

In the hotel and outside, the little old lady from Pasadena was sometimes a familiar political character, the little old lady in sneakers. Little old gentlemen wear sneakers, too, for the same good reason, to get the traction that protects brittle limbs from slips and falls. I saw one Huntington Hotel tiny old mink-topped guest hurrying along in brightly striped regulation NBA basketball shoes. Maybe she sported the Rick Barry specials only during Rose Bowl week, when she and her elderly friends were all but blotted out by Big Ten and Pacific-8 Conference mesomorphs crunching in and out of the old hotel.

Life in the Huntington Hotel didn't stop for the Rose Bowl, though as headquarters for the press and conference officials it became a slap-on-the-back cheery reunion frat house, playground for public relations people, conference officials, alumni nostalgics, and retired cheerleaders past their best handspring weight. The lobby was a crest of blazers, a gray of flannels, a repp of striped school ties, a dale carnegie of smilers.

Woody Hayes and Ohio State were playing John McKay and USC in the 1972 Rose Bowl—"wondrous Woody," Paul Hornung, turned Columbus sportswriter after forced early retirement from the NFL, shamelessly called Hayes. The coaching confrontation was supposedly allegorical. Woody Hayes was a Vietnam hawk coach, a collegian's own Vince Lombardi. Woody sometimes behaved like an army general in, say, *Doctor Strangelove*. John McKay wasn't totally cynical about this pop "Pop" Warner, yet couldn't pretend he was delighted to be playing a team rooted in nineteenth-century fundamentalist football fundamentals. After the game he and "wondrous Woody" somehow contrived not to meet for that "Well done, old man" minisecond midfield brush-by, a good thing, too, considering McKay's unusual post-game press conference. To the print-out questions, "How'dja do it?" etc., McKay replied:

"We just kicked their ass; it's that simple."

When some guy asked:

"Did President Nixon call?"

"No," McKay said, "and I didn't call him either."

The Huntington Hotel, days before the game, filled with Big Ten and Pacific-8 newspaper people. Outside it was sunny, warm, inside the pressroom dark, and bluish from a huge out-of-focus, weird-color TV screen. On screen was the take-off of some 1,400 planes recently returned from a routine bombing of Hanoi and Haiphong.

The press people were all drinking gin and California orange juice, chewing on peanuts and pretzels, ignoring the Vietnam shots as they wouldn't an airplane commercial. They were waiting. Harry Truman's funeral was going to be shown live on television.

"Harry's the one," said a man wearing an Ohio State eyeshade, "Harry was the whole ball of wax."

"Harry taught the country to really stand up to the Communists," said a man in a reddish T-shirt. "You got to give that little guy a lot of credit."

"Without Harry, our President today wouldn't be standing tall," said the man in the eyeshade.

"Real hardnosed," a voice said from a corner, "look how Harry handled Uncle Joe Stalin. Nobody in the whole world could control old Joe. Only old Harry."

"There's a lot of old Harry in old Woody," said the man in the eyeshade.

Between Miami Beach's political spectaculars and the Rose Bowl came the Munich Olympics, in September, live television guerrilla theater ending with dead Israelis and dead Palestinians. In November, just as the polls all had indicated, Richard Nixon was easily re-elected—in spite of Watergate, the ITT disclosures, the milk fund disclosures, and war continuing in Vietnam, Laos, and Cambodia.

The Los Angeles *Times,* a few days before the Rose Bowl, ran an Interlandi cartoon of Henry Kissinger flapping two empty sleeves and cackling his best one-liner, "Peace is at hand." Telford Taylor and Joan Baez had just returned from Hanoi to describe the carpet bombing of North Vietnam and the destruction of Bach Mai Hospital. The Pentagon's press spokesman, Jerry Friedheim, who always acted as if press briefings were interrupting an urgent trip to the men's room, explained that any damage Taylor and Baez had seen was caused by North Vietnam missiles shooting into the sky—and missing.

The war had fortunately hung on long enough for the Tournament of Roses grand marshal, John Wayne—selected many months earlier—not to have to be connected with anything as sissy as peace. The Tournament of Roses Committee had selected John Wayne not simply because he went well with the "Movie Memories" parade theme. Everybody everywhere knew that John Wayne was hardnosed.

Rose Bowl publicity outlined some of Duke Wayne's qualifications to be grand marshal of its pastoral flower show, among them the following awards:

1. U.S. Government War Agencies Plaques
2. U.S. Marine Corps Iron Mike Award (oddly characterized as the "highest award that can be given a civilian")
3. American Legion Americanism Award
4. Veterans of Foreign Wars Americanism Award
5. West Point Society of Los Angeles Duty, Honor, Country Award

An added homey touch told how hardnosed old Duke, when not making hardnosed movies, "gets away for fishing or just relaxing on his converted minesweeper, *Wild Goose*."

All the 1920s Fitzgerald dreams went into the making of a Rose Bowl spectacular—football heroes, Hollywood splash, and the very rich living out their unaffected *imitatio* of royalty-at-play. Woody Hayes and Ohio State may have been a little crude for Fitzgerald's Princeton-dropout taste. USC was perhaps a trifle too rah-rah for a West Coast world that couldn't come up with a socially OK Rose Bowl team like Stanford.

Unlike a Louisville transformed by the Kentucky Derby, or Indianapolis during the weeks of the "500," Pasadena proper was almost unrippled by the Rose Bowl. The Huntington Hotel was only one of the well-kept buildings and mansions that set Pasadena's cool tone. In spite of commercial production numbers and punch-out publicity programs, the Rose Bowl retained a closed "this is *our* thing" quality. The Tournament of Roses had headquarters on posh Orange Grove Boulevard in a huge mansion once the home of William Wrigley, the chewing-gum king. Wide green lawns on a tree-punctuated street kept the Rose Bowl tightly zoned for its white flannel and red-rosed officials. Pasadena cops in this setting gave the impression they were some private security force working this, as they did most well-heeled areas of the country, to discourage breaking and entering, invasions of privacy, and the intrusion of that rough element so disruptive to millionaires' neighborhoods.

In 1973, for instance, the city of Pasadena erected bleacher seats on a 300-foot parkway which, for the preceding twelve years, had been traditionally—and unofficially—occupied by local blacks living in the vicinity of the Rose Bowl. Elderly black people would be set up in seats early and be served food and hot drinks by young community blacks during the parade. The black community had established squatters' rights to that particular spot in 1960. The area they used had grown steadily till the 1972 Rose Bowl Parade, when about seventy people were accommodated.

When the black community protested the disappearance of their seats, the city's defense was that California freeway robbery took away about 10,000 parade seats. To cut that 10,000 by seventy "black community seats" seemed, to white Pasadena, only just and right.

I asked one of those neat nice country-club white Pasadena cops why he thought the city had suddenly decided—only a week before the parade—to put up those bleachers. I wondered why nobody had told the black community what was happening.

"Hell, they were killing Pasadena's image," the policeman said. "Some TV cameramen showed them last year—messy, wrinkled, old. And noisy. Paying no real attention to the parade—just drinking, and eating. Hell, my Daddy told me we *never* had *Tobacco Road* in Pasadena, even during the Depression, so why have it now? Nobody wants to see a bunch of old Negroes bugaloo first thing New Year's morning."

At a last-minute conference with Pasadena's assistant city manager and the Tournament of Roses' liaison man, the black community settled for sixty tickets in a reserved section that left no room for bugalooing.

Pasadena didn't completely escape the violence (and antiwar feeling) of the rest of the country. During New Year's Eve, which was cold and harshly windy—down to the low forties and high thirties—a thirty-three-year-old man stepped on the foot of a teenager. In the argument that followed the man was stabbed, and died an hour later in Huntington Memorial Hospital. In another incident, police rushed a group of fifty to sixty young people, and the usual response—a "barrage of rocks and bottles"—followed, a "mini-riot," as the police called it. Part of the 1,100 force of Pasadena police and sheriff's deputies had the riot well under control by 3 A.M., hours before John Wayne and Mrs. Richard Nixon took their places in the Pasadena fun parade.

The Tournament of Roses Committee first announced on March 21, 1972, that the 1973 parade theme would be "Movie Memories." Otis Blasingham, president of the Tournament, said, "When I looked back through our records I was astonished to find we'd never had a movie theme before." The official Tournament Association puff was bland: "We think 'Movie Memories' will lend itself to a spectacular parade in '73. All of us have fond memories of motion pictures."

If Michigan, with its big big big Big Ten band, couldn't make the Rose Bowl, Ohio State, with its big big band, could, and did. Though Woody Hayes and Ohio State football hadn't acknowledged the twentieth century, the "O" band gave signs that Elvis, *Hair,* and the ancient (i.e., pre-Altamont) Woodstock cult had worked some changes in Columbus. Brushcuts had all but disappeared among male band members: their sideburns were a little longer than a West Point cadet's; real mustaches sneaked in, even if rather thin and sketchy. Band women abandoned the tight tight perm. Continuity, however, was guaranteed by the fierce military uniforms, the franchised march patterns and unspontaneous play. Here, too, things looked wondrously allegorical—the Midwest paramilitary spats-on-parade, the West Coast's USC Trojan War costumes absurd as *Ben Hur.*

Five firms—Festival Artists, Floatmasters, Donald J. Bent, Coleman Enterprises, and Herrin-Preston—made over 90 per cent of the floats in the Rose Parade. They were year-round commercial enterprises able to design, construct, and decorate the floats assigned to them.

I was less interested in these commercial floats than I was in community involvement with the Rose Bowl. A couple of days before the parade I drove out to a tent on Mission Street where the South Pasadena float on the theme of "The Perils of Pauline" was being built by the Mission Street community. It had financed the float, designed it, built it, and now was decorating it. Kids were up on the float, dozens of girls and boys around seven or eight, and lots more teenagers. It was a happy working crew of Michelangelo helpers up on scaffolding, covering chickenwire and wood, hollering for flowers, greens, and paint. Older people were working on "Pauline's" rocking canoe of red camellias; a steam engine bearing down was being covered with white and yellow chrysanthemums. Chunks of recently discarded Christmas tree added green and once-green touches to the float.

A mother-of-eight rushed past me.

"I've got to hit them up again—oh dear, those poor merchants. We're always after them for something, doughnuts, Cokes, paper cups—and money. They're generous. We're in this together."

Downey, California, had its own float association; so did Burbank and Sierra Madre, and Cal Poly had an ongoing yearly university float project for its design students. The rest was done by those commercial float-builders or by outfits like Walt Disney Enterprises.

The Mission Street kids behaved like professionals, craft workers who took their milk or Coke breaks with backs to the tent's small food stand. Their eyes were constantly fixed on the rising "Perils of Pauline." Nobody under the tent was a drone. Some swept the ground clear of snipped wire and cropped leaves. Others were either up on the scaffolds, climbing all over the frame, attaching or handing up and fetching. A few teenage girls sat at a sawhorse table wiring flowers together one by one.

In the dump of a parking lot behind the tent, kids in imitation of some ABC "Wide World of Sports" special whizzed their bikes up an Evel Knievel ramp improvised out of warped boards leaned against a cementblock cesspool. From time to time a parent would run out of the tent to take down the dangerous boards, but in no time at all the kids would set up more warped lumber and the stunt driving would start all over again. Not even when a boy's wobbly wheel slipped off the boards and slammed him to the ground did the stunting stop. The boy, crying to himself, got up, looked at the rear bike wheel still pointlessly spinning, the bike frame and front wheel now a mess of twistage, then limped into the tent, sat down beside a crew of flower-wirers, who, without a word, handed him some work. Outside, the kids straightened the ramp boards and resumed their dangerous stunting.

Through the day, mothers and older teenagers periodically left the tent to lead young children on a door-to-door canvas for nickels, dimes, quarters, and dollar bills. Excited, happy kids dumped jars and baskets of small change on the snack counters. Everyone cheered. During the year the float was being prepared, the Mission Street community raised money through raffles, cake and garage sales, small fairs, special community events. The Rose Parade had been going on longer than the Rose Bowl football game—eighty-four years by 1973 (to fifty for the played-in-Pasadena football games, fifty-nine for the games all told). In that time traditions had been established, and some had disappeared. South Pasadena kept its community project going long after most others had either stopped participating, or had turned responsibility for floats over to the pros. Participation in the *preparation* was obviously as important to Mission Street as the Parade itself.

Similarly, in Indianapolis, family traditions made the "500" trials as significant as the more famous race. Community participation in Mardi Gras made the day something privately special for New Orleans' residents. Local communities, generally not caught up in the spirit of commercial rip-off, resent or ignore the invasion of their town by tourists, campfollowers, spectaculars nuts, and attendant hokery.

Pasadena's unique situation made the Tournament of Roses different from the other spectaculars in one significant way: Pasadena was located in the most thickly populated area of the United States, Southern California, and so did not depend on people from the rest of the country coming to its parade and game. Pasadena and Los Angeles were always automobile-oriented; Louisville, Indianapolis, Miami Beach, New Orleans had massive parking problems and automobile-access problems. Pasadena's traffic was just part of modern American automotive madness. Most people coming to the parade and the game lived within fifty to eighty miles of Pasadena and didn't usually need hotels and motels. Tournament of Roses followers therefore didn't add much revenue to local commercial enterprises—most of which were closed on New Year's Day anyway.

Trinkety souvenirs were part of the Rose Bowl package, peddled half-heartedly, almost as an afterthought. Just as the Tournament of Roses Parade comfortably considered itself the "granddaddy of all parades," so the Rose Bowl, confidently the "granddaddy of all football bowl games," had a relaxed national stance. Being "Number One" among bowl games was more than an honorary designation and kept the Rose Bowl, and its parade, Number One in lucrative television network contracts. The Rose Bowl and its parade had the highest and most pleasurable "identification" rating in the nation. Like the Kentucky Derby, the Rose Bowl was hardly affected, nationally, by the quality of its participants.

The Rose Bowl could say its parade began in 1890, its football championship in 1902 (Michigan vs. Stanford). Or it could stress continuity by giving 1916, its second start, as the origin of continuous New Year's Day play. It could be even more modest and choose 1923, when the Rose Bowl was first set in Pasadena, as its true beginnings. Generosity was easy. No matter how Pasadena counted, its rivals lagged far behind. The Orange Bowl (originally called the Palm Festival) didn't get started till 1933, didn't move into Miami's Orange Bowl Stadium till 1935. The Sugar Bowl, played in New Orleans' Tulane Stadium, also began on January 1, 1935; the Cotton Bowl, in Dallas, didn't start till 1937, and its current practice—of automatically sending the Southern Conference champions to the Cotton Bowl—wasn't set policy until 1941. The Sun Bowl began in El Paso, Texas, in 1935 as a Texas high school game (switching to the college level in 1936); the Gator Bowl in Jacksonville, Florida, began in 1946; Houston's Bluebonnet Bowl (named after the real—not "yellow rose"—state flower of Texas) began in 1959, the same year that the Liberty Bowl was played in Philadelphia for the first time (it moved to Memphis in 1965).

The Rose Bowl obliquely dramatized an American sport allegory Fitzgerald and, in his own way, Hemingway would have recognized: the private gentlemen's colleges, best exemplified by the Ivy League, and even better by the Big Three—Harvard, Yale, Princeton—acknowledged one West Coast institution, Stanford. The University of Southern California was too big, too new, allegedly too lax in its academic standards, too Hollywood and flapper to be considered a serious Stanfordian enterprise. Then there were the public state universities. The 1902 game between Michigan and Stanford, which ended with Michigan winning, 49–0, was a contemporary boys' book view of life. Stanford was full of good young men from good families: Percival Percival, Jr., who had barely time to remove his spectacles and white flannels and tennis sweater marked with the scarlet letter, "S," before the midwestern state university unacademic ringers fell on him and pounded him unconscious. State university toughs outweighed him, outnumbered him, outcrafted him in a tasteless demonstration of what no-brow gashouse democracy could do physically to America's gentlemanly aristocrats. In the boys' books the gentlemen always won: in the record books they had the shit kicked out of them.

Once, in 1920, when the last Ivy League team to make its appearance in the Rose Bowl, Harvard, was ostensibly being beaten by the University of Oregon, the referees called Oregon's last-second victorious field goal "wide," and gentlemanly Harvard won for the upper classes its last allegorical do-or-die tussle with the western masses. That other aspect of the Rose Bowl game, the contest between the "East" and the "West," stood as the Rose Bowl formula till 1947 when the Big Ten-Pacific Coast Conference game was established.

The Rose Bowl leaves little to chance. Add the number of Pacific-8 and Big Ten alumni living in Southern California—or along the West Coast: schools with annual enrollments of between 20,000 and 45,000 (plus old-school-tie part-timers) can take up most of the 104,500 (1973 capacity) Rose Bowl seats in no time at all. The Rose Bowl, with this alumni base, doesn't have to get into the business promotion game that works so well for the Kentucky Derby, the Indianapolis "500," or the upstart professional Super Bowl. Using its television ratings and the commercial exploitation possibilities of its parade, it can charge 1972 parade rates of $32,000 a minute, and sell Rose Bowl game commercial time at

$135,000 a minute. Market research claimed that of every ten TV sets tuned to the parades in 1971, eight followed the Rose Parade; in 1972, seven out of ten were said to be tuned to the Rose Parade. The audience was stated as 110,000,000, making the Rose Bowl and its parade easily the most successful commercial spectacular in the country.

More than any other spectacular, too, the Tournament of Roses calculatingly uses commercial America's mix—militarism, patriotism, nostalgia, celebrities (including sports superstars), regionalism (equestrian teams big on the Old West theme, and bigger yet on expensive old Mexican and American silver saddles), free enterprise, right-of-center politics (while claiming to be nonpartisan *and* nonpolitical). Since 1947, the year the Big Ten pact began, Tournament grand marshals, for example, have included the following: Bob Hope (twice), Richard Nixon (twice as Vice-President), the late Senator Everett Dirksen of Illinois, General Omar Bradley, General Eisenhower, Major General William F. Dean, Secretary of Defense Charles Wilson (the only cabinet minister and the only department ever represented), Captain Eddie Rickenbacker (Eastern Airlines and numerous far-right organizations), Commander Perry Brown of the American Legion, Walt Disney, Billy Graham; and, representing the "center," Paul G. Hoffman (for his various international roles), Earl Warren, the University of California's Chancellor Robert Gordon Sproul, and Washington Governor Albert D. Rosellini. Not till 1975 was a black grand marshal named, Hank Aaron, who, without a single bugaloo, apolitically and unmilitarily broke Babe Ruth's lifetime homerun record.

Of the Rose Bowl queens who presided over the parades and games since 1947, three were named Nancy, three Pamela, two Barbara, and two Virginia. Of the women in the 1973 court, "Queen" Salli Ann Noren and her six "princesses," Michele, Gayle, Melanie, Janet, Jimmie Lou, and Caryn, most listed sewing among their hot hobbies; defying that Equal Rights Amendment stuff, they all wanted careers as either good homebodies or good secretaries, stewardesses, nurses, elementary schoolteachers, social workers. Only one mentioned an unfeminine pursuit—law—but covered her daring with added domestic reassurances, "bread baking and knitting."

All spectaculars are programmed to project Good News, and only good news. Of all compulsory optimisms the most optimistic is the Tournament of Roses Parade. The military-industrial-political-entertainment complex provides an invisible supreme Grand Marshal, no matter who happens to be the nominal marshal in any given year. In the midst of the Depression, "America's Sweetheart," Mary Pickford, was chosen to project the blissful untroubled image of 1933. In 1935, America's not-Chaplin (i.e., not-political) funnyman was made grand marshal, Harold Lloyd, a conservative man with proved double-entry bookkeeping accomplishments; sandwiched between romance and comedy was 1934's security grand marshal, Admiral William S. Sims. In 1939, dimpled Grand Marshal Shirley Temple, still smiling like a proper child star, flashed the necessary "all's right" message.

If one looks carefully at the Rose Bowl and its parade as a model of the nation's spectaculars, big games, big public events, one sees how the majoritarian power structure controls seemingly insignificant fluffy entertainments. During that 1930s Depression, for instance, Hollywood studios fought against pictures with a controversial anticapitalist political point of view and made what it insisted "the public wanted," musical extravaganzas with casts of happy thousands. Slowly, during World War II and after, directors and actors broke into the Hollywood "dream factory" to produce movies about poverty, demagoguery, discrimination, bigotry, corporate dictatorship.

But the Great American Spectacular Parade and Half-Time Show has not been at all affected by those Hollywood changes. In 1973—and indeed in 1976—the images still being projected on the country eliminate dissent or old people bugalooing, or anything not consonant with the majoritarian view that in this, the best of all possible worlds, everything is always coming up roses. Again, the Constitution reflected in the great American spectacular does not separate church and state but rather joins public prayer with public military displays of allegiance to the flag, the President, and other icons of pure power.

Dissent and antiwar demonstrations, Lyndon Johnson said in

the mid 1960s, were the work of "extremists." In those same 1960s, the NCAA, which presides over all intercollegiate sports including Bowl games, began referring to NCAA-sponsored activities as a "counterforce" to "protests" and "campus unrest." America the Happy, according to the majoritarian credo, didn't have dissenters (just as, for a long time, America officially didn't have more than a "handful" of "draft dodgers" and "deserters"); therefore the intrusion of anti-Vietnam War and "Free Angela Davis" demonstrations during the 1972 Tournament of Roses Parade was subversive of the parade happiness theme—a higher value than even Lyndon Johnson's or Richard Nixon's "national consensus."

A black UCLA student told me that the black community parade seats of 1973 disappeared as the penalty Pasadena and the Tournament of Roses people imposed for the 1972 Angela Davis demonstrations. Hunger and poverty were "not what the country wants to see" in the 1930s movies; demonstrations, poverty, old age, and dissent were "not what the country wants to see" in the 1960s and 1970s spectaculars. The country obviously *wanted* to see exactly what the Tournament of Roses Parade provided, starting with John Wayne and Pat Nixon.

There's a special prose that goes with souvenir programs. During television lulls—when the Tournament of Roses Parade is slowed down, or stuck—a commentator might even read some of the stuff. It's written in the language of publicity handouts, official dispatches of the Ministry of Good News and National Consensus. Franchised sentiments and opinions are not an important part of the New York *Times* or the Los Angles *Times*. Franchised free-enterprise editorials, sports-builds-character and prayer-in-the-schools columns, however, circulate through the country daily and are picked up and frequently reprinted verbatim in small weeklies or tiny-staffed dailies. Slightly larger daily papers and, say, fraternal order magazines use much more of the prepared prose than is commonly recognized.

The military-industrial-political-entertainment complex in 1973 pushed the usual patriotic happiness themes of the franchised editorials and "news" columns. Knott's Berry Farm, source of extreme right-wing pro-Vietnam War and pro-Richard Nixon propaganda, picked on "Patriotic American, George M. Cohan" to be its parade hero as "portrayed in the award-winning film, *Yankee Doodle Dandy.*" More prose followed:

> The float depicts our American heritage in documents, historical scenes and symbols of patriotism to past and present generations as well as hope for the generations to come. . . . The patriotic Cohan songs testified to his deep devotion to American ideals.

The Occidental Life Insurance Company's ill-fated float, "Premiere," understandably avoided the unhappy insurance motif of death and instead fixed on the premiere as a "glamorous institution of the Land of Make-Believe." Walt Disney Productions led off the float parade with a salute to itself—"50 Happy Years"—a "block-long cavalcade of more than 100 famous Disney cartoon characters . . . in a fanciful atmosphere of make-believe." In front of the Walt Disney float rode motorcycle riders, not Hell's Angels but fraternal Elks from Huntington Park. The Long Beach Mounted Police followed the Disney float in a "posse of thirty Palominos" patriotically "displaying the massed red, white and blue colors of the United States."

Nowhere in the parade were any of the testy local issues found—polluted water, or Cesar Chavez's lettuce boycott (which only Senator Edward Kennedy mentioned at either the Democratic or Republican national conventions). The float sponsors were almost solidly pro-Vietnam War and pro-Nixon, and included the following:

1. Anheuser-Busch's "crowd-pleasing Clydesdales" in support of the City of St. Louis's float, "Stagecoach," described in the program as "the movie that launched Grand Marshal John Wayne on a career that has not been equalled in cinema history."
2. Union Oil Company, a pre-*Checkers speech* friend of Richard Nixon, which stayed on a noncontroversial non-offshore drilling theme, "Keystone Kops."
3. McDonald's hamburger chain, a huge contributor to the Nixon campaign of 1972 and, like the milk lobby, charged

with making illegal contributions which coincided with a removal of price controls and subsequent sharp price rise. The happy McDonald's-Pepsi Generation parade image was projected by "McDonald's All American High School Band" representing "The United States of America, All 50 States." All bandmembers wore "the uniform of the high school . . . they represent with matching McDonald overlays and caps."

4. The Bank of America which used the "Ziegfeld Follies" as a reminder of the make-believe image Americans "wanted" during those depression blackouts of anything but "Hollywood musical extravaganzas."

5. Sunkist Growers, Inc., which not unexpectedly sidestepped union themes in favor of "the Arabian Nights, mixing fantasy with the world of realism."

6. Eastman Kodak stayed on that fantasy wavelength with its float, "Anna and the King of Siam," and attendant "visions of exotic lands, adventures and romance." The Farmers Insurance Group reinforced the Anna image with its float on the theme of "The King and I."

7. The Gillette Company used "A Star Is Born" as its theme and explicitly linked the Tournament of Roses Parade with another idealized pure entertainment vision, the Miss America pageant. "Appearing on the spectacular" Gillette entry, said the program notes, was "Miss America 1973, a rising star in her own right." Gillette was TV sponsor of the Miss America Show.

8. The Association of Motion Picture and Television Producers representing the "entertainment" component in the military-industrial-political-entertainment complex explicitly stated its function through its float theme, "The Movies—Memories in the Making." An oversize length of movie film was supposed to represent "the technology of the industry [and] the glamor of Hollywood."

9. Native Sons and Daughters of the Golden West, an outfit well to the right of the D.A.R., doodled a responsible pastoral Smokey the Bear on the movie backdrop, "How Green Was My Valley."

10. Al Malaikah Shrine Temple's theme, "The Happy Ending,"

made explicit another important part of the "Good News" credo.

11. The Odd Fellows and Rebekhas used "Love Thy Neighbor" in a float with the "central motif [of] a huge helping hand of love, which revolves continuously."

12. The Salvation Army float theme was "The Greatest Story Ever Told." The float's "focal points are the Christ Child in the manger . . . and the huge open Bible. . . . A large cross of white chrysanthemums stands amid a golden wave of cascading roses." The Salvation Army float was followed by its 145-piece band "whose music," said the program—a trifle apologetically—"lends a note of reverence to the festivities."

13. The Lutheran Layman's League, not to be outdone by Rebekhas-Odd Fellows and the Salvation Army, used "King of Kings" as its float theme. "The floral scene rendered in exact detail," said the program, "is Christ's triumphant entry into the city of Jerusalem on Palm Sunday. The figure of Christ is seated on a donkey, passing underneath a huge arch of gold chrysanthemums. . . . All of the waiting figures are in authentically detailed floral robes."

Cowboys, even those characterized as a "posse," were supposedly apolitical, and could therefore be part of the American happiness syndrome; religion was another accepted part of the happiness syndrome, evidently; most important of all, fantasy and fun *were* the happiness syndrome. Fantasy and fun were what the movies—in the industry view—were all about. No *Citizen Kane* float appeared. Nor did any float reflect the political complexities of, say, *All the King's Men*. That *Tobacco Road* the Pasadena policeman and his father found offensive was similarly ignored— along with *Cannery Row, Gentleman's Agreement, Watch on the Rhine,* or the gently political *Mr. Deeds Goes to Washington.* Disney images, *Kismet* and *Arabian Nights* images, Keystone Kops images, colossal Christ images, circus images, cowboy images constituted the seemingly apolitical, noncontroversial, Okay, All-rightnik American consensus view which only in the very late 1960s began to be recognized as the country's most coercive political projection.

10

The Golden Bowl

Spectaculars celebrants don't wait for the Big Day sun. Real Rose Bowl, Indianapolis "500," Mardi Gras aficionados don't go to sleep the night before and don't bed down till late the night after. The awaited day is forced beyond a mere twenty-four hours. Spectaculars breed instant traditions. Anything done once sets a fixed pattern for future doing. It's not enough to be *there:* one has to be in some exact spot at some precise time. Then spectaculars magic can work properly.

Someone who has spread a blanket on the Churchill Downs infield green five or six years in a row regards the spot as something owned. Withdrawal symptoms attend its disappearance. No hotdog stand can go up, no stage, no comfort station, without someone's traditional way being shattered. Worse yet is a take-over by poltroons ignorant of why Druids draw spiritual circles. Being up early frequently translates as getting *there* first. Only from that very place can one see the Derby finish, or watch the most expert "500" jockeying, witness the significant Rose Bowl touchdown, snatch the best Mardi Gras trinkets flung in New Orleans air.

Veteran spectaculars-followers are brilliant inventors and adapters, wise about primary matters—wind, rain, dust, heat, cold, hunger, thirst, ablution, elimination. Every camping trick is displayed, every ordinary bit of equipment turned to special spectaculars needs. A Thermos may be filled with everything from still-warm mother's milk to a 15-1 martini on flawless square rocks. A hibachi set up on a tiny patch of ground glows a barbecue in places oxygen barely reaches. A garbage bag, skillfully cut, is the fastest way out of the rain, or sun. Folded newspapers become sunhats, cushioncovers, extra-layer diapers, windbreaks, tablecloths, or higher animals, sailboat and airplane toys. Sterno, the rummy's last refuge, will boil an egg, heat a tin of babyfood, warm feet and hands on a cold May or January morning prelude to an eighty degree afternoon.

Perhaps the only defense against spectaculars room-rental ripoff is the sleepingbag. A one-person bag sometimes serves two, but the two-person bag is frequently used to offer shelter and comfort the way a car takes on a hitch-hiker. Under any spreading tree during most spectaculars a double sleepingbag offers lovers public invisibility. What man and woman, woman and woman, man and man have joined, it's hoped no cop will sunder. Frisbee-chasers, though, are another matter, or kids playing tag, scurrying squirrels, nosing dogs, cool photographers, Peeping Toms, Nosey Parkers. For those in the bag, loveplay's the thing, even if it means missing the big, suddenly secondary, spectaculars event.

With or without sleepingbag, the motorcycle pair comes to the spectaculars separate or in unmuffled blackleather packs. Mirrored sunglasses, heavy studded boots, armless jackets, helmets flashy as pinball machine beacons go with extended handlebars, bananaseats, skulls and crossbones, swastikas, tattoos, stenciled snakes and dragons that terrify the locals and provide immediate *lebensraum* for Harley-Davidsons, Rickman-Metisses, BSAs, and less menacing Hondas, Kawasakis, Yamahas, Suzukis. Stockbroker clerks, nurses, delivery boys and girls on their noisy middleclass scooters share the revulsion American normalcy feels for anything barbarously motorized. If a cycle sounds, a Hell's Angel can't be far behind, goes one bourgeois fear; and where there's one Hell's Angel, a hundred more are sure to follow. Usually the roaring weaving pairs in gaggle are some tame parochial *imitatio* of Angels with charmingly parodistic clubnames like Rosemary's Babies or Satan's Wheels. During *Ramparts'* days of biker chic, the mean wisdom of Sonny Barger seeped into distant parishes, helped along by educational television and/or *chicsters* Dick Cavett, Geraldo Rivera, David Susskind.

Pasadena and New Orleans saw hundreds of silent two-wheel bicycles trimmed in colorful crepe paper, flying flags, pennons, pennants, buntings. The Tournament of Roses Parade passed through residential areas kids and grownups could pedal up from easily. Frequently at an Orange Grove Boulevard or Colorado Street intersection bikes trimmed in USC, Ohio State, or USA colors stood wheel by wheel as in a showroom display. Bikes served as pedestals for parade-viewers to lord it over the unladdered bipeds down below.

When 1973 finally arrived in Southern California, it came by way of a bowdlerized sky. A newspaper star-watcher decided not to tell his family readers what a nice Greek god like Zeus was really doing to Europa. "Taurus, the Bull, crosses your local meridian this week," Sherman Walker wrote in the Los Angeles *Times*. "It is easily identified by its appearance although only its head and horns are visible. . . . To find the Bull, face southward at 9 P.M." Mr. Walker then explained that "in Greek mythology, Taurus is the milk-white bull into which Jupiter [sic] changed himself in order to carry [sic] Europa from Phoenicia to Crete."

The year 1973 arrived on powerful Santa Ana hurricane-force winds gusting up to 80 mph on top of the San Gabriel Mountains—site of the Mount Wilson Observatory and northern backdrop for the Tournament of Roses Parade. Those Santa Anas were responsible for the cold dawn, the ten-foot waves smashing boats in Avalon Harbor. Not far from the Rose Bowl itself, winds blew at 40 to 55 mph. Dust and sand whirled up over the highways, filling the sky above parade-bound traffic with strange brown light. Close to the parade route, several campers were overturned, trees knocked down. For some 250 houses, 1973 came in as a power failure.

The year 1972 had ended with Roberto Clemente, the all-star Pittsburgh Pirates outfielder, crashing to his death in a cargo plane in Puerto Rico. Organized for the relief of Nicaraguans suffering from a disastrous earthquake, Clemente's group chartered a plane either unfit or overloaded. It disappeared into the ocean within sight of San Juan's luxury hotel "Strip."

On New Year's Day three Pierce College students described how and why they had stranded a fraternity brother in the Angeles National Forest just before Christmas. They had decided the 270-pound, 5'10" young man, who, like a character in *Lord of the Flies,* "wore glasses," was "obnoxious," and "needed to be taught a lesson." The young man, in total darkness, fell over a 500-foot cliff. His body was not found till December 31, at roughly the same time Clemente was killed.

On New Year's afternoon in the Huntington Sheraton the Ohio newspaper people gathered once more to watch television, this time the East-West Shrine game. Players' skins glowed yellow, the turf pale mauve, and shadows a grayish green. The man with the Ohio State eyeshade grinned at a news announcement about some Italian Pittsburgh Steelers fans who sent their Super Bowl team a Pentagonian communiqué directing them to wipe out the Miami Dolphins as though they were enemy Viet Cong. The Miami Dolphins motel had been "bombed" with leaflets.

"That's real cute," said the man in the eyeshade. "Some people think of everything."

A short news release from Hanoi showed a pilot recently shot down during the renewed bombing: his message to the American people was, "Merry Christmas, Dick."

By noon, Sunday, it was California gold rush days all over—a swarm of campers and bivouackers putting up canvas and nylon tents. Then the Rose Bowl party began in earnest, and went on till game time, Monday. Tent-hopping, van-hopping, camper-hopping was the thing to do New Year's Eve. Cops tried to stop dancing in the streets, honking horns, whistle-blowing, and barefoot square-dancing and touchfootball in the forty-degree cold darkness.

Passing headlights picked out T-shirted revelers laying over car fenders like shot deer. Tipplers with peristaltic complications lurched and spasmed to some mysteriously choreographed St. Vitus dance. The inevitable exhibitionist pissed un-nautically into the forty-mile Santa Ana winds sweeping the parade routes.

By sun-up the drunk and the stoned had been piled into inconspicuous spaces. A few who were still high squinted in the glaring post-New Year's Eve light. More and more younger children turned up to line the streets. Stands were beginning to fill. In no time only a few seats were still empty. Traffic along the Ventura Freeway was almost stopped. Fair Oaks Avenue, Lake Avenue, Sierra Madre Boulevard were jammed with cars, buses, trucks, and trailers.

By 7 A.M. most of the floats and bands were ready to go in the Orange Grove Boulevard formation area. Again, as at the "500," bandmembers were yawning, red-eyed, dragging their instruments and their asses.

Once the parade began, the Raymond Burrs, the Betty Whites, the Bob Barkers, the June Lockharts found themselves trapped in the emulsive official program prose. The Tournament of Roses Parade began rolling to march tunes and superlatives: America was *first,* and *number one,* and *mighty on the moon.* Every band that won an award instantly chaired its leader—that guy in glasses, with the white gloves, who paced my nightmare sousaphonist from Louisville through to New Orleans.

I once watched a steward on the exit ramp of a full 747 say "Thank you for flying with us" to every person leaving the plane. Winking at me, he cranked at his ribs as though he were an old-fashioned gramophone, and kept on with the exactly unvaried farewell line. There were a lot of awards in Pasadena, and opportunity for a lot of rib-cranking.

I referred earlier to the Occidental Life Insurance Company's float, "Premiere." After "Premiere" had been judged, and awarded the parade's "Grand Prize" (which, nobody familiar with spectaculars language will be surprised to learn, means coming in second), it developed a split rim on one of its front casters. Tournament officials called for a tow truck; one—ordinary-sized—appeared, and painfully dragged the huge float off Colorado Boulevard onto Craig Avenue. James Coco had been riding "Premiere," which was pushing the 1972 Coco movie, *Man of La Mancha,* and, luckily for him, got off, and so did Margo Lynn Johnson (Miss America 1972), and several models. The parade had been stalled by the "Premiere" breakdown, but got moving again, and never looked back.

The "Premiere" scene changed instantly to *Day of the Locust.* On Craig Avenue, onlookers gathered, watched, and, suddenly, turned into a mob, taking over the float, ignoring the driver, Bob

Hammond, who had only his wife to help him ward them off. In Hollywood, people who take chunks out of anything are called souvenir hunters. Cops less romantically think of such people as vandals. Nathanael West, in *Day of the Locust,* recognized the souvenir hunter and autograph seeker as a potentially murderous force.

That Craig Avenue scene, which changed "Premiere's" make-believe into nightmare reality, was analogous to what happens after an airplane crash, when ostensibly souvenir-hunting crowds start picking up bits of fuselage, seatbelts, cushions, upholstery, then switch to rings, watches, wallets, luggage, clothes, hearing-aids.

Nothing in the Rose Bowl Parade was more make-believe than "Premiere," with its vintage open cars flashing a message of wealth and lavish excess. Marquees reinforced the Premiere image, and thousands of chrysanthemums, calendula, arthuriums, orchids set among rose petals and silver leaves. It all reminded me of Mrs. C. V. Whitney's Lexington party. Festival Artists had charged $35,000 for the float. Four related sets of spinning pink and white carnation disks gave the illusion of spotlights. Better than anything else—from the mob's point of view—were giant, colored, flower-seed poster portraits, particularly those of Peter O'Toole and Sophia Loren, eminently removable.

Massive generators and batteries which lay out of sight and, a mechanic told me, weighed 300 pounds or more, "them bastards hauled away like they were flowers." Unlike the scavenging ghouls that roach into planecrashes, this mob wrecked what it could not steal. Sledgehammers suddenly appeared to escalate destruction. The generation gap broke down with every communal smash at an inanimate object. Old people, middle-aged people, young people, children—male, female—joined in grabbing, tugging, cutting. One man produced wire snips in order to steal lengths of seemingly useless chickenwire.

People who lived on Craig Avenue told me one woman climbed to the top of the marquee, risking a fall, ripping her dress, exposing her underwear:

"An old dame—you wouldn't believe it. Her and a hundred more. They were like crazy."

"That driver," a thirteen-year-old girl from the neighborhood told me, "kept begging people to go watch the parade—to go home. We were all sure the cops would come any minute. Someone told the driver a bigger tow truck was on the way. Nothing good came—only more and more wild crazy people—with tools—screwdrivers, wrenches, crowbars, hammers. My uncle told the driver and the woman with him to get out of there before the crazy people tore the clothes off their backs."

The word spread quickly, I was told. First it was dozens, then hundreds, and in all a thousand or more people taking turns at plucking clean or smashing "this glamorous institution of the Land of Make-Believe."

"They kept yelling things like, 'I could use a picture frame,' or, 'I could use some two-by-fours.' The worst were the ones that kicked something in and then climbed higher just to kick some more. It was like in gym. Someone would do something and someone else would match it or do something crazier. The tearing sound was the most terrible. And the way they fought each other for a stupid sprayed carnation. I was afraid they'd break off and turn on us. My uncle said it was enough parade for this year. He made us go into the house, lock the doors, and watch the rest on TV. Nobody even mentioned what was happening to this poor float."

On the football field, the gratuitously violent and irrational acts were left to Woody Hayes, builder of character. A fifty-five-year-old Los Angeles *Times* photographer, Art Rogers, wearing all the official Tournament of Roses credentials, moved to photograph a huddle Hayes was conducting about five minutes before game time. Rogers, kneeling, had his long-lens camera to his eye when Hayes suddenly broke out of the huddle, jammed the camera's eyepiece back against Rogers's forehead, and, according to Rogers, hollered:

"That ought to take care of you, you son of a bitch."

A mortal doing the same thing would have had his ass kicked—literally, not just as John McKay described the 42–17 whipping of Ohio State soon to follow. Or someone might have called a cop. But "wondrous Woody" was a "real hardnosed" football coach, and thus exempt from normal expectation. Hardnosed Woody had promised to close the Ohio State dressing room to reporters after the game—and, gee, he did. And for twenty whole minutes. He also slammed the dressing room door in the face of several of his own players who came off the field late. They weren't made to stand in the corner—only the corridor. Earlier Woody had forbidden his players to speak to the press at all. Sports characters don't abound in the 1970s; so the press makes do with whatever mean-spirited goofs it has around.

After that twenty-minute locked door treatment and a little chit-chat about the game, Hayes was asked to describe what had happened in the incident with Rogers. He responded by throwing the interview microphone on the floor and hollering:

"Oh for Jesus Christ's sake, forget it."

That was the end of his interview. The newspaperman with the Ohio State eyeshade was terribly miffed.

"Look how that Los Angeles punk went and upset the coach," he said.

In the pressroom before the game a small, yellow, four-page publication, *Rose Bowl Players Speak Out,* was included among the items laid out on the press tables. It was, unprofanely, "for Jesus Christ's sake." Eight *Rose Bowl Athletes*—as they called themselves officially—four from Ohio State, four from USC (three whites and one black in each case), were declaring themselves for Jesus *before* the game. I looked through the pile of Rose Bowl handouts to see what other political or religious groups had been invited to add a leaflet to the press kit: those California grape-pickers or lettuce-pickers, say, or the California Committee Against Prayer in the Schools. I found nothing.

One of the Ohio State *Rose Bowl Players* to *Speak Out,* John Smurda, testified:

> "Before I personally received Christ I was more concerned about myself and my own goals. Now I have become warmer toward others."

And toward the bench, Smurda, a spare, might have added. Another Ohio State player, Harold "Champ" Henson, a starter, couldn't keep his good news statistics out of his statement as Christ's witness:

"I've had a lot of success at OSU—beating Michigan and leading the nation in scoring [twenty touchdowns]. But I can honestly say that accepting Christ is the greatest thing that has happened to me. Life is now more full and worthwhile. Christ provides a new adventure, different from the humdrum of everyday life. For example, I used to think only about myself, but now I am more considerate of others."

The Players' statements concluded with a promise:

"You can have this same relationship with Christ that we have if you will acknowledge to Him that you have sinned and need His forgiveness."

A form with three boxes was provided for Rose Bowl fans who wanted to make this a lasting spectacular. Under "Comment," one was asked to choose among three positions:

[] I have just asked Jesus Christ to be my Savior and Lord.
[] I would like more information about how I too can have a personal relationship with Christ.
[] I already know Jesus Christ in a personal way but would like some information on how I can live a better Christian life.

Outside the sanctified pressroom window the Santa Ana winds, not yet subdued, whipped the dry palm trees into nature's soundtrack, in competition with the cheerleader's loudspeakers echoing "One two, one two." From time to time wind would gust, the pressroom sway as if from an earthquake.

At 12:45 the Ohio State quarterbacks and centers came out on the field—traffic, at that moment, was backed up three miles on Ventura Boulevard. While the paired centers and quarterbacks were practicing snaps and shadow-handoffs, Ohio State's cheerleaders and pompom girls ran out on the field with warm-up stretches, cartwheels, flips, splits, somersaults, backbends, handstands, high kicks.

The quarterbacks had separated from the centers and begun a game of ovoid pepperball when the entire Ohio State squad jogged out on the field. At 1:10 USC's squad came out. Then USC left and, for a few minutes, the field belonged to the bands.

It was that spectaculars moment again, like the one which preceded the playing of "My Old Kentucky Home" at Churchill Downs, or the call of "Gentlemen, start your engines" at the Indianapolis Speedway, or the first announcement of "The clerk will call the roll" at a presidential nominating convention, or that extraordinary stillness before Rex moved out to start the official revelry of Mardi Gras Day.

"I couldn't believe it," I was told in Pasadena, and everywhere else, "that I was actually *here*." The Rose Bowl—the Kentucky Derby, the Indianapolis "500," Democratic or Republican National Conventions, Mardi Gras.

I also heard something else: those attending somehow felt they represented their families, their communities, their cities.

"Nobody from my hometown that I ever heard of was at the Rose Bowl," the woman next to me in my non-pressbox seat said religiously.

She was from the Cold River area of Washington State.

"This is my dream!" she said. "It's everybody's dream."

At 1:18 Ohio State came back on the field, sprinting now, followed, two minutes later, by USC. Ohio State went through a series of set calisthenic drills. A lineman would crouch, another lineman lean on him. Two guards or tackles would rear up against each other like rampant heraldic lions. For an instant they would hold their frozen poses. Then a lineman would grab up another and carry him ten yards stifflegged as a post-race jockey standing up in his stirrups.

At 1:40 the USC band in its wacky Trojan War outfits crisscrossed with its team which entered stage left, whooping, fists thrust in the air. At 1:43 the game officials appeared on the field, followed by "Tommy Trojan," the USC mascot on his white horse, behind him, Mrs. Richard Nixon, smiling and waving. As she climbed into the stands, a mass of tiny flags suddenly appeared, saluting Mrs. Nixon as if she were a successful moon shot. Duke Wayne, the grand marshal, at this moment was having trouble hanging onto his macho hairpiece in the high Santa Ana winds.

At precisely 2 P.M., with that wind blowing hard down on the field, Anthony Davis of USC kicked off and Ohio State scrimmaged from its own 28. Neither team looked very good in the first half, but Mike Rae's USC touchdown pass to Lynn Swann in the first quarter might have prepared everyone for what was going to happen in the second half.

In the third quarter, with the score 7–7, the slaughter of Woody Hayes's supposedly well-drilled innocents began. Mike Rae completed passes every time he seriously tried (he was 18 for 25). Ohio State would get ready for a goal-line stand, and USC's fullback, Sam Cunningham, would soar over into the end zone—four times, for a new Rose Bowl record. When Ohio State worked at pass coverage or tensed for Cunningham, Anthony Davis ran the ends (for 157 yards).

The style of Woody Hayes was best illustrated when his team, down 14–7, kicked a field goal, on fourth down. USC was offside. Taking the penalty—and giving up three points—Ohio State would have had a first down close to the USC goal line. Gutsy Woody declined.

No wonder, then, that Jim Murray, in the Los Angeles *Times,* captioned his game column "Stone Age Football," and said things like:

> Well, I can see why Woody Hayes kept his Ohio State team hidden. He should have locked them in a closet on game day, too. . . . Woody Hayes, who's a great student of military history, must have gotten his game plan from Mussolini. . . . He gave the impression he was running out the clock. On the opening kickoff. . . . Behind 42–10, with only a few minutes left to play, Woody sent in a series of line bucks. . . . They put the lights on in the fourth quarter, but . . . Hayes' team . . . can play . . . in a dark alley or in a coal mine.

Murray wasn't satisfied to knock Woody Hayes. He had something to say about the Rose Bowl itself—in contrast to what area newspapers did for all other spectaculars in the way of build-up and drumroll:

> For those of you unlucky enough never to have been to a Rose Bowl game, you can get the same effect by putting your car on the Ventura Freeway, surrounding it with a lot of buses with guys in them wearing lampshades and doing the hula and spilling martinis all around. Arrange for your

> car to move 10 feet every 15 minutes. Have your house 50
> miles away from the bowl so you have to leave at sunrise and
> still miss the 2 o'clock kickoff. . . . Now, if you're lucky,
> when you get there, Roy Riegels [of California] will run the
> wrong way or the Four Horsemen [of Notre Dame] will
> run the right way. . . . If you're unlucky, Ohio State will be
> there. . . .

Murray wasn't the only one in the *Times* to work the Bowl
game over. John Hall in his column referred to it all as "The Rose
Charade":

> . . . the great Rose Bowl wind of 1973 . . . died shortly af-
> ter halftime and so did the great windbag from Ohio State,
> Woody Hayes. . . . Away from the eyes of the public, the
> mighty Rose Bowl is a creaking relic that should be exter-
> minated along with other undesirable creatures of the dark
> ages. . . .

Hall was upset by John McKay being "clawed and pounded on the
neck on his way to the dressing room." "I'm not going back out in
that madhouse," McKay had said once he made it inside. "Getting
back to the dressing room was the toughest thing we had to do all
day."

Again the contrast between McKay and Woody Hayes took on
sociological and political implications. Hayes was against permis-
sive coaches. McKay felt that players were grown-ups who could
talk to or not talk to whomever they pleased. Lynn Swann of USC
said he and his teammates had "kinda laughed and cracked up
about" Woody Hayes's rigid pre-game restrictions. "Players are
more mature today," Swann said—McKay's point of view. "They
don't have to be told again and again 'You can't do this, you can't
do that.'"

Woody Hayes and creaking Bowl customs aside, the people
leaving Pasadena after the game didn't, on the whole, feel what
Jim Murray and John Hall felt—that the Rose Bowl was an institution whose time had passed. Just as the Kentucky Derby operates
more or less independent of the special quality of any year's
horses, so the Rose Bowl could not be summed up by an objective

evaluation of its participating teams. Few people attending a Great American Spectacular want the mystery explained or disturbed.

In a few hours, the pre-game Rose Bowl traffic jam turned into the post-game traffic jam. The winds had calmed, but the dust raised by the Santa Anas still darkened the sky. A buffgray sunset forced inch-worming cars to turn on their headlights. Rose Bowl spectators, unlike the "500" infield people, who, after the race, wanted to stay on, and on, rushed away—into trapping Ventura Boulevard traffic.

A few campers were left in the parkinglots, a few vans, the odd chartered bus. On the Tournament of Roses parade route, the stands looked like bared metal construction rods, sculptors' armatures set for the winding on of wet plaster. Streetcleaning details tidied Orange Grove Boulevard. A couple of occupied sleepingbags lay unmoving under parade-route trees. Another cold night was coming. Tomorrow the Rose Bowl would be quiet. And empty. In the Tournament of Roses headquarters, a 1974 parade theme would have to be selected; the float builders would yawn and start again; the machinery of the great college football spectacular would be oiled, not overhauled, and begin to grind out the obvious Rose Bowl message—"We're Number One!"

11

The Mardi Gras Ball Within a Ball Within a Ball

As Wallace Stevens said of blackbirds, there are at least thirteen ways of looking at a spectacular. Socially, as I've been indicating, the spectacular is complex. That complexity extends to the spectacular politically, economically, sentimentally, commercially, culturally, even religiously and mythically. The Day of Misrule celebrated by New Orleans' Mardi Gras is much older than Mardi Gras. Greek, Roman, Hebraic cultures all had a version of the Day of Misrule in which hierarchies were inverted and criticism was free. For one short day the powerful acted powerless, and the powerless pretended to have power. What was done on the Day of Misrule was not held against one when that day was over. Lear's Fool had twenty-four free hours to set the old fool straight, and thousands more to realize that his truth didn't take.

Mardi Gras psychologically and politically is a release, a final fling, the last oats-sowing before Lent ashes mark the penitent brows of those who celebrated Fat Tuesday with special homage to each of the Seven Deadly Sins. Though New Orleans is still a Catholic city, Mardi Gras has become secular. The French Roman Catholic families who celebrated Mardi Gras in the nineteenth century have fewer Catholic descendants in the 1970s. Few family members now speak French. As in our society generally, ritual has turned into routine. Religion went social. Mardi Gras in the 1970s is clubby at its core, and private. But nobody can keep a spectacular private for long.

At its silent social center, every spectacular is run by a familiar power combination—political figures, industrial and commercial organizations, professional associations. Mardi Gras is at once the most obvious and most interesting microcosm of a spectacular at work. Its hierarchy is clear—at the top, white, old-family, financially established, politically and professionally elite. Mardi Gras makes explicit what the people of New Orleans live with all year round—fraternities call it the "bounce system," a recognized social structure with a powerful top and a not-so-powerful drop-off in the many gradations below. A series of "Ancient Krewes"—parade and social organizations—are headed by the most exclusive, Comus and Rex. Dozens upon dozens of Krewes form a hierarchy ending with Comus and Rex parodies like the Krewe of [Friar] Tucks, which is "Fort Lauderdale's" own contribution to Mardi Gras.

The Krewe of Tucks confines its parade to the university area (St. Charles, Broadway, Freret, Palmer, South Claiborne streets), where, presumably, the Day of Misrule is allowed that extra latitude so essential to sophomoric predictability. The usual Mardi Gras doubloons, beads, trinkets, and wooden nickels are thrown to a beer-drinking sideline crowd. In 1973 Chuck Berry's "My Ding-a-Ling," a great favorite with college and university audiences on this continent and in Europe, became a smirky double-entendre parade theme to go with an assortment of fraternity toilet jokes—e.g., a "Dukes of Dung" float featuring four college boys asquat on toilet thrones. King Tuck V was a New Orleans cop who in 1972 had steered the parade the wrong way.

The point about the Krewe of Tucks is participation—the Mardi Gras thing. The Fort Lauderdale gang peripheral to the Kentucky Derby, the Indianapolis "500," the nominating conventions, the Rose Bowl is absorbed into Mardi Gras. The T-shirted Greek-lettered beer-drinkers can stand along the sidewalks catching trinkets or climb up on the floats.

Louisiana State University students come from Baton Rouge to join with LSU at New Orleans students, Tulane students, Loyola students, USL students in their own Mardi Gras ball. Such mock marching bands and mock floats as Tucks Precision Drill Team, Ruby Bagonia's Marching Band and Health Club, the Ragin' Cajuns, and the Million Dollar Kazoo Band go through the usual

Mardi Gras maneuvers. The Bay Area Bombers do a street parody of the roller derby and water skiers.

In the New Orleans power structure, at the top of the society ladder, Mardi Gras is the most significant social event of the year— the coming-out ball for white debutantes. The season's debs, their daddies, their escorts are introduced to phony kings, queens, dukes, and duchesses. From time to time a comparatively real duke or live duchess is brought from Europe to meet "King" Rex and be around at the climactic Comus-Rex witching hour. Before Rex goes to the Comus ball, the unofficial Mardi Gras theme song, "If Ever I Cease To Love," a/k/a "The Song of Rex," must be sung. This "Auld Lang Syne" of Mardi Gras uses the music of a burlesque, *Blue Beard,* first sung in 1872 by one Miss Lydia Thompson for the Grand Duke Alexis of Russia. The music—take my word for it—fits the words of Rex's theme song:

> *If ever I cease to love*
> *If ever I cease to love*
> *If ever I cease to love*
> *If ever I cease to love*
> *If ever I cease to love*
> *If ever I cease to love*
>
> *May the Grand Duke Alexis*
> *Ride a buffalo through Texas*
> *May fish grow legs*
> *And cows lay eggs*
> *May bow-legged rats*
> *Chase one-eyed cats*
>
> *If ever I cease to love*
> *If ever I cease to love*
> *If ever I cease to love*

I know of no version by Chuck Berry.

Between the powerful Mardi Gras Rex-Comus organizations and Friar Tucks fall about a hundred different krewes and reveler societies, most of them in New Orleans, some in other Louisiana towns and cities. Unique is the Cajun "Run Mardi Gras" held in the Cajun town of Mamou, made up not of floats but people on horseback. In contrast to the purple, green, gold fluff and tinsel of citified Mardi Gras, Mamou riders wear hideous fierce-toothed, swollen-lip devil's masks, ape's masks, witch's masks, ass-heads, and even Ku Klux Klan headpieces.

The point of "Run Mardi Gras" is to bring the Day of Misrule to farm families. The masked posse, full of brew, rides through the Evangeline parish town of Mamou after its unmasked leader, *le capitaine,* lays down ground rules for his clown posse. No busting up property. No shooting off guns. No personal hip flasks or bottles: all boozing is to be communal—poured straight off the revelers' guzzle truck. Anybody who starts a fight is booted out of the posse along with anybody too drunk to sit a horse.

"*Biens?*" shouts *le capitaine.*

"*Allons!*" he himself, joined by his cavalry clowns, responds.

The captain carries a *corne à vache*—cow's horn—he blows to alert a farm family the Mardi Gras revelers are at hand. The captain himself—always someone wellknown—asks permission for his crew to enter.

"*Voulez-vous recevoir le Mardi Gras?*" is his ceremonial greeting.

"*Oui, monsieur,*" is the expected reply.

Any girl coming out of the house can be grabbed and freely kissed by the hundred riders of misrule. The visit/raid is actually a quest for ingredients to go into the community gumbo. The riders try to earn the *poule grosse* with their version of a Halloween "trick or treat," the famous *faîtes de macaque*—songs, dances, acrobatics, magic, sheer clowning around. The farm family responds not by giving but by turning loose a live speedy creature "for the gumbo"—usually a fairly tough old chicken. This is the *poule grosse* the men on horseback try to catch. Such sorties leave men not only very drunk but covered with sheepdip from the run through the farmyards. The Mamou Fat Tuesday communal gumbo contains all the catches of *poule grosse,* and other things. Cajun music—not Rex's "If Ever I Cease To Love" theme—fills Mamou till Lent closes out most of the partying.

Mamou's Mardi Gras is far different from New Orleans' socially striated spectacular. The right sentiments, the proper traditions, the correct tone are set by the establishment organizations, Rex and Comus and Momus and Proteus and Bacchus. Once the Mardi Gras parades were private processions on their way to exclusive white-only balls. Those excluded—the whites, that is; Louisiana blacks in the post-Civil War era didn't count—looked on the balls as insults. Attempts were made to crash the swank parties. Parades were then thrown to the populace to get them off the mummers' backs. Plebeians were supposed to accept watching a parade as total participation.

Historically, though, enmity continued between the paraders and the watchers. From their height on cars and floats and horseback the official revelers could not only socially but literally look down on the watchers. Some couldn't resist a few misrule tricks of their own—like dousing the watchers with water, or powdering them with choking flour unloaded from float-held sacks. Retribution wasn't long in coming: the watchers retaliated by stoning the riders and their horses, trying to pull revelers off the floats and wagons. Stones gave way to bricks and bottles. Every warring exchange was a potential no-fun mob scene. The paraders considered it their social privilege to be able to douse the people on the sidelines—a Mardi Gras version of *noblesse oblige,* doubtless.

The Mardi Gras switch to "throws"—people on floats, wagons, and horseback tossing harmless trinkets and doubloons—was an obvious attempt to bring peace to the parade. Now the parade could be anticipated for beads or souvenirs.

While the nature of the exchange between reveler and watcher was undergoing significant changes, the degree of parade participation itself began to change. In 1973, for instance, the Krewe of Tucks was having only its fifth annual Mardi Gras while the invitation to Rex's ball read:

> *The Grand Ball of His Majesty Rex*
> *1973*
> *In the 102nd Year of His Reign*

Krewes were easily formed, and just as easily disappeared. Mardi Gras did not operate with a fixed quota of parade organizations. In time all-black parades became part of Mardi Gras, first confined to black areas, then venturing on to the regular parade routes. In time the establishment parades were followed by truck

floats—huge trailer truck beds with, for the most part, only the simplest designs and superstructures. Trade unions could now join the
Mardi Gras festivities, small communities, fraternal societies, even
families. A truck float, for example, could establish itself instantly
by throwing more and better stuff. Word gets out fast. Watchers
will always bunch where the unusual throws appear.

Usually, the same old things are thrown—Italian beads, American plastic beads, and, once in a while, those beautiful glowing
Czechoslovakian glass beads. Doubloons are valued not for their
metal but are ranked according to the place of the throwers in the
Mardi Gras power structure. Rex and Comus doubloons are the
most sought after by collectors. In 1973 Proteus doubloons became instant collectors' items when the Proteus parade was can-
celed because of foul weather Mardi Gras eve (thus no Proteus
doubloons were actually thrown).

The whole Mardi Gras collecting game is fascinating. People
stand for hours to catch the junk jewelry and "money" they
wouldn't bother to pick up the other fifty-one weeks of the year.
Mardi Gras magic makes people push, dash into the path of on-
coming floats, fight over a string of beads or a bracelet as if it were
a piece of heaven's manna. Twenty-four hours after Mardi Gras
only collector freaks care at all about what was snatched or how
much was hoarded. During parade week everybody must have
something. Some must have a full set of establishment doubloons.
Some must have at least a hundred throws. Kids peddle their
catches to the unlucky and the slow-of-hand on the sidelines.
Women and men walk around wearing several dozen necklaces.
Beads are tied in the hair by men, women, and children, hands
covered with rings, blouses with doubloon brooches. Pockets ring
weighed-down with doubloons. Special cloth doubloon bags are
knotted at the top to prevent not-so-chance pilfering.

Adults, as well as children, covet the throws; yet, except for the
dated doubloons, it's hard to separate a 1973 ring from one caught
in 1972 or 1962. So it is with the beads and other junk pitched out
of barrels and sacks and boxes by masked revelers.

Mardi Gras is the model of the great American spectacular
adopted, adapted, converted, inverted by adults and children, old
and young, white and black eager to become part of a significant

event at a certain time of year in a very important place. Diversity is the potential theme of the great American spectacular: everyone is capable of picking up at least some part of the action. Mardi Gras provides the maximum opportunity for watchers to become doers, inventors, creators. Parade themes and krewe floats are boring and dull, but there are ways for innovation to thrive during Mardi Gras. Those who can't be *in* Comus can parody Comus. Those contemptuous of a society debutante ball may hold a "He-Sheba" costume contest to mock Comus, Miss America, Coco Chanel all at once.

Groucho Marx's famous wisecrack, that he wouldn't want to belong to a club which would have him as a member, doesn't fit the serious social ambitions rampant in New Orleans. Everybody who wants to be somebody in New Orleans society has a definite *arriviste* goal in mind, some club or organization in which membership would count as a social crown of bays. Comus is the most prestigious social group not only because it is the oldest Mardi Gras organization but because the families in Comus are New Orleans' oldest. In New Orleans any socially distinguished old family is obviously "pre-Civil War." The elegant balls of Mardi Gras almost all celebrate the antebellum style—elegance, lavishness, the romantic *Gone With the Wind* stuff in which night-parade flambeaux substitute for the fire of Tara.

Comus began in 1857, pre-Civil War, but celebrating Mardi Gras, New Orleans society people believe, dates back to 1699 when Pierre le Moyne, sieur d'Iberville, founded the first Louisiana settlement he called *Point du Mardi Gras* to mark the day of his discovery. Rex didn't appear till after the Civil War, in 1872, when Momus also appeared, followed ten years later by Proteus. In that special form of promo-history attached to most spectaculars, "elegance" was allegedly introduced into New Orleans by the Marquis de Vaudreuil, who wanted Carnival to be the grandest gala outside of Paris and pre-French Revolution Versailles. The Mardi Gras Parade, according to some historians, began in the late 1830s. Its needed shape and essential order followed on the formation of Comus.

Pre-Civil War New Orleans, "antebellum plantation fairyland," was also, of course, a place and a time of functioning slavery. New

Orleans, "The City That Care Forgot," was the most important slave market in the South. Care perhaps forgot the city's powerful (many of whom were in Comus), but undoubtedly remembered their black plantation slaves. Elegance and graciousness were, as most Mardi Gras handbooks don't stress, supported by the paternalized slave economy. The oldest and most socially powerful families in New Orleans established their power on elegant graceful slave plantations.

In his *Study of History* Arnold Toynbee refers to "Archaism" as "an attempt to remount the stream of life . . . in the hope of regaining one of those quiet upper reaches that in 'Times of Troubles' are regretted the more poignantly the farther they have been left behind." On one important social level, Mardi Gras is southern society's celebration of a way of life which Civil War defeat did not totally destroy. Toynbee, without reference to New Orleans, underlined the "pathological exaggeration which is one of the characteristic notes of Archaism in all its manifestations."

Mardi Gras is made up of Old Line organizations with serious social ends—parties, costume balls, formal balls, the presentation of debutantes, the designation of certain debutantes as Mardi Gras queens. Everything is worked out with striational social accuracy. If a certain young woman is chosen to be Queen of Comus, it's a clear indication of how her family stands in the *current* New Orleans social hierarchy. Mardi Gras is the southern version of Opening Night at the Met.

"One of those pretty little fillies," a New Orleans social observer told me, "would want her daddy to horsewhip everyone in [x] or [y] if she didn't end up the highest in every reckoning."

The Rex organization, on which I chose to focus for Mardi Gras, had many members far more concerned about the social, private Rex ball than the public parade. The *ends* of Rex were social, the parade an elaborate *means* which, to the commoner, looked fancy enough to be Rex's only end. The parade, though fun, seemed, at times, a sop to the populace. The real Old Line social business of Rex and Comus and Momus and Proteus and Oberon and Nereus and Mithras and Olympians was to celebrate the past lavishly. My helpful Rex guide, it turned out, was also the father of Rex's debutante queen. No matter where we went, gray-suited business and professional men came forward to shake his hand and congratulate him for "the great and deserved honor" bestowed on *him*—through his daughter.

In the New Orleans *Times-Picayune* for Sunday, March 4, 1973, two days before Mardi Gras, a three-column *color* print at the very top of the front page featured "Her Royal Highness, The Mystic Queen." Mystic, though not a nineteenth-century organization—1973's was only its fifty-first ball—was decidedly Old Line. The "ball held in honor of Marie-Joseph-Paul-Yves-Rock-Gilbert du Motier, Marquis de Lafayette," was, in 1973, recreating *the* social event at the Theatre d'Orleans in 1825. The New Orleans Municipal Auditorium was converted, for this one night, into the Theatre d'Orleans. A huge French tricolor canopy (much preferred to the tricolor stars and stripes, I was told) covered the entrance to the ballroom. The walls were decorated with tricolor cockades and bunting. Twinklelights such as Mrs. C. V. Whitney used so cleverly in Lexington sparkled in a crystal chandelier (during Mardi Gras, the two Municipal Auditorium ballrooms were in constant use—each time decorated in some fitting historical style).

The *Times-Picayune* writer gave a detailed description of every gown, but really full was the description of the Mystic Queen herself:

> Her Majesty made a charming picture in a gown of imported golden lace, with an underskirt of dove gray satin and a bodice of dove gray velvet. . . . Sleeves were huge and puffed.
>
> A metallic thread highlighted the design of the golden lace while an irridescent, metallic thread-trim accented the broad neckline and the regal waistline.
>
> The queen's golden crown was studded with topaz and diamond "stones." From the back of the crown extended a golden-threaded net train, a gold and topaz brooch, golden drop earrings and elbow-length gray satin gloves. . . . In keeping with her role as the [1825] mayor's wife, Her Majesty carried a fan instead of a scepter.

After the New Orleans matrons, who were the queen's ladies-in-waiting, had had their gowns described, the writer turned to the thirteen star debutantes chosen for presentation:

> The debutantes . . . were arrayed in satin gowns, which varied in color. In keeping with the style of the early 19th

century, the frocks were made with close-fitting bodices and full, ankle-length skirts to achieve an hour-glass effect. . . . Silk and velvet roses, bows, tassels and satin flounces adorned the "debs'" dresses while on their feet were bright-colored dancing slippers. White gloves and white stockings completed their ensembles.

The *Times-Picayune* story was carried over to page 8; on page 9, facing it, was a five-column tale captioned:

Per Capita Income Rank of Louisiana Is Declining.

Ungilt, unbeaded, unsequined, a second fact stood out: Louisiana continued as "the South's leader in functional illiteracy."

For the "Krewe of Mystery" Ball, the chosen setting, according to the *Times-Picayune,* was again, in the spirit of (Toynbee's) "Archaism," a "summer house and garden of an ante-bellum plantation." Where, in the Mardi Gras festivities, a carrier of dangerous liquid fire flambeaux was required for historical authenticity, a young black always got the job. In New Orleans the descendants of slave owners would have no difficulty in finding blacks directly descended from antebellum plantation slaves.

Mystery, like Mystic, was a twentieth-century significant society Krewe to which genuine Mardi Gras debutantes had to be presented. The *Times-Picayune* writer perhaps thought the Queen of the Krewe of Mystery inadequately gowned, and so ignored her costume, but not her mother's. Also "noted wearing lovely ballgowns were," said the writer, listing—not in simple alphabetical order—fifty or sixty women by their correctly spelled names.

Photographs and gown descriptions were a social code language any seasoned society observer could translate instantaneously. A real genuine part-of-the-ruling-hierarchy queen had to appear in living newsprint color (like the Mystic Queen) or, if printed up black and white, occupy a minimum of one fifth of a page full face or full figure. Debutantes in Old Line or near-Old Line "courts" had to have their gowns, their hair-dos, their day frocks, and their out-of-doors costumes minutely detailed. The *Times-Picayune* and the *States-Item* obviously knew their readership well. Such social coverage seemed obligatory.

A member of Comus who had spent time in New England academies told me that a debutante of "good family had to be queen of something" during Mardi Gras, and that the somethings were as rigidly differentiated hierarchically as the descending offices of the Roman Catholic Church. Being queen didn't end a debutante's obligations and privileges: she would also be a member of two or three other courts whose queens might well be maids in *her* court. In addition, she was presented formally at all the other socially significant balls. A separate ballgown for each fete was, of course, the absolute minimum: three, four, or ten other special dresses, costumes, and suits were needed to complete Mardi Gras. Tradition had it that a debutante queen entertained at supper after her ball: two or three hundred guests were not unusual.

"In all," I was told, "four or five thousand dollars, ten, perhaps more—not counting our membership, our charities, and our other obligatory and quite heavy ad hoc outlays."

The two highest social designations for Mardi Gras are, in ascending order, Queen of Rex (which means being Queen of Carnival) and Queen of Comus. In 1973 the Queen of Rex was also an attendant to the Queen of the Elves of Oberon (Old Line); the Queen of the Krewe of Mystery and the Queen of the High Priests of Mithras (Old Line) were attendants at the court of the Queen of Rex; the Queen of the High Priests of Mithras had in her court the debutante who was also the Queen of Proteus—etc., etc.

The New Orleans papers listed every Old Line matron and Old Line family debutante in town, it seemed. Long after New York, Boston, Chicago, Los Angeles, San Francisco, and other papers have all but abandoned society reporting and the "Society Section," New Orleans, uncoerced, made "Society" perhaps the strongest voice in the paper. Eastern bluebloodery, on the other hand, has all but deeded coming-out parties to Pentagon generals, beribboned admirals and their sometimes socially registered wives.

The unofficial historian and social explainer for Rex and Mardi Gras in New Orleans is Charles L. "Pie" Dufour, a local social observer who appears regularly in a column headed "Pie's A La Mode." The Sunday before Mardi Gras, Mr. Dufour answered what he said were the three most frequently asked questions about Carnival. The second was, "What do Rex's colors mean?": though a meaning had been attached after the fact—green for faith, purple for "Imperial Justice," and gold for power—the colors had probably been chosen simply "because they are bright and gay," said Mr. Dufour. The third question, "What is a 'krewe'?" elicited an answer Toynbee might have written: "The founding fathers of Comus wanted to create an archaic sort of title, so they started off with 'Mystick' and that led them to do tricks with 'crew' changing it to 'krewe.'"

The first question was quite the most interesting: "What does it 'cost' to be Rex, King of Carnival?"

Mr. Dufour's ideologically proper answer came first: "Nothing. The honor is bestowed by the School of Design—that is the official name of the Rex Organization—upon a citizen in recognition of his civic activities" (in 1973 that honor fell on Dr. Howard Raymond Mahorner, past president of the American College of Surgeons).

"There are some expenses," Mr. Dufour went on to explain, "but these are rigidly controlled by the School of Design." He then went on to list—I should add, partially—the expenses of Rex:

> A handsome gift for his consort, the Queen of Carnival, and gifts also for the maids in Her Majesty's Court. Gifts are also provided for the young men who serve as dukes to escort the maids at the Rex ball and during Rex's traditional visit to Comus and his court. There is a gift, too, for the little girl who traditionally presents the King of Carnival the key to the city at City Hall.
>
> There are flowers for his queen, flowers for his wife, champagne at the Rex Den with which former Kings of Carnival salute Rex before he mounts the king's float to lead the parade. All of these expenses are undertaken by the King of Carnival, but the amount he spends has been stabilized at between $600 and $800.

Mardi Gras, I was told by a local participant and observer, "offers grand opportunities for displays of *largesse*," far in excess of Dufour's "stabilized" top of $800. "Some of us—mere mortals who will never become Comus or Rex—spend more than $800 dressing up *ourselves,* and our horses. I have friends who spend almost $1,000 on throws alone—though $100 to $200 is a more usual expenditure." Rex and Comus, I was told, *meant* Mardi

Gras *largesse:* "We never choose a Comus or Rex who might find expenditures of several thousand dollars the tiniest bit burdensome." The further suggestion was that neither Rex nor Comus harbored penurious or niggardly creatures.

During the time I spent at Rex headquarters, the Rex den, the Rex "garage," where the freshly painted Rex-owned floats were kept, and at the Municipal Auditorium where Rex's gilt emblems were being set up for the grand finale Mardi Gras Carnival Ball, I met dozens of men, all volunteers. They were doing what was expected of them—taking time from their professions, callings, businesses to help the few paid electricians, sound-men, and carpenters set up the papier-mâché opulence of Rex's court.

"If you had to pay these men their hourly rate," the Captain of Rex told me, "it'd go you $1,000 or more. And here they are setting up chairs. They could be keeping appointments for real dollars instead of doing this doubloon-pay work."

None of these men much resembled a dashing courtier. Standing awkwardly amid the decorative blank masks of comedy and grinning gilt death's heads their Municipal Auditorium appearances contrasted with what many of them looked like a day or two later, on a caparisoned horse, proud, helmeted, booted, plumed like cavaliers. Rex volunteers, mostly in their fifties and sixties, were big on collar pins, tie clasps, the odd pinky ring.

"Comus won't take in the department store manager or the top insurance company man in town," a Comus member who also belonged to Rex said to me. "Rex will. The plumber and butcher make it into Rex. No way they'll ever dance at a Comus ball."

W. J. Cash in his *The Mind of the South* uses Virginians as his Old South models, but his observations fit New Orleans. Cash could have focused on Mardi Gras for its dramatization of southern power and post-Civil War image-making. Though the lowly Rexes I saw were without visible sparkle, others, members of both Rex and Comus, belonged to that "hell of a fellow" category dedicated to drink, bragging, wenching, dueling, and, eventually, disaster. Extravagance was the pre-Civil War southern aristocrat's mark. He could drink more, wench more, ride faster, horsewhip harder—and, on the whole, care less—than anybody not his social, or acre-owning, peer. In fact, being *who* he was, he had no need to *do* anything—better, or at all.

Since the Civil War, Comus and Rex, internally, are little changed. Mardi Gras, on their level, still affirms the values the Civil War did not kill off in the Old South. A visiting photographer —waggishly, I assume—asked a Rex member if the organization had any blacks in it.

"Any what?" said the Rex member.

"Blacks."

"Blacks?"

"Colored folks—you know—the people you've been referring to as niggers all afternoon."

"The niggers have their own."

"Their own Rex?"

"Their own Carnival."

"On the same day you hold yours?"

"I do believe so."

Nobody in Rex I spoke with, including my guide, referred to blacks as anything but "niggers," but always with a very special meaning. The black standing out on the street wasn't a "nigger." He wasn't anything. "Nigger" referred only to those blacks who were around to *shlep* and carry. For example, it didn't matter where one parked one's car outside the Rex float compound during a torrential rain because one could "easily find a nigger to tote these throws inside."

The master-servant archetypes of pre-Civil War New Orleans were still being honored in most exchanges. Ritually, the Old South celebrated itself in front of the local populace under the delusion, perhaps, that national and international society was watching, too. The Old South lost its war, but retained its superior way of life, it believes. And it is that way of life which society's Mardi Gras puts on display. The seventeenth-century and eighteenth-century models for southern aristocracy fared much worse, after all: the English Cavaliers, for example, lost their Rex, Charles, forever. For the next eleven puritanical years courtiers went into a depressing decline. The French models for the grand life had, alas, been guillotined by trashy sans-culottes. But here, in

1973, were the descendants of 1857's Krewe of Comus, still very much in charge.

Some things had changed: for instance, the invitations to Rex's ball used to be delivered personally by a man on horseback, and the acceptance sent back the same way. The invitation was always elaborate, and always—in the early days—accompanied by some expensive souvenir—an inkwell, a vase, a letter opener. The invitations were sometimes huge, almost always in French, and frequently shaped like a fan or a guitar, a dragon, a bell, an elephant, or a deck of cards. Among the most sought-after collectors' items in New Orleans right now are those invitations to the Rex or to any other of the Old Line balls.

Rex and Comus and society may dominate the newspapers during Mardi Gras, but the holiday itself is celebrated by hundreds of thousands—white, black, young, old—who know nothing more about Comus and Rex than that they stage the best Mardi Gras parades—one at night, the other during the day. Mardi Gras, after all, exists for both Labelle's "Creole Lady Marmalade" and her gray flannel man, who might, indeed, be a member of Rex and Comus. He knows little about her Mardi Gras, she less about his, but both hers and his contribute to make Mardi Gras the best party in the entire country.

An old man from Wisconsin, now retired, started to come to Mardi Gras thirty Rex parades before 1973. He arranged his vacations to coincide with Mardi Gras.

"My wife used to like Mardi Gras almost more than me," he said. "She died one Twelfth Night. I felt I owed it to her never to miss Mardi Gras. That's over ten year ago now. We got no kids, so Mardi Gras was always bigger with us than Christmas. We didn't give each other much Christmas so we'd have a little extra something here."

He didn't read the New Orleans papers. The rooming house he stayed in didn't provide TV—or even a radio. His Mardi Gras was the streets. He sat on a bench off Canal Street, seeing only those floats high enough to loom above the massed crowd.

In the outer reaches of the Vieux Carré, off Esplanade Avenue, off Governor Nicholls Street, I met a black man of eighty-three who said he remembered Mardi Gras from around age two, when his family, that had gone off to Oklahoma after the Civil War, moved back to New Orleans.

"I don' go roun' too much," he told me. "Now the Mardi Gras come to me."

He motioned out into a hardly paved heave of street where seven- and eight-year-old Creole children were rubbing rouge on their cheeks to make themselves Carnival Indians. Every tiny house was unpainted. In the city that care forgot, almost every house sagged downward with finality. Piles of beer cases stacked in the backyards, rickety card tables spread with party napkins, covered pots of food, whiskey bottles. Several cars rested on rusted-out hubs, the glassless doors open for kids to run in and out. In their yards a few adults wore parts of a costume—mostly too-large or too-small hats crowned with paper flowers, devil's heads, skulls, or Pepsi cards. A local soul station was grooving on a long long chicken commercial.

"You be here when it dark," the old man said. "See the real Mardi Gras—right there—there—dancin', no need go t' Canal Street. I use' do that dancin'. They call me 'Flamboo.' You know flamboo? Hot krazine. Man, I moo-oove."

He had been sitting on an old beach chair with rusted-through base, bolts missing on one side, plastic straps frayed, some already torn and hanging. Somehow, spurning my hand, he fought that chair to a draw, struggled up, bent low, his hands hefting an imagined flambeau as his doubled-over body began to gyrate, dancing. From time to time he mimed a glance up at the flaming kerosene, then made a swift first-baseman's scoop out of the dirt, coming up with an imagined dime, maybe, or nickel, or quarter.

"Get so's I could hear silver. Real silver, in the dark."

He motioned to the kids in the street. Now they were sticking badly creased cardboard feathers into their beaded headbands.

"Come back when it dark. 'Flamboo' do flamboo."

My cabdriver hadn't approved of the drive through the black district.

"All these hardheaded niggers're drunk or worse. Dope. You blow your horn you liable to have trouble with 'em."

A black woman on Governor Nicholls toasted us with a whiskey bottle.

"The niggers trying to scare the white people," he said. "So's they can have Mardi Gras to theirself."

By late Saturday night and early Sunday, New Orleans resembled the Indianapolis infield on Race Day. In the French Quarter every bar, stripper joint, jazz spot had dozens, even hundreds, of people trying to get in, out, or simply see what was happening. By 1973 the decline of jazz in New Orleans was a staple of summer news broadcasts, a film-clip fill-in, decline-of-America item. Footage would show "decayed" Vieux Carré exteriors owned by, say, a lawyer and her stockbroker husband making, between them, a cool hundred thousand per.

Around Jackson Square at noon, Vieux Carré strippers were hurrying from joint to joint, made-up, carrying huge bags—as they did in New York, Chicago, London's Soho. Mardi Gras speeded up their usual action. More shows in more places, more circuses exchanged for bread. The girl dragging the L.L. Bean bag full of pasties and G-strings in 1973 was as likely to be a full-time graduate student as a part-time waitress.

In the French Quarter those vans I had seen in Louisville, Indianapolis, Miami Beach, Pasadena lined up next to curtained, customized campers. Chased out by a cop, the out-of-state pickups drew into traffic, made a turn, slowly climbed a sidewalk till another cop hollered, "Aright, mistuh, moooove!" For the young, crossing Canal Street out of the French Quarter—even to the university section—was admitting cultural defeat. The French Quarter was where it all hung out. One didn't go to the Kentucky Derby to spend one's time in downtown Louisville. All those legends about the French Quarter had to be witnessed first-hand—perhaps experienced: what *was* the best corner to meet the whores? Where were the queers congregating? Which were the *real* transvestite bars? Did people *really* fuck on the streets during Mardi Gras?

The locals had prepared for the invasion: stores in the French Quarter were advertising specials on Boone's Farm wines, ice cold double-six packs—in drizzly March—vitamin E, granola, brown rice. Someone had obviously been reading underground newspapers. The same places pushing fermented grapes and blueberries stocked postcards, porn books, cut-rate nudie calendars, slides, centerfolds. Five paces away, the real thing flashed out of open doors. Women hawked themselves on the corners and in doorways, wearing short fur jackets, platform shoes, thigh-high boots. Few were "Creole babies." Many made the New Orleans trip each year—from Memphis, Biloxi, Mobile, Galveston, Chicago: some had worked the Derby and the "500." I was sure I had seen one of the women at the Eden Roc in Miami Beach.

"Where?" she said.

I repeated myself.

"I may'a been there, honey. I visit everywhere one time or another."

Mardi Gras, generally, speeds up the interdependencies of what's original, what's imitated, what's parodied, what's put down: in America, Monday's high art may become Tuesday's schlock, Wednesday's high budget movie, Thursday's comedy send-up, Friday's TV series, Saturday's ten-second commercial, Sunday's documentary on the fate of serious art. In New Orleans, during Mardi Gras, all these things happen, simultaneously.

There's a black Zulu organization aping Comus with a gentle toss of gilded coconuts (and memories of a *black* power slave society). Outside of New Orleans there's the Krewe of the Slidellians (in Slidell, Louisiana) and their burgher-like Women's Civic Club "Le Bal Magnifique," similarly imitating Rex and Comus. The identities of the ball king and queen, for instance, were kept "secret" until the grand entrance—a staple of the society balls. The King and Queen Samaritan XXIV were a balding, pudgy gentleman and an unrelated, full-figured, grandmotherly woman in swept-up coiffure and butterfly eyeglasses. They were surrounded by Slidellians playing the parts of:

The Margrave and Margravine of Germany
The Marquis and Marchioness of Italy
The Royal Lord and Lady of England
The Archduke and Archduchess of Austria
The Conde and Condesa of Spain
The Baron and Baroness of Prussia
The Prince and Princess of Russia
The Grand Duke and Grand Duchess of Poland

In the French Quarter there were transvestite duchesses galore, and enough campy dukes to cover all the dance floors of the Municipal Auditorium. A woman wearing a leather jacket with "Biker Dike" on the back led five or six other jacketed women in an elbowing shouldering sweep of Bourbon Street, hollering—oblivious of its discordant consequences for Gay Liberation—"Out of my way, you fucking fags!" At an unscheduled stop at a strip joint the women shoveled young kids out of their way like fallen cricket-wickets.

The guy giving the stripper pitch made no attempt to confront the women: his caution suggested he had experienced the exciting follow-up on such action. In time the women grew bored, turned, and resumed their "front four" assault on male passers-by looking for the topless, the bottomless, the fabled Vieux Carré *café au lait*.

Outside the French Quarter, the square tours were arriving, watchers in search of Mardi Gras "sights." Mardi Gras indulges everyone's delusions. The French Quarter levels vertical distinctions by accenting horizontals. Right outside the Royal Street walls of Comus (at Number 127, where the organization was founded), its insistence on "manners," "honor," "graciousness" means little. The Vieux Carré street scene doesn't keep women and men forever dressed up for a formal or masked ball. The fabled society daddy of debutantes, the model husband, the civic standout "hell of a fellow" will pack his wife off to bed and return to a private club, set-up, or shared Vieux Carré accommodation to continue Mardi Gras (according to the sexist code which says hot-blooded aristocrats can't be surfeited by white women of breeding). Mardi Gras, that is, resembles all other New Orleans nights—only better.

Mimes on Royal Street mime for their money; others join the old black jazzmen in a dancing turned-on zigzag through narrow Bourbon Street. As usual at spectaculars, pushers do some fast trading—anything from a single stick to a whole stash, some "reds," Seconal, "'ludes," or, slightly more guarded, cocaine. St. Louis Cemetery Two is where one buys and, perhaps, spaces out. Everybody knows the best tombs to use when getting in out of the rain or cold. St. Louis One, because Marie Laveau, "Queen of Voodoo"—a big item in the Vieux Carré—is supposedly buried there, receives delegations of visiting covens and coveneers. Black candles (preferred for voodooistic death-wishing) are peddled in Vieux Carré shops and spooked on the streets, along with cock-wilt powders, turn-on Tristan-Isolde philters—the usual stuff. Nothing special is brewed for Mardi Gras. *In*corcists and exorcists divide evenly: the Devil during Mardi Gras is just one more "hell of a fellow."

The tour bus brings the southern and northern smalltowners and city folk through the cemeteries where problem drinking and shooting-up translates as local color. The re-use of tombs built above ground causes many "oooooghghgh's" before every tour bus is reloaded. Cameras may catch the odd foot, pair, or two pair protruding from a tomb. Tour people, like pigeons, are hardly noticed as they wheel in and wheel out.

A black "hell of a fellow" in white sombrero was watching the tour buses come and go outside of St. Louis One. He wore shades, a goatee, rhinestones sewed into the braid of his wide white lapels, a white ankle-length cape tastefully speckled with tiny blue stars, and carried a white umbrella with gold grinning ape's-head handle. He stood about six and a half feet tall, and thin, but his white patent-leather boots had high platforms. He resembled the plantation put-on I had seen at the Derby or, more recognizably, a New York pimp come to check out the receipts at the corner of Broadway and Forty-sixth Street. He claimed to be a graduate student at Southern University in from Baton Rouge for "whatever comes to pass." He said he had been born in New Orleans to a servant couple working in a "Comus" mansion whose "owners," he pointed out, weren't his.

"Don't get me wrong, man," he said as one tour bus pulled out, and another in, "I take. Inside Massuh's slave sty I's yo' very best yassuh nigger. Massuh loves me. Like everytime he sees me he asks, 'What you studying, Rastus?' 'I's studyin' t'be Rastus X, Massuh,' I *don't* say."

He threw back his head and cackled like Stepin Fetchit. A woman in blue-tinted plastic rainhat, see-through plastic raincoat, paused on her way out the bus door, blocking those coming out behind her. The fabled New Orleans above-watertable dead weren't worth this trip into wickedness.

"Understand Mardi Gras, man," he said. "First comes Massuh on his horse. Massuh never burned or strung up anyone. Not by his own hand."

Again his head went back, with no sound. He raised the shades off his eyes for a second.

"Bet you think the bus tour hires my act to get it on for the honkies."

He tapped his umbrella ferule against a corroded twist of wrought iron.

"Banana trees grow best in cemeteries," he said to me, "and truck floats full of blue collar Klan members. Remember: nobody's violent in the French Quarter. Last time a person got mugged here was at least a hundred . . . minutes ago."

Bored, he opened his umbrella, did a flambeaux dancer's skip, shuffle, twirl.

"I scarin' you, man?"

The lady in the plastic rainhat stepped aside to let the rest of the tour out.

"Heeyah!" the man in the sombrero shouted, baring his teeth and fencing viciously in the direction of no one. "Oh, man, we are co-or-rupt here. We are degenerate, eee-vil, deeebauched, full of unrepentant sin. Tonight all your college-boy John Deans and Jebbie Magruders going to be following Al Hirt and Pete Fountain and our best struttin' banjo niggers. I-i-i-gnore that shee-ut, man. I-i-i-gnore it, I say. Our Creole babies who been hauling whitey's ashes for centuries, man, follow them. I mean female Creole babies, male Creole babies, and 300 other sexes—countin' what got changed by surgery."

The tour bus began loading again. Another bus had already chugged in behind it. The man in the sombrero stood tiptoe to wave a lordly fingerflexing goodbye at the lady in the rainhat.

"I could give them a tour," he said as she and her bus drove away. " 'An' here, ladies an' gen'leman, the finest slave auction. Look careful. Behind every plantation column is Massuh's slave block.' "

He stopped.

"It's all a bunch of shee-ut, man. This *was* a mean place, and still is."

Any number of walking tours passed us as we stood there. Up on the second floor wrought-iron balcony on the other side of the street, people were hanging pennants and bunting, French flags.

The French Quarter during Mardi Gras didn't change its residential character in the noncommercial streets. Like every other charming old section of a North American city—Boston's Beacon Hill backstreets rising to Louisburg Square, old Brooklyn Heights, even Cobble Hill, and Chicago's Old Town—what could have been slum was now haven for young successfuls. Bigger houses had been taken over by private clubs. Their elegant courtyards were full of small shiny sportscars. At the door of most of the left-as-is Vieux Carré façades stood a European car, sometimes two. A few residents, disregarding tax consequences, had restored even the outside of their landmark houses, and added swimming pools. An early nineteenth-century wrought-iron outside lamp, elaborate doorknob, stylized numerals, mail-slots, or fully restored front doors were other semaphores that success had taken over the Vieux Carré.

The *apartheid* of the plantation world, of Comus and other Old Line social groups doesn't extend to the French Quarter, and never really did. In this zone of misrule, blacks drink and live next to whites, churches abut whorehouses and pornshops, beggars crowd a rundown slum next to a restoration full of Impressionist paintings, designer furniture, Old South antiques.

Sex levels all in the Vieux Carré. During Mardi Gras, French Quarter permissiveness spills over into the rest of New Orleans. For the most part, Mardi Gras is show biz during its last post-vaudeville gasp. Somehow something vital breaks out of an overwhelming silliness. Mardi Gras is a continuous off-key march in sunlight and darkness. The country's worst half-time stunts have more originality than 95 per cent of the official Mardi Gras parades. The whole thing seems, in retrospect, absurd. Not a single Mardi Gras float could make it into the Tournament of Roses Parade, not even its King Bacchus one stocked with a Bob Hope. But all this, again, is irrelevant. Disbelief and critical standards are suspended for Mardi Gras. Parade floats, like a hundred-plus deck of cards, year after year are dealt out, only modestly departing from random. Rex, I'm certain, could run exactly the same parade year after year and most people would hardly notice: those who notice would hardly care.

Costume balls, perhaps, require "flair" and variety, but I suspect they, too, could be repeated year in, year out. The debutantes are different every year, and in the Old Line krewes only social matters like debutantes count. Different society elders can similarly be honored in set ways.

The Mardi Gras cry is already ritualized: no matter what is thrown, the aspiring catcher on the sidelines always shouts: "Throw me something, Mister!"

The catchers, by now game-wise, have ritualized the way they handle what is thrown. Aficionados know not only who throws the best stuff, but where. Techniques may be personalized, but everyone, after a while, belongs to a certain category:

The Waiter—who stands motionless till the beads and doubloons are in the air, then shoots out a fist like a seal head snapping at thrown fish

The Canny Interceptor—who picks out the prettiest woman the showboating throwers will try to pitch to, then cuts in front of her to grab stuff before it lands

The Alongsider—who will dodge cops and sneak right up to the float to make a personal appeal

The Beggar—who will stand in front of the best catchers and whine "I got nothing"

The Scavenger—who will trail after the successful catchers, knowing something has to drop

The Trader—who knows the absolute values in the hierarchy of collector doubloons and will pass off worthless but flashy truck throws in exchange for a Comus, Momus, Rex, or Proteus

The Crook—who will plunge his hand in a sack, bag, or pocket and come up with Old Line throws

More interesting than the catchers are the throwers, and what moves them to conspicuous distribution. Random pitching is not the way of Santa Clauses. Those who participate in *noblesse oblige* want a specific catcher to acknowledge their *largesse*.

Truck floats, properly plebeian, avoid fancy historical subjects in favor of basic everyday themes like, say, gambling in Las Vegas. A façade may be decorated with a flashing royal flush, some dice, a roulette wheel, a slotmachine jackpot. Truck floats may decide on "The Pull of Fate" as theme. Everyone is a costumed orange, lemon, cherry, or gold bar. Similar stuff could fit "One-Arm Bandits," maybe, in which everyone on the float has an arm in a sling during a very long parade.

What binds together all parades is that sense of Mardi Gras as community effort. Just as other spectaculars peak the year for working people in search of "something special," so Mardi Gras serves to climax fifty weeks of preparation for thousands of individuals and families. Mardi Gras gets its special energy from that community participation. Those Rex "volunteers" are perhaps dragooned, pressured, or slyly co-opted, but nevertheless do put in their time—and their labor. Rex's executive secretary told me she takes her vacation right after the Rex ball, but the day she gets back immerses herself in the usual complexities that end only the year following, on Ash Wednesday.

In New Orleans and out of the city, Elks organizations the weekend before Mardi Gras were putting the last touches to their community truck floats. Some were the work of cousins, or people living on the same street, belonging to the same church, working in the same factory, members of the same union. Middleclass bonding imitated the togetherness which kept Comus and Rex homogeneous.

No matter what truck group I spoke with, the one sure way to break them up was to pass along "Pie" Dufour's figure of $600–$800 as the cost of being King of Rex.

"Pie's typewriter run out of zeroes maybe," a man who belonged to the Elks Krewe of Orleanians told me. "Hell, this here po' boy float runs us maybe three and a half, four thousand—that's one caviar 'n champagne Rex breakfast."

"I tell you somethin'," said a woman pasting cardboard bubbles on a float. "They never yet named a poor man King o' Rex. If they did, the feller'd have to kill hisself."

"Rex don' have no poor men," said the man; "rest easy."

"Ain't no real poor folk truckin' either," said the woman. "We ain't high society but you better believe we got as many doctors and lawyers as Rex."

"Ours," said the man, "is the ones what make house calls."

Trucking is like being a volunteer fireman, a Little League coach, or a member of some fanatic bowling league. There's the ritual activity, the almost-scripted kibitzing, the mandatory beer—weekly. Sundays are spoken for, and, as Mardi Gras gets closer, many other days of the week. Two or three outlets in New Orleans sell beads and other throws by the gross, the box, or the barrel: truck float builders know all the sources, and, also, where to get cloth, paper, glue, paint, sequins, braid, two-by-fours, plywood, chickenwire, wigs, masks, fans, wands, balloons, doubloons.

"A reliable truck," said the truck float man, "is gonna cost a little somethin'—maybe that same $800 Rex lays out."

"That's without the *in*surance," said the woman.

Their trucks carried theme names such as "Pink Squirrel," "Hawaiian Adventure," "The March Wind Doth Blow," "On The Good Ship Lollipop," "Wheeling and Dealing," etc. Between 160 and 170 Orleanian trucks rolled out for 1973, each one full of men, women, and children throwing.

"I know for a fact," a woman said, "that people on the street respect what we throw. Rex an' Proteus people take anythin' a salesman plumps down. Billie and me know quality merchandise."

"What *really* costs," said her husband, "is film. Go to the Boston Club Tuesday when Rex comes, and see them princesses with their hats and gloves and fancy cameras taking pictures of people taking pictures of them."

"They says Philadelphia Mummers invented our parades," his wife said. "I think both got invented by the camera."

Mardi Gras is a perfect mark for American Express scare commercials. Everybody knows the French Quarter must be full of muggers, rollers, panhandlers, purse-snatchers, pickpockets, conmen, conwomen, so any tour guarantees an encapsulated trip starting in a sealed airplane. When one lands in New Orleans, one transfers to a sealed charter bus that chugs to a sealed hotel. If a tour member pokes a nose outside, it's to enter another sealed bus that continues the tour assault-proof, pickpocket-proof, hustler-proof.

Wickedness, always a great tourist attraction, looks best from a high bus seat protected by double-thick tinted glass. Porn-postcard shops are usually proscribed; tours favor postcard-lunch stops at franchised eateries. One passes Antoine's, Galatoire's, or The Court of Two Sisters, *must* stops in the guidebooks, before returning to, say, the Jung Hotel coffeeshop, where, still sealed, the tour member can partake of average, unpushy, general American food.

If the people at the Jung Hotel want to see a parade, they have only to step outside, in daylight or in darkness. A few yards from the hotel entrance on Canal Street, as some parade comes by, you can snap a full 120 roll of film and establish proof that you are *there*. If paraders, throwers, or catchers get too boisterous, you can sneak right back into the safely encapsulating hotel. Tour members observe all the "don'ts." Participation in something so openly raunchy as Mardi Gras thus becomes difficult. But the tour-stops along Royal or Bourbon or Basin streets almost guarantee the tourist one black-and-white couple (even in the far-out Quarter that means, 99 per cent of the time, a white male with a black female); at least one jazz band, one jazz strut; two transvestites, a romp of "queers" and "lesbians." Tourists have to snap the—then—unfinished Superdome, the French Market, the Lee Circle statue of General Robert E. Lee, St. Louis Cathedral in Jackson Square, the Rex float, the Boeuf Gras float, the Comus float, the Bob Hope Bacchus float, one truck float, and the tour's a success. In the Quarter, Miami Beach's "Tanktop" wouldn't rate a camera click, even if covered with *Nixon* buttons.

Basin Street Blues, years before the Warren Court school decision, promised that in "New Orleans, The Land of Dreams," one could see "dark and white folks all meet." That has not changed.

As Mardi Gras approached, the Vieux Carré became less important. Parades went on all over New Orleans, and in outlying suburbs and towns. The Sunday before Mardi Gras, for instance, the following krewes paraded in New Orleans, or the suburbs of Kenner, Gretha, Metaire:

The Krewe of Thoth—its theme, "Man's Quest for Knowledge," included a float under the heading, "Medieval Superstitions"
The Krewe of Venus (all women)—its theme, "The Powers Behind the Throne," pushed Queens Isabella and Cleopatra, familiar figures in many a Mardi Gras Parade

The Krewe of Mid-City—its staple theme, "Walt Disney's World," was one extended animated film commercial

The Krewe of Bacchus—its theme, "Bacchus Goes to the Movies," saluted the same movies and the very same stars who showed up in the Tournament of Roses movie parade—Bogart, Hepburn, Wayne, Gable, Hope, and Crosby

The parades went on and on. But even repetition was irrelevant: the climax was coming, Mardi Gras Day.

12

The "Thereness" Is All

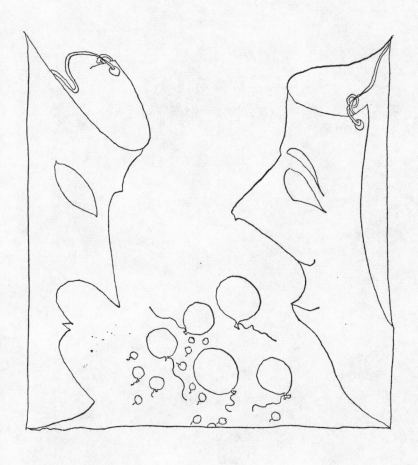

Once in New Orleans, I began to hear the Mardi Gras voice-print, sound reverberations, spectaculars signature distinct as the roar-past of "500" cars. First it rumbled in the distance, indistinct as an approaching summer storm. As I left Tulane Avenue and drove onto Canal Street it reverberated, like thunder in a canyon. Some-one blind, told what was happening, could, forever after, associate images of motion with the rise and fall of a parade's passing. Someone deaf, once instructed about a parade's roar, could, for-ever after, read signatures of sound in the gestures of parade-followers rushing toward the floats, arms upraised, open mouths calling out the unheard:

"Throw me something, Mister!"

A parade could be delayed one hour, two, or longer, disappoint children, make them cranky, but, for most others, only change the action. Instead of watching, one improvised. Along Canal Street and St. Charles, spontaneous mini-parades crowded the sidewalks. Strangers fell into shuffling step, or danced, skipped, whirled behind anybody setting the pace in "Follow the Leader." If a rival "parade" looked more promising, one easily switched over without missing a step.

Kids from nine or ten into the early teens were never deflected from their main catching action. No matter how long a parade was delayed the children used their time well—to jockey in ahead of the massed would-be watchers, slip past policemen trying to pen the crowds up on the sidewalks. Some child would run into the street, see the parade looming up from the direction of the French Quarter, and shout another Mardi Gras signature cry:

"Here it comes!"

Instantly all side games stop. A split second hush interrupts the continuities of sound. Then the first float shimmers into view. That insistent clamorous Mardi Gras roar begins. Anyone in a nearby house or hotel room, hearing that sound, could be out on the street in time for the first float's arrival, and its horseback riders, its twirlers, handspringers, clowns, drum-laden mules and camels. The float pulls into sight, riding high, a landship, a movable circus. Band music slips in and out of that rising crowd roar, sometimes two or three bands at once scrambling tunes in clashing keys. Rear sidewalk areas are deserted; everyone presses forward, hands upraised, fingers extended. Knowing watchers tie handkerchiefs to their fingers to attract attention, and leave hands free to catch the throws.

In the sudden rush of sound is a yet louder chant:

"Throw!

Throw!

Throw!"

This cry is the ultimate Mardi Gras sound. It goes with the rising applause and cheering that greet the first notes of "My Old Kentucky Home" or the Indianapolis call of "Gentlemen, start your motors." It's as distinct as the bullhorn-punctuated roar that drowns out the last bar of the "Star-Spangled Banner" before the Rose Bowl kick-off. It has the same surging rhythm of celebration and recognition I heard at the presidential nominating conventions when everyone realizes, in the midst of a state being polled, that a candidate has attained the number of votes needed for nomination.

All along the parade route that chant passed wave after wave, city block by city block:

"Throw!

Throw!

Throw!"

Crying "Throw me something, Mister" is a ritual proof that you are *there*. At a there that is there. *You* are present *at* Mardi Gras, one of those great events you were always dying to attend. Some souvenir—physical proof of attendance—is needed, but even more essential is the great American spectacular existential proof, The Anecdote. It can be as ordinary as "I was less than two feet from Bob Hope on the Bacchus float—he looked right at me." The ultimate Spectaculars success story, however, stresses getting into something terribly "private," "exclusive," or "secret." Most Mardi Gras anecdotes epiphanize the "wild and crazy" chanced on at a "wild and crazy" hour.

My own experience of Mardi Gras began simply enough—a long delay on my flight out of La Guardia Airport socked in by early morning winter fog. There I noticed a grinning man in thick bifocals, glenplaid hat, glenplaid overcoat, glenplaid jacket. He had missed the entire underside of his chin shaving that morning, and, probably, a few mornings before. He was sitting next to a woman almost invisible under costume jewelry. Her husband stood at a payphone, one ear covered by the receiver, the other by his cupping hand. He insisted on spelling his name out, slowly, loudly.

"You ain't got my reservation?" he kept yelling. "I made it with you—you're the Royal Sonesta, ain't you?—last August."

"Such a liar," the woman muttered.

"What day in August?" her husband hollered. "What kind of a question is that? What *day?* A Tuesday!"

"Ask if they've got a reservation for Smith," the woman said. "It betters your odds."

The man hung up.

"Don't worry," he said. "We get there I'll slip that lousy clerk a double sawbuck."

"During Mardi Gras?" the woman said. "A double sawbuck gets you half an Alka-Seltzer tablet."

"I'll slip somebody a C-note then," her husband said, "or a double C-note. You forget already that Rolls dealer in Indy? Did he or didn't he get us the best suite in town?"

"When he starts with the remember," the woman said to the man in bifocals, "it means we're lucky if we end up in a Holiday Inn."

"Did you know the biggest Rolls-Royce dealer in the whole

country is in Indianapolis?" her husband said to the man in bifocals.

The man in bifocals shook his head.

"Here's one," said the woman, looking through a guide. "The old Desoto—now Le Pavillon—where Huey Long used to operate. And the Roosevelt—big suites, it says here."

The man in bifocals grinned. He began to bounce excitedly in his seat.

"Oh, you're going to love Mardi Gras," he said, clapping his hands together. "Everyone goeth wild and crazy! You'll love Comuth, you'll love Rexth, you'll love Momuth and Proteuth and Bacchuth and Potheidon!"

His voice grew loud. His pixie lisp cut through the sleepiness of the lounge. Again and again he pronounced the names that seemed to have been invented for him alone.

". . . Rexth and Comuth and Momuth and Proteuth . . ."

Suddenly everyone in the lounge seemed to be awake.

"They throw trinketth and doubloonth and cupth engraved Rexth."

The woman thumbing the guidebook wore several rings on every finger, half a dozen waist chains, four or five linked thicknesses round her neck. Her bare wrists and blouse arms were covered with bracelets and bangles.

"Which one's best and biggest?" said her husband to the man in bifocals.

"Rexth," said the man in bifocals without hesitating.

"Write that down, honey," the man said to his wife, "Rexth."

The man in bifocals was elated. He began to recite Mardi Gras history, "rules," disasters. He paused only once to open his briefcase and pull out a wrinkled many-times-refolded paperbag. He fished up two white hardboiled eggs, two slices of buttered white bread, an envelope of excessively white salt. He alone had come prepared for La Guardia fog.

Behind me a young woman and young man began to sing softly —not unkindly.

> *"Comuth and Momuth and Proteuth and Bacchuth*
> *Bacchuth and Proteuth and Momuth and Comuth*

Comuth and Momuth and Bacchuth and Rexth
These are a few of my favorite yecchhth"

Not till almost an hour later was the flight called; every waiting minute the man in bifocals packed with Mardi Gras lore. The couple trying for reservations were still getting no reaction on the payphones.

"Sport," the woman said to her husband as they were boarding, "I have a feeling we'll be sleeping under the table at some all-night Burger King."

"Tell me just one thing," her husband countered, "did you ever once have to sleep out on the streets since you know me?"

"Before the *Titanic* went down, it didn't go down before either," the woman said just as two smiling stewardesses reached for their boarding passes and chorused:

"Welcome to Mardi Gras."

Beside me on the plane was Bob, a young man from Massachusetts who worked Louisiana offshore oil rigs (and cleared $800–$900 a month.) He was returning to New Orleans after a visit home. His girl was an undergraduate at Tufts.

"I'm glad somebody's excited about Mardi Gras," Bob said, nodding toward the man in bifocals. "New Orleans has only one honest thing about it, its initials, N.O.—nothing. All that hype. What a crock. New Orleans is a city—like Athens and Detroit and Fitchburg, Mass. After the Bourbon Street bit, it goes sour fast."

"Oh dear," his friend said, "Bobbie, you're such an idealist. Everything's rip-off these days. Some rip-offs happen to be more interesting than others."

Of the spectaculars I attended in 1972–73, only Mardi Gras took place with the United States out of the Vietnam War. The weekend before Fat Tuesday, C-141s stood by to carry American prisoners of war out of Hanoi. In Khartoum the Black September Palestinian organization had killed two Americans and one Belgian and were holding hostages, bargaining for asylum in Sudan. In harsh cold South Dakota, the Siege of Wounded Knee was going on, while in Camp David, Maryland, President Richard M. Nixon was still a few March days away from the delivery to Judge John Sirica of James McCord's now-famous letter "telling all." From Camp David the President issued a taped message which slyly applied a resisted Vietnam tack to the domestic situation. Vermont Senator George Aiken had been suggesting for years that America *declare* the Vietnam War over, *declare* itself the "winner," and thus be quit of Vietnam once and for all. President Nixon adapted the suggestion to the war on poverty, and announced that "the hour of [urban] crisis has passed." In the year 1973, said the President, "city governments are no longer on the verge of financial catastrophe."

Locally, a bankrobber observed the New Orleans season by holding up the Mercantile Bank and Trust Company appropriately costumed in Mardi Gras mask. The local papers carried the usual predictable police blotter items—people whose pockets had been picked, whose handbags had been snatched, people who had been rolled, or mugged or, while watching parades, had their hotel rooms burgled. Burglars with an interior decoration kink stole chandeliers from a row of stately mansions empty because of Mardi Gras society revels. Shigellosis, a nasty intestinal disease, struck New Orleans a few days before Mardi Gras.

New Orleans came at me first in a blur of Tulane Avenue's office buildings, franchised hotels, motels, restaurants, structures just torn down so others duplicating them could instantly go up. Rubble and parking plots, as in the rest of the country, commemorated change-over.

At an entrance to the Fontainebleau Motor Hotel on Tulane Avenue, several buses unloaded people in the party hats and funny get-ups chronic in studio audiences of "Let's Make a Deal." Franchised-costume partygoers were off to some franchised commercial outfit's franchised party. At times the whole city looked like a studio audience unleashed to celebrate a contest in which nobody loses.

Cars and taxis, buses and vans, trucks and motorbikes converged on the parade streets of the city. Near Canal Street cars were diverted. Drivers looked lost. The familiar parking game was being played near all the parade routes: across from the Jung Hotel, for instance, an unfinished parking ramp was jamming cars in over sand heaps, piled bags of cement, knocked-over sawhorses, smashed barricades. Off La Salle a parking come-on said, "Parking, $10. Police towing $50 + +. You choose!" Kids helpfully guided drivers into no-parking areas, took their money, disappeared.

Mardi Gras is largely a walking spectacular. Walkers, costumed, uncostumed, followed every parade, crowded every street, carrying campstools, stepladders, pulling kiddywagons stocked with children and/or coolers of beer. Tiny children, bigger children, all ages and sizes of women sat on the shoulders of men to mark the margins of Mardi Gras marches.

Everyone, it was instantly apparent, could have the Mardi Gras of her or his choosing. Old people propped up on chairs in doorways saw only the very tops of passing floats, but that was a Mardi Gras. All backs—backs solo, backs joined arm-in-arm, backs stacked two-tier, backs atop stepladders, backs leaned against light-poles. On a signal, the hands of those backs would rise in the air, stiff waving arms create an image out of Nuremberg. Seeing almost nothing, the old people still applauded every passing tip of every invisible iceberg. Vendors ignored them. A call to a seller of iced drinks rarely got a response. But theirs was the best Mardi Gras going. Several wore tiny paper hats or waved washed-out flags. Some who sat alone were wreathed in beads kind passers-by shared. Those beads were everywhere, wound around cops' guns, cops' hats, cops' motorcycle grips.

Children's Mardi Gras may be the loveliest Mardi Gras of all. Unlike Halloween, Mardi Gras has no cut-off date, no age at which one becomes too old for costumes. Almost everyone who lives in New Orleans dresses up on Mardi Gras Day. Women in costume nurse infants in costume. Whole families dress in harmonized colors, stylized themes.

Parents in or out of costume frequently jogged beside their costumed parading children, ready with cold drinks and food whenever a parade stalled. One woman carried a folding stool she slid under her sweating ten-year-old flag-bearer son at every halt. In the middle of Mardi Gras show biz, social elbowing, and pomp came many a smalltown Scout or Brownie parade sans Rex, sans Comus, sans the King of Zulu.

In Audubon Park a motorcycle club gathered under the park's water oaks soggy with black Spanish moss. They looked like movie

Hell's Angels, their sleeveless jackets neatly ripped by a wardrobe mistress, the stencils on their backs readable, the scattered beaver hats full of stage plumes and feathers untouched by mustard, ketchup, bike-grease, french fries, blood.

The park grass was covered with standing water from heavy rains, which didn't deter anybody. Children in masks and costume were being pushed on swings by adults in costume, or being helped down slides, or at play in the sodden sandboxes.

In addition to the usual franchised five-and-dime costumes, the children in Audubon Park and elsewhere throughout New Orleans wore Pooh outfits, Piglet outfits, were Kangas, and Roos. Children's books turned up live, and moving, not only in the plastic Disney images dominating the floats. Three Alice in Wonderlands I counted in one Audubon Park picnic, one a lovely Creole child with poetically licensed long black hair. Near her was a black and beautiful Queen of Hearts. I saw a Tweedledum and Tweedledee—one white, one black. Humpty Dumpty turned up everywhere, once as a huge dressed-up balloon mounted on back of a pick-up truck and surrounded by kids throwing on Fat Tuesday the trinkets and doubloons collected early in the holiday.

Not just kids' books came alive during Mardi Gras. Comic books, comic strips loosed hundreds of Lone Rangers, Tontos, Batmans, Robins, Supermans, Superwomans, Superchildren, Superpups. Pirates leaped out of comic strips *and* New Orleans legends about Jean Lafitte. Picasso harlequins and Pierrots appeared on the streets beside Degas balletmasters and pink organdy dancers one could never be sure were women. The imitation turned parody could, with just one more twist, go all the way over to drag. Somebody witty, or unconscious, for instance, scheduled Robert Penn Warren's *Band of Angels* on New Orleans television the night before Mardi Gras. On the Bacchus float there was this enormous plastic Clark Gable head, from *Gone With the Wind* (as it passed I heard people holler, "Burn, Tara, burn!"); on television, in *Band of Angels,* Gable reigned again as a dashing scoundrel, this time up to his ass in the New Orleans slave trade. On the floats plastic Marie Antoinette was peppered with plastic moles, and very flouncy; off Bourbon Street Marie Antoinette, like

Isadora Duncan, was a favorite persona of drag queens, along with Jean Cocteau's silver face drag Beauty and drag Beast.

In 1973 drag queens were more and more being reclassified as "transsexuals," their idol Christine Jorgenson, who attained the once unattainable female selfness with the help of science, surgery, and hormones. But "she" who suffered a sex change must find a doctor or street clinic willing to change dressings and dispense massive doses of trans-sexifying hormones so that *mirror, mirror, on the wall* can play back, "Dougie-girl, you're a living doll."

All year round, New Orleans is a drag-queen haven, and Mardi Gras a kind of semi-formal drag queen convention. During the weeks of misrule, drag queens are guaranteed an even greater freedom from police hassle. Extremes of dress and behavior reach a limit police observe with special holiday tolerance.

"That is because some of our best femmes are policemen," a drag queen existentially located midway between Isadora Duncan and Mick Jagger told me. "Our motto for cops and everybody is— *If You've Got It, Flaunt It*. My God, if I was a jungle bunny and wanted to straighten my hair, who would *want* to stop me? Or all those ugly supermarket mummies in their rollers that are supposed to friz them up, or people who bob their noses or have plastic surgery for small chins or no titties. If you don't like the genes you were dealt, we say, don't just stand there. *Do* something."

The speaker waiting to "go on" in the He-Sheba contest was wearing a gilded slave bracelet on the upper arm, a spaghetti-strapped backless silver evening gown, a rose-colored organdy scarf wound round the neck and reaching down to the floor. Jackie Curtis "red lipsticks" and Warhol "Holly purple" were everywhere. Gold and silver mascara on eye, cheek, forehead. The commercial frills Women's Liberation spurned and discarded, drag queens picked up to exaggerate. Dime-store tiaras, feather boas, Jean Harlow wigs, ostrich plumes, flamingo fans, Theda Bara headbands, towering Ziegfeld girl headdresses, Busby Berkeley shorts and high heels, black star-specked tights, string-bikini halters.

"Everybody's in drag one way or the other," my informant— "her" name was Daphnée—said. "We can hardly compete with Richard Nixon coming on honest. And all the squares and straights go crazy during Mardi Gras. We live *Star Trek* all year round. Sci-fi, *c'est nous!* We like to go like everything—animal, vegetable, mineral. We're *funny,* hilarious all the time."

One measure of drag queen identification, Daphnée said, was who used the women's and who the men's washrooms.

"It's as much fun seeing reactions in one as in the other," Daphnée said. "We only give points to those of us who use the ladies'."

Shakespeare, according to Daphnée, was the grandest drag queen of them all.

" 'She' would have loved Mardi Gras. Can you imagine getting *hired* to be Ophelia or Juliet or Queen Bess?"

Mardi Gras, more than any other spectacular, offers nonconformities an illusion of refuge, an unhassled eye in the majoritarian American hurricane. As paint-by-numbers uniformity expands, and the pressure to be middleclass in everything builds conformity compounds, the inverse desire to live in status-less tatters burgeons. Vietnam escalated coercion toward consensus, and minority rejection of anything Lyndon Johnson, or Richard Nixon, was for.

Even after Woodstock changed into Altamont, the Woodstock dream persisted. For self-styled "freaks," Mardi Gras was as much a refuge as New Orleans was, generally, for drag queens and gays. In the French Quarter one could smoke, otherwise turn on, groove, undress, make love, with little or no interference from "the authorities." At Woodstock, Altamont, and the numberless rock festivals of the late 1960s, instant Mardi Gras was a theme. *Where it's at* became *where you won't be hassled.* In their desire for freak "order" totally secure from establishment police, for instance, the Rolling Stones bought Hell's Angels to guarantee "crowd control."

"Out there," a college student from Iowa told me—indicating the world beyond New Orleans—"if I don't wear a bra it has something to do not with me but with men. But Mardi Gras runs by *our* rules. I was here last year. I'll keep coming back as long as I have the bread because Mardi Gras offers one place where what I do is *my* business."

The Fort Lauderdale sect, too, believed that Mardi Gras was invented for its delectation. For students who read *The Sun Also*

Rises in freshman English, canny Vieux Carré merchants stocked brown plastic wineskins (trimmed in bubblegum pink). With a wineskin, a Fort Lauderdale male not only had something he could fill up and drink from but use in a sophisticated water-pistol fight. Otherwise, Fort Lauderdale Mardi Gras relied on standard clown miniaturization or magnification—male heads covered with tiny black bowlers, tiny firechief hats. False noses, Groucho Marx eyebrows, mustaches, glasses were favorites, and oversized baseball mitts, combined with tiny baseball bats. Fort Lauderdale women were instantly recognizable in wine-drenched sweatshirts left over from sexist crucifixion scenes (four macho males press a woman against a wall while a fifth jets purple juice at her out of a wineskin).

For their Mardi Gras, Shriners matched Fort Lauderdale's mesomorphic jinks. Expensive motorized kiddy-cars propelled through street parades, the drivers waving loaded water pistols. Nobody left Mardi Gras feeling her or his thing hadn't been completely realized. For squares it was the best of times. For society, too. Those who came merely to ogle, ogled. Those who came to snap pictures simply did that. Who wanted to march, marched; who wanted to throw, threw; who wanted to collect, tried.

The outside world wasn't totally eliminated from Mardi Gras. Rex's unreal plumage—metallic purple, green, and gold contrasted with Black Power primary red, bright green, and black. Just before the Rex parade began, two men in Black Power colors drove up Canal Street, salaaming, pretending to take a formal salute. Cheers were faint, booing fainter. Rex's Boeuf Gras got a much more enthusiastic response.

Parade images confounded actuality and fantasy. While the Wounded Knee situation remained serious and dangerous, a Mardi Gras "Indian" spackled with drag queen bodypaint wardanced in front of some anachronistic Russian-bloused marchers in the midcity parade. A young black girl flaunted her T-shirt before passing floats and throwers, on it the stenciled word "SLAVE" above two black footprints. At the corner of Canal Street and La Salle, two young white women in sweatshirts printed "PUSSY POWER" bobbled extravagantly at every man throwing.

On Mardi Gras Day nothing was held back. Out came the

freshly pressed costume, the best dress, the best suit. The moment Rex's parade came into sight, an old white-haired black woman tararaboomdeyayed ahead of Rex's float, her ruffled dance-halldress raised up to show her authentic historical frilly white pantaloons. An equally old white woman in a Santa Claus mini-skirt linked arms with the black woman just before a cop chased them both out of the parade's path. This left a very fat old woman wearing a "Grandma Loves Men" sign free to shuffle into the Rex line, waving a huge nippled bottle labeled "Gin."

The one Mardi Gras figure who summed up the celebration of 1973 was a tall beautiful woman in a nun's black coif, nun's bib, extremely short skirt, black pantyhose, buckled shoes, wearing a huge Women's Liberation symbol dangling where a nun would have had a crucifix. Wherever she went, she was followed—by women, men, children. People in floats leaned far out of their re-straining harnesses to call to her, to try to reach her with their trinkets and doubloons. She warded off the shower of flying beads, still walking, still followed, still being thrown to.

On Mardi Gras Day obscene acronyms appeared in parades and street banners. Oversize codpieces and mammoth balloon-bosoms tamely mimed the Roman saturnalia in which upperclass matrons (such as in New Orleans belonged to Comus) paraded beatifically under a thirty-foot phallus. The traditional overtly sexual rites of Priapus couldn't be matched by any Mardi Gras mummers, even those who carried signs they considered daring, like, for instance:

*F*ree
*U*s
*C*aptain
*K*ennedy

A mock-cleanup truck carried its message this way:

*C*ommittee
*R*ecycling to
*A*void
*P*ollution

The message everywhere in New Orleans—from the mayor down —was, "If you can't *do it*—whatever it is—during Mardi Gras, you can't do it anywhere in the world." Mardi Gras was *absolute possi-*

bility, the one chance in a lifetime. "Not doing it" was, then, either a failure of the imagination or a failure of nerve. As Mardi Gras wore on, the "what do I do now?" look appeared in the company of "where do I go?" The search for The Anecdote fell behind the urgent desire for The Experience. Early Fat Tuesday morning, I began to see that "I was robbed" expression on unlucky faces. Those who gave up on adventure fell to turning on or boozing. Some who had tried too hard too early had nothing left for the Mardi Gras Day finals. They turned up for the Rex parade subdued, bruised, scraped, bandaged, looking made up by Central Casting for a scat filming of *Marat Sade.*

Mardi Gras brought on Mary Poppins floating under tiny umbrellas or helium-filled balloons in the middle of culturally scrambled messages: a Bacchus float, for example, in which Al Jolson as *Jazz Singer* was an oversized blackface golliwog lording it above real blacks being thrown phony doubloons by real whites in blackface. Or the all-black Zulu parade with its floats decorated by paintings of white women. Or a marching band of pirates playing the bagpipes. Or three Frankenstein heads wearing Three Musketeer costumes. Or a ha-ha sneer at Women's Liberation in the Bacchus "Queen Kong" float featuring a lady "gorilla" in hair ribbon and bra.

The stock spectaculars mix of the church and the military was, as usual, added to by the "third force," show biz, in the person of a most devout Mrs. Bob Hope, who, while still plugging the stopped Vietnam War (along with Bacchus guest, General Westmoreland), disclosed that happiness back home in Los Angeles came from our "lovely archbishop who's been made a cardinal."

Political, historically aware blacks could watch blacks doing a strut they associated with slaves shuffling and the "opiate" of gospel dancing. "Happy darkies" were all over New Orleans, doing a shackle gratitude slide behind an imaginary master's imaginary wagon.

Dozens of Mardi Gras gorillas jostled the parade crowds in search of pretty young girls to rock with. Early morning hustlers in toe-length capes flashed flesh at startled passers-by. On Mardi Gras Day even the television master of ceremonies wore a costume. Everyone everywhere pretended to be a participant.

The pressure of circuses on ritual and routines, a constant in cultural evolution, showed itself during Mardi Gras. The Bacchanalia which made drama religious ritual and religious ritual drama—in Greece and Rome and medieval Christian countries— anticipated New Orleans churches and synagogues trying to adapt or co-opt the spirit of Mardi Gras. A synagogue on 'St. Charles Avenue announced:

> "LAUGHTER, FUN AND SONGS ARE KEYS TO
> WORSHIP."

The Jewish Community Center on the same avenue tried to one-up Mardi Gras with an announcement that, in less than two weeks (March 18), it would be celebrating the real thing, the "Festival of Purim." Numerous churches announced Mardi Gras (sometimes muted to "pre-Lenten") sermons on themes such as "Christ and Joy," or "Frolic Begins in the Heart," or "Man does not live by bread alone."

By noon Tuesday, when Rex was ready to roll, and Mardi Gras moved into its last twelve (semi-official) hours, two different responses were evident: one, the Indianapolis "500" infield response, that the party just mustn't be allowed to end; the other, that the party had been going on far too long. Those with no other spectacular to look forward to in 1973 differed from those anticipating future frolics and festivals. The drag queens who sang a camp "Good Night Ladies" to each other bewept the passing of Mardi Gras, but in New Orleans could experience a Fat Wednesday as garish as their Fat Tuesday.

When Rex began his parade, New Orleans was clammy, the sun hidden behind clouds. The night before, the Weather Bureau's department of Mardi Gras good news had announced a "20 per cent probability of showers" at the moment rain was washing out the Proteus parade. At 12:50 P.M., just as Rex reached the Boston Club to toast his queen, and be toasted, a high wind lifted visors up off heads, whipped at skirts, cassocks, overhead banners, shutters, flagpoles. While Rex was being praised for "having opened the hearts of all New Orleans" with his (Dr. Howard Raymond Mahorner's) "professional skill and kingly charm," the sky darkened, and stayed dark even as Rex toasted his queen—sheltered on the balcony of the Boston Club—for her "beauty and youth [which] are symbols of joy to the people of New Orleans."

Rex's public toast was instantly imitated along the streets of New Orleans. After his toast, Rex cavalierly dashed his glass to the ground, the band at the Boston Club began yet another chorus of "If Ever I Cease To Love."

Suddenly the air was full of bullhorns, noisemakers. The response to other parades had been loud; the Rex float got a soaring crowd roar, noisy and lasting. Out marched the bands, out trotted Rex's mounted lieutenants, on came Rex and his pages, Rex's band, his Butchers of the White Bull. An army drill team—fresh from Florida Senator Ellender's funeral—swung militarily into the fantasy hike. Real jets flew overhead, real navy cars joined the parade.

Rex's theme was "Kings and Queens of Fantasy and Fact." What one saw on the sidewalks were serendipitous parallels to what showed on the floats. Someone on the Henry VIII float might pitch a handful of doubloons to a street Henry VIII displaying a bloodied head of Anne Boleyn. Ignoring throws, people drank, bumped, shimmied on the sidewalks, touched pelvises with utter strangers.

The Philadelphia string band marching with Rex got an appreciative handclapping response. The group that woke up the watchers was an all-black marching rhythm group from St. Augustine High, "The People's Band," playing their trombones and trumpets Archie Shepp's way. Every booh, bah, booh, bah beat sent the crowd rocking. Not even the "Streetcar Named Desire" float with a resident live Dixieland band up on top got that wild reaction.

Shortly after one o'clock, a few raindrops fell on Rex's parade, but hardly anyone noticed. In Jackson Square, around the old French Market, the rain came down harder—on drunks, snorers, and sleepers. Thunder had an immediate effect. Once leisurely, the Rex parade now sped through Canal Street. By 1:30 it had made its turn for home, moving fast. Throwers, like salespeople at a close-out, unloaded their merchandise by the handful, as if baling water out of a sinking ark.

As soon as the Rex parade ended, the Krewe of Orleans truck floats began to rumble. For many, Rex was *the* parade, the only parade. Activity switched to the sidewalks. A dozen men and women with toy instruments gave a silent "concert," surrounded by a huge crowd. Behind them, the trucks on Canal Street sounded like the pace-car parade of the Indianapolis "500," and a passing army convoy. Music off the floats came through distorted and wonderfully tinny.

Someone had built a plywood double highchair for two kids strapped in on top of a tall stepladder and wreathed in beads. Parents, siblings hung throws on tiny feet or stuffed shopping bags hanging from the highchair. On the truck floats small children throwing usually couldn't reach the upheld hands of those left to yell

"Throw!

Throw!

Throw!"

Police generously swept up the throws and tossed them into the crowd.

The end of the Rex parade for many meant siesta. Soon Comus would usher in Mardi Gras Night, and the wildest revel. The truck floats for many were a manifestation of parochial dullness filling time between the twin excitements, Rex and Comus. Darkness was coming. Everything that hadn't yet been done might still be done. Once night arrived one might:

1. Crash a big society ball
2. Attend the greatest New Orleans jazz set ever
3. Ball and get balled wilder than ever before
4. Get drunker or turn on higher than ever before
5. Groove at the grandest Storyville cat-house before crashing at the toniest plantation party New Orleans ever saw
6. Eat the perfect Creole meal
7. Hold off Ash Wednesday forever

By 6 P.M., just before Comus began to roll, the streets of Mardi Gras 1973 filled up for that big "one more time." Those who still needed a parade, or still felt an urge to shout, "Throw me something, Mister!" were few. The Mardi Gras roar had steadily lost decibels since the Rex parade. Rex's parade-watchers formed up in lines outside Pete Fountain's, or Al Hirt's, or Antoine's, or

Galatoire's. Crowds massed in front of any open door, any place offering a glimpse of moving bodies.

In the day's intermittent rain, America's spaced-out children, who had struggled to get to New Orleans for Mardi Gras, huddled obliviously in Vieux Carré doorways, already far gone, or fast going. The "thereness" *was* all. Whoever made it to Mardi Gras had grasped the Grail, surfed on a tidal wave, touched the tip of Everest. Once one got "there"—to Mardi Gras—one could pass quietly into a private "there" which in space, and time, was nowhere.

Jesus Freaks, when the party grew wildest, didn't forget their business, nor did followers of Krishna, Buddha, the National Rifle Association, Richard M. Nixon. Voodoo rites snaked through the streets where solitary flambeaux dancers grooved on music spilling out of tacky bump-and-grind joints. *La Strada* at the corner of St. Louis and Bourbon was hemmed in by a carny-looking uncostumed gang fascinated by a sign promising a "Perfect 34-24-34" inside. Barkers mixed hints of orgy with homey guarantees of "ice cold beer." At Boy Dodd's the usual "Topless and Bottomless" come-on attracted begging Krishnas and smiling Jesus disciples. On North Rampart the Odd Fellows themselves were having a ball.

Once the parades ended, that Mardi Gras roar disappeared. The dominant sounds now were bullhorns, band instruments doing solo riffs, police, fire, and ambulance sirens, screams and shrieks and squealing tires. By ten o'clock both Rex and Comus had gone through all the ritual call-outs and rites of their respective balls. People still stood shivering outside the Municipal Auditorium ballrooms, as though waiting for a promised gala Hollywood premiere. Inside, Rex went over to the court of Comus, signaling the beginning of the end of Mardi Gras 1973.

From time to time, cars sped by, still getting rid of throws and doubloons. By midnight, there were no takers. Garden parties on St. Charles Avenue ended, or moved inside. Thousands upon thousands of people crowded every hustle street in the Vieux Carré. The flambeaux dancers disappeared. Street musicians closed their fiddle and banjo cases.

Later, on my way back to New York, when all the images of

riot and revel were receding fast, I looked at some of the throws
and doubloons I had caught or been given. On the plane they were
—junk. In New York it was almost impossible to make anyone understand that this cheap string of beads, the day before Ash
Wednesday, could turn someone on.

But Rex, King of Carnival, on that plane would have simply
looked silly. Any costumed Bourbon Street swinger would have
looked equally foolish. In New Orleans, though, doubloons seemed
real, and beads magically changed.

Space, like time, I realized, declares its own Ash Wednesday.
Mardi Gras, which suspended the ordinary, was over. Outside of
New Orleans, there was no wild or feigned recognition between
strangers, no hugging, no "Texas" rhyme for "Alexis." The party
was over—for the ruling classes of New Orleans and their dreams
of gracious Sambo-served antebellum days. Ash Wednesday
changed debutantes into mere socially eligible young women. Rex,
on Wednesday, was only a surgeon. Horses were unplumed, and so
were their riders. Without bands, without bongo-laden mules and
camels, without throwers, floats lay in dark barns and dingy garages, signifying nothing. The trucks were stripped of decoration,
bare hauling structures down on their wheels. Buses carried the
last Mardi Gras tourists out of the French Quarter. Hotels emptied
out. Conventions of salesmen returned, anxious to hear tell of yes-
terday's wild wild naked Mardi Gras.

Ahead lay the unpeaked months of 1973, or perhaps one would
be lucky enough to make 1973's Kentucky Derby and begin yet
another cycle. One could perhaps turn to America's natural
wonders—Niagara Falls, Carlsbad Caverns, the Grand Canyon,
Yellowstone Park, the Grand Tetons, the redwood forest, the
Great Salt Lake, the Rockies, etc. One could visit the flashy places
—New York, Chicago, Los Angeles, Las Vegas, San Francisco, or
the pseudo-pleasure domes, the Disneylands, plastic safaris,
junglelands, adventurelands which guarantee the togetherness of a
family rip-off.

For some, cultural events peak the year—the opera, the ballet,
the stage, museums, galleries, libraries—or those American arenas
of enjoyment, the bowling alley, the roller rink, the movie house,

golf course, tennis court. For the rest, there's always television, and a chance to participate in secondhand joys.

If religion was an opiate—in Marx's estimation—and a massive hindrance to revolution and economic reform, what, applying his parameters, can one say about Mardi Gras or man's other circuses and spectaculars? I've tried to indicate that, existentially, these circuses cannot be written off as mere opiates or as anything *secondary*. Conservative moralists, who glory in the poor always being with us, at the first sign of crisis want to close down the circuses— to the poor. Yet nobody in this or any other land lives by bread alone. Not even those on welfare. As spare a civilization as China's is full of real and metaphorical circuses. If *circuses* are the opiate of the people in the U.S.S.R., they operate full time and keep any potential revolutionary spirit slumbering.

If the year is a string of Ash Wednesdays, one day, at least, falls to Mardi Gras. One day offers the hope or illusion of breakthrough and bustout. Every civilization has had and will undoubtedly continue to have its gala days, its festivals, its days of misrule, its spectaculars. In America such times and such places set the larger goal of identification. The thereness is all.

"All through the Rex parade I kept pinching myself," a woman told me. "I couldn't believe that *I* was actually at Mardi Gras."

The line, by then, was familiar to me. It was the characteristic unbelieving response to being miraculously "there."

Great American Spectaculars Tote Sheet

	FIRST TIME	ATTENDED	REVISITED		PLANNED
Kentucky Derby	[	]	[	]	1977
					1978
					1979
					1980
					later
Indianapolis "500"	[	]	[	]	1977
					1978
					1979
					1980
					later
Rose Bowl	[	]	[	]	1977
					1978
					1979
					1980
					later
Mardi Gras	[	]	[	]	1977
					1978
					1979
					1980
					later
Republican or Democratic National Nominating Convention	[	]	[	]	1980
					1984
					later

SCHOOLCRAFT
COLLEGE LIBRARY